Pedalling
to
HAWAII

A human-powered adventure

STEVIE SMITH

1st Edition, signed and
personally dedicated
copies of this book are
available from
www.p2hi.com

PEDALLING TO HAWAII

Copyright © Stevie Smith, 2005

The right of Stevie Smith to be identified as the author of this work has been asserted in accordance with sections 77 and 78 of the Copyright, Designs and Patents Act 1988.

Condition of Sale
This book is sold subject to the condition that it shall not, by way of trade or otherwise, be lent, re-sold, hired out or otherwise circulated in any form of binding or cover other than that in which it is published and without a similar condition including this condition being imposed on the subsequent publisher.

Summersdale Publishers Ltd
46 West Street
Chichester
West Sussex
PO19 1RP
UK

www.summersdale.com

Cover photographs © Expedition 360

Author photograph © Seb Joli – Exp!osures of Salcombe

Printed and bound in Great Britain

ISBN 1 84024 446 1

This book is dedicated to Ray and Sylvia Shortman.
Your constant generosity and loving support created the ideal
environment in which to write a book.

Contents

THE DALAI LAMA

FOREWORD

I have been happy to support Steve Smith and his friends since they first proposed a project to "circumnavigate the world using human power alone to promote environmental responsibility and international understanding," nearly ten years ago, because I believe it is important in our era of cars, trains and aeroplanes that we are reminded what human beings can achieve using their own strength and resources.

I have always admired those who, in addition to expressing well-intentioned words, actually do something practical to further their cause. Undertaking a human-powered journey around the world takes great courage and determination. I am reminded of the many journeys on foot made down the centuries by people in Tibet. They were mostly going on pilgrimage or on their way to join a monastery to further their education, but like these adventurers they too would dedicate their efforts to the welfare of others.

January 14, 2005

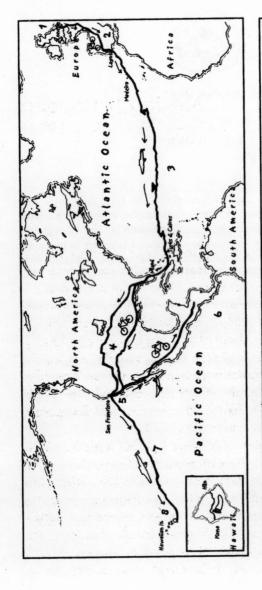

Pedalling to Hawaii

Chapter Locations Marked 1 – 8

Route Legend:

| Bicycle | Walking | Skate | Pedal Boat | Kayak |

1. Making It Happen
(June 1991 – July 1994)

A Third-Life Crisis
Paris: 26 June

A great tension has built up in me over recent months, a dilemma now so ever-present and pregnant that it threatens to explode and overwhelm me. I think a lot about death. I realise it's a bit premature, approaching my twenty-fifth birthday, to start thinking about death. But I can't help it. There's something about that looming quarter-century milestone that raises a ghastly flag of mortality on the far horizon and the distance from here to there – let's say fifty years – becomes quite shockingly and neatly calculable. It is only twice again what I have lived – an entire third that appears to have come and gone in no time at all.

I'll call it a 'third-life crisis', since it comes at the threshold of my 'primetime', the central, life-defining third. The dilemma, then, is not about death but about life – what to do with it. The standard model, which my friends are pursuing with great enthusiasm and almost without exception, couldn't be clearer and goes as follows: newly independent men and women go forth and make their mark on the world, find homes, partners, make babies and earn money for as comfortable a life as possible (not forgetting to put enough aside for old age).

OK fine, but why? Because that's what life is for? Because that will make me happy? It doesn't strike me as too unreasonable a question to ask before devoting the rest of one's life to the effort. Don't I owe it to myself to be convinced?

I am not convinced. I just can't seem to buy into the whole comfort-and-security scheme. I only wish I could, it would make life so much easier. I could fit in and feel normal, at home. But I'm not, because what I see, day after day, are captured lives, half-lives, dedicated to a mirage of fullness that never comes. And I wonder why we keep falling for it.

My greatest fear is of mediocrity and of a slow, unremarkable acquiescence to society. As Leo Tolstoy once remarked, there are no conditions of life to which a man cannot become accustomed, especially when he sees them accepted by all about him. And I fear that fifty years from now, when I'm rocking in my chair in fond reflection, I'll have this terrible revelation: as pleasant and worthwhile a life as it was on the whole, it wasn't really mine. I never owned it because I never truly chose it and how could I have, when I never even questioned it? I just went ahead and did it. This life, my life, was yet another solid performance of, or conformance to, that lifelong cabaret entitled 'What People Do'.

8.15 a.m.: the morning ritual: wash, shave, choose one of two suits and one of five ties. Grab case, slam apartment door, walk briskly to the station, buy a newspaper and wait for a double-decker train along with other impassive cyborgs in suits holding cases and newspapers.

Disembarking at Avenue Henri Martin, I hurry across the boulevard before the traffic lights release their next batch of impatient drivers and continue to my destination – a vast, unlovable block of offices set back and separated from the street by a white chain-link barrier and a dull expanse of asphalt. I dangle my identity tag before the guard at the entrance and lean into the revolving door. I pick up a coffee and pastry in the foyer café and enter the elevator for the sixth floor. A second guard at the entrance to the International Energy Agency recognises me and, seeing my hands filled with breakfast, waves me through.

Dozens of reports are stacked on my desk in separate piles marked 'UN', 'Global Warming Data' and 'Emissions From Cars'. I place my pastry and coffee on top of them and switch on the computer. The familiar whirring of the hard-drive signals the start of another day at the Organisation for Economic and Cooperative Development.

The OECD is like a gentleman's club for rich countries. Unlike the United Nations, OECD membership doesn't bestow any great privileges or the power to create internationally binding laws. It simply enables member countries to talk together in pleasant surroundings, plan mutually beneficial schemes and share information. My department was hastily established in the aftermath of the mid-1970s' oil crises to monitor and evaluate world oil markets, but its remit has since expanded to include energy-related environmental concerns. My role here is to help calculate the likely contribution of vehicle fumes to worldwide emissions of so-called 'greenhouse gases' by the year 2010. It is interesting work and very worthwhile, to a point – the point at which the economists take over, which they invariably do. An inhabitable planet for future generations is a lovely idea, they sympathise, but we simply can't afford it.

I am an outsider here for thinking otherwise and for seeing the tragic irony of being considered naïve by those whose 'realism' rests on such shameful absurdities.

Still, I am proud of my modest achievements and have enjoyed being part of this important study. And I absolutely adore Paris, from the fabulous boulevards and imperial façades to the shabbiest back alleys, even to the surly waiters and dog-fouled public parks. I abandoned London and all that it had become for me – the network of friends, the habitual rounds of pubs and drunken conversations – some three months ago and came to Paris to discover something new.

My life now is certainly different: my closest friend is my elderly landlady, Mrs Misson-Ducot, with whom I enjoy long evening meals while listening to her reminisce about her beloved Pays-Basque, as she sits wrapped in a black lace shawl. I'll spend a day walking alone from one end of Paris to the other and stumbling upon all sorts of delights – garden fêtes, forgotten cemeteries, eccentric shops, church recitals or ordinary Parisians doing ordinary things that I find momentarily captivating. Most importantly, I have found space.

There's something about Paris that compels one to question, to dig really deep and then to let it all burst through. What is it? Why am I not happy to carry on like this?

Standing at my office window, I stare vacantly out beyond the grey slate roof of the Chateau de la Muette to a distant tuft of trees in the Bois de Boulogne. What am I doing here in this ridiculous uniform, this dismal office, with red eyes transfixed to this computer screen all day long? What if I were free to do absolutely anything? What would I do then? What is the greatest dream I have for myself?

Adventure. That is what immediately comes to mind, adventure, something really simple that requires no great expertise. On the other hand I feel a tremendous desire to achieve something grand, something epic and extraordinary, like a journey around the world. I could ride a motorcycle around the world – but then I should never hear anything above the noise and besides, I'm useless with engines; perhaps a bicycle then, or even on foot through more difficult terrain – mountains, deserts, jungles and so on. Yes, that sounds more like a real adventure and keeps things simple and self-sufficient, even so far as relying on my own power.

That's it! A human-powered-around-the-world adventure. What could be simpler and yet more extraordinary than for a man to circle the planet using the power of his own body? It's a fantastic idea, a Eureka moment! Every cell of my body tingles with a previously unimaginable sense of purpose.

2.15 p.m.: kayaking would be another great way to travel. I ponder this for a while. It is hopeless trying to focus on work. My mind is flooded with images of a kayak slicing through white surf in a windswept bay. Seizing upon an idea, I leave my office and march vigorously to the end of a long corridor and turn into the agency library.

Elizabeth the librarian is on a coffee break. I take an atlas of the world, sit cross-legged with it on the hard linoleum floor and begin taking wildly inaccurate calculations of distances with my thumb, recording them onto the back of a cigarette packet.

4.30 p.m.: I write in tiny scrawled letters, '80,000 miles – approx. 10 years' along the base, just above the words 'Seriously Damages Health'.

6.30 p.m.: I close the atlas and leave the office. The computer is left on and the reports remain neatly stacked in three piles.

I remember nothing of the train journey home. I am paddling past dhows anchored in sparkling seas somewhere in the Arabian Gulf.

A Willing Accomplice
Paris: 15 August

'Have you ever been in a kayak, Steve?'

'Sure, a couple of times on school trips – loved it.'

'And you want me to come with you?'

Jason Lewis, with whom I was at college, has been in Paris for less than thirty minutes, on a weekend visit. I have been bombarding him with my new obsession from the first.

'Well, yes. It's such a massive project. I don't think I could manage it alone. You're the best person I could think of. What do you say? Up for an adventure?'

'Yeah, I'll do it; sounds incredible. When do we start?' There is no hesitation. I look for any sarcasm in his stubble-faced grin. There is none.

'Well, um, 1994 feels about right. I have some work in Brussels. I'll be back in London next summer. We could start on it then, giving ourselves two years to raise the cash and organise visas and stuff.'

'And learn how to kayak!' He laughs and raises an eyebrow.

'Oh yeah, there's that. And how about you? Had enough of cleaning carpets and singing in a rock band?' I study Jason's face – remembering well that disarmingly confident gaze, dark features and flushed cheeks – and realise that I miss his company. After graduating from university I had moved into central London to study for my master's degree, while Jason had devoted himself to his music, his live-in girlfriend and his job as a contract cleaner. They lived not so far away in Tooting but I rarely saw him. The last time we met before I moved to Paris was in early spring, just after he and his girlfriend had suffered a difficult break-up. We went on a two-day hike and pub-crawl in the Chilterns to help him take his mind off her.

'The music is going pretty well, actually. We changed the band's name to 'Psi Jamma'. It's more of a Seattle grunge feel...'

'Oh, no! I thought 'Dougal Goes To Norway' was the best! All those huge wigs and Viking helmets.'

'Student days mate, things change.'

'The outside world isn't so drunk and idiotic, you mean.'

'Yeah, exactly.'

We leave my apartment near Clichy station for a tour of the city by metro.

'So, has anyone tried this before, you know, going around the world by human power?' Jason shouts as the metro shudders noisily past La Gare du Nord. He leans casually into a vertical steel bar, wrapping one forearm around it and letting himself swing from side to side while his other hand is wedged comfortably into the back pocket of faded black jeans. He stands absorbing the impact of the rattling train as though he were riding on the tailgate of his father's tractor in deepest Dorset. His face also reminds me of that ancient county with its smooth, well-rounded contours, slightly swollen, like a boxer who's stayed on his feet one round too many.

'No, we would be the first as far as I know. Incredible, isn't it? Think of all the other great firsts – first to conquer Everest, first man on the moon, first to reach the poles – and all the expertise and technology that required. This may very well be the last great 'first' left to be done. It's a kind of ultimate human challenge and it's never been tried! Vast yet simple. Maybe that's why no one ever thought of it, because it's so simple.'

'Lots of people probably thought of it!' Jason snorts. 'But nobody simple enough to do it! By the way, have you ever noticed there's a dirty great gap between Europe and America? How are we supposed to kayak across that?'

'The Atlantic? Oh shit mate, it's only what, a few hundred miles between Scotland and Iceland! Not even that to Greenland; around there, another couple of hundred across the Davis Straights and you're pretty much there.' I jump up, extend my arms and perform an exaggerated kayak-paddling motion to a bewildered metro audience. 'I mean all you have to do is that! What's the problem?'

'You're insane, ha-hah!' Jason's roar reverberates through the carriage.

One Year On, An Expedition Takes Shape
London: 18 July

I stride purposefully in the darkness, north through Hyde Park. Veering off the path into long grass, I head towards the north gates. The blue neon sign of a bureau de change is my navigational beacon to Queensway.

The gates are already locked. I climb over the park railings instead, land with a thud on the pavement and scurry across Bayswater Road. The rain is lashing hard now. Cars whip up a spray as they pass. Drenched, I jog down Queensway, dodging the rucksacks and umbrella spikes that swarm between late-night food joints and cheap luggage stores.

My father's flat sits above a supermarket opposite Whiteleys Shopping Centre and is reached via a dank stairway. Stuart, my father, opens the door and we hug warmly. Jason has already arrived. From his crater in Stuart's enormous sofa he hurls me a can of Kestrel Super (a favourite among homeless drunks) with the greeting, 'Here you go. This'll put hair on your teeth!'

After dinner we migrate into the kitchen and the conversation turns to our evolving thoughts on the expedition.

Thus far we have agreed to shelve the idea of kayaking around the world, partly because it would take too long (at least ten years, whereas we're hoping to finish it in three) and partly on account of that 'dirty great gap between Europe and America'. Besides, why limit the possibilities of a human-powered circumnavigation to the coasts when we could also cycle through countries or go on foot, experiencing so much more. We've decided to travel east across Eurasia and will be practically halfway round before we meet the North Pacific, our first ocean.

The oceans present the greatest challenge for human-powered travel because you need a boat big enough to store food and water for several months but which is small and light enough to row. We are both studying accounts of previous trans-oceanic rowing expeditions and have been uplifted to discover that no fewer than twenty-five attempts have been made to row across the Atlantic Ocean, twenty of which have been successful and the first as far back as 1896. Scores of people, it seems, have already cycled across continents and others have rowed across oceans. But no one has combined the two into a human-powered journey around the world. With the need for a heavy rowing boat to tackle the oceans, comes an element of motorised support in order to transport the boat from one ocean to the next – and the bikes from one continent to the next – but that is unavoidable. As long as we personally are travelling under human power that's good enough. Surely no one would expect us to strap an inflatable Lilo to our pannier bags, or carry bikes on our backs as we paddled on our stomachs across oceans!

Neither of us have any experience of cycle touring, of boating, or of expeditions of any kind. We are supremely unqualified and have very little money. As an eleven-year-old schoolboy I was taken to see a presentation by the explorer Colonel John Blashford-Snell, who made an indelible impression on me, but from that day to this I've never met anyone similar. And yet despite this comprehensive ignorance we are equally confident, for reasons I cannot fathom, and quite determined to go through with it. That's why I asked Jason to be my expedition partner. We have a history of following things through together – silly student things mostly, but we've never let each other down.

I hated him at first. We met in our first week at university. One day I returned to my room and found it full of drunken strangers – Jason among them, this bellowing, rude farmboy sprawled across my bed with some girl and a half-empty bottle of gin, spilling it everywhere.

He claims to have been a shy child who hated school and suffered from a terrible stammer. But instead of just dreaming of being able to defend himself from the inevitable abuse he got a black belt in karate. Instead of cursing his impediment he took speech therapy and became the lead singer of his own rock band.

I suppose we became friends because we fed on each other's taste for extremes, and being typical students this often meant being extremely drunk or stupid, usually both. But we were also creative and could rely on each other to actually do the things that others agreed at the bar and forgot by morning. If Jason suggested climbing a Welsh mountain we'd drive there overnight and climb it the following day; when HRH Princess Anne, the college president, came to visit it was Jason who helped me make and erect a two-metre high 'pink cock and hairy balls' welcome for her on the college spire; during the geography field trip to Dartmoor it was Jason who woke me each morning at five o'clock to poach trout; and last year, after we had all graduated and gone our separate ways and many friends promised to visit me in Paris, it was only Jason who came.

Pedal Power
London: 5 August

8.15 a.m.: It is well into the morning rush hour by the time I cram everything into a rucksack, grab my gloves and helmet and slam the door of my studio apartment. My motorbike fires up on the second kick. I turn onto White Hart Lane heading towards the river Thames at Barnes, then ride north past a long line of cars waiting to cross Hammersmith Bridge.

Twenty minutes later I dismount at the entrance to the Centre for Environmental Technology, where I work, feeling a bit dizzy from the engine vibration; my jaws ache from all the teeth-clenching concentration. I feel mightily relieved not to be wearing the passenger door of a black minicab that stopped outside the Natural History Museum just before I passed it.

There is a brown envelope lying in my mailbox. I attack the paper and rush upstairs to my office with great excitement knowing that the package, labelled 'Boswell Designs', contains my future.

Several weeks ago I telephoned the Exeter Maritime Museum in Devon, hoping to speak to anyone who might know of a sturdy rowing boat for sale. As luck would have it, a museum volunteer called Alan Boswell answered my call. Alan happened to be a naval architect and enthusiast of human-powered vehicle design. I told him our entire plan to circumnavigate the world by human power and listened to his expert opinion, finally replacing the handset forty-five minutes later. To my delight, Alan not only shared my enthusiasm, he offered to design us an ocean-going, pedal-powered boat.

The package, containing a lengthy letter and design sketches reads:

'Dear Steven

Thank you for your letter and details of your expedition. I would be very interested in designing the boat for you, and I enclose an outline drawing showing some of the key features I think should be included. Taking as read such essentials as self-righting ability, easily driven hull form, covered living space, etc., I think the important points are:

Light weight.

Low windage: A propeller driven vessel eliminates the windage of oars.

Easy steering: I anticipate steering by lines running to a tiller. Simple but effective, and it will allow you to pull against them while pedalling, which I think will feel most natural.

Fresh water making and gathering: fresh water is the heaviest but most essential commodity you will be carrying. This design enables you to use the whole area of the boat for catching any rain that falls.

Fishing: allows for towing a lure and retrieving fish.

Pedalling: another advantage of a pedal-powered vessel is that, since you will be cycling across continents, you will be fantastically fit for pedalling, but not for rowing, when you get to the ocean sections. I think it is pointless to set up a tandem pedalling system, as the important thing is to maintain the pedalling for as close to 24hrs/day as possible, not to have brief bursts of power being soaked up by the rapidly climbing resistance curve at higher speed. Therefore, your strategy should be to take turns at pedalling, with the 'off-duty' person sleeping and when not sleeping doing the cooking, communicating, navigating, fishing, water collecting, etc.

Materials: the lightest option would be a carbon/Kevlar/foam sandwich. If you are really short of money it would be possible to build the boat in plywood. This would be the cheapest option by far and quite satisfactory.

This design provides a good starting point incorporating the lessons I have gleaned from the reported experiences of a variety of ocean rowers, and from a study of the boats we have at Exeter Maritime Museum.

I look forward to hearing your reaction.'

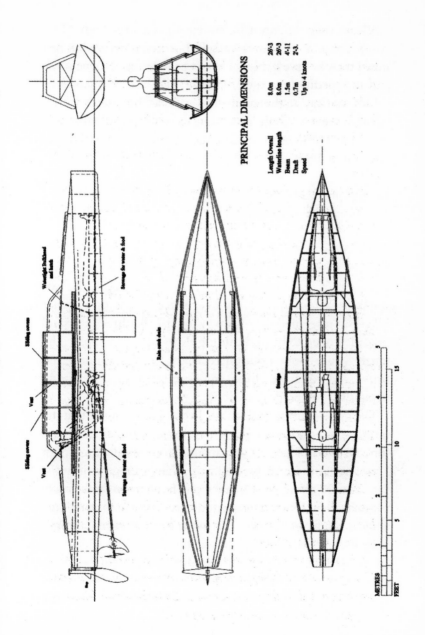

PRINCIPAL DIMENSIONS

Length Overall	8.0m	26'3
Waterline length	8.0m	26'3
Beam	1.5m	4'11
Draft	0.7m	2'3
Speed	Up to 4 knots	

Watertight Bulkhead and hatch

Storage for water & food

Sliding covers

Vent

Sliding covers

Vent

Storage for water & food

Stem

Rain catch drain

Storage

METRES

FEET

A huge surge of adrenalin sweeps through my body. 'This will happen,' I whisper to myself. I've said it before but just now I truly believe it. Now I have a boat design, a vague route and an expedition partner.

I sit staring at the plans and re-reading Alan's letter, dissecting every detail, imagining how the vessel will look, what it will feel like to pedal on the ocean. But how will I ever afford to build it?

Pissing On My Fireworks
Near Nantes, France: 23 October

A few months ago I decided to cycle to the Sahara Desert. Strange decision on the face of it, considering that I was totally unfit, had only previously managed to cycle the two miles to school and hardly ever since, and didn't own a bike. But it seemed the only way to raise the three thousand pounds I need to begin building Boswell's pedal boat. The entire route from London to Marrakech is about 1,700 miles and to make things more interesting I'm giving myself seventeen days to do it.

The cycle-touring enthusiasts I've spoken to insist that my target – a hundred miles a day for seventeen days – is unrealistic and I haven't met anyone to contradict them. But I can't honestly see the big deal. Surely, any averagely-fit cyclist can trundle along at ten miles per hour, even with heavy panniers: therefore all that's required is to do that for ten hours a day – say from seven in the morning until seven at night with an hour for breakfast and an hour for lunch – and you're laughing! Not that I tell my sponsors that, of course. I just show them the brochure with the maps and distances, and London to the Sahara by bike in seventeen days does look damned impressive, although I expect most people I know will be generous enough to support me just for finishing inside of a month.

I don't have a month. I've only arranged two weeks off work. Nor do I have three hundred friends waving ten pound notes. I have about fifty friends and instead of simply asking them to sponsor me I've asked them to take a brochure and become fund-raisers. I'm hoping they can meet a target of fifty pounds among all their friends, and anyone who donates at least ten pounds will have their names permanently inscribed on the pedal boat – once it is built.

I am now on the second night of the London-to-Sahara cycle ride, having made camp in a small copse next to the road, twenty miles north of Nantes. The opening day's ride from London to Portsmouth amounted to seventy miles of continual heavy wheezing, sweating and periods of self-doubt that rose to a feverish panic. The raw excitement of being on my way got me through it. I slept on the overnight ferry to Saint Malo and began the French section with very stiff limbs and a wicked headwind that continued throughout the day, often accompanied by torrential rain. The initial excitement is now all gone. I still believe I can reach Marrakech within the seventeen days, but a hundred miles a day is proving to be a lot harder than I thought. There are so many extra complications and delays I hadn't thought of, including these headwinds, having to keep finding water (and how damn heavy the stuff is!), cooking food, packing and unpacking pannier bags, repairing inner tubes, taking wrong turns, looking for sheltered places to sleep and wood to burn.

I am starving, low on water and slightly edgy in the pitch darkness. I frisk myself for the torch and unload cooking supplies from my pannier bag: noodles, cooking pot, chocolate, tea, an apple and two tins of tuna. There's also a one-pound bag of raw kidney beans, which I brought along partly because beans are good energy food and partly because I watched too many cowboy films as a child. I've no idea how to make these rock-hard pebbles edible. My family had never even entertained the idea of a camping holiday when I was young and I'm ashamed to admit that I've never pitched a tent before. It's just as well that I didn't have room for one on this trip.

'Camping? Nothing to it,' I mutter to myself as I gather dry twigs into a large pile. Plenty of Ronsonol lighter fluid should do the trick. I fumble for the matches.

'Furruummm!' Instant fire, marvellous! I pour most of the water into the pot and open up the bag of noodles while envisioning the hard days ahead: a hundred miles per day, every day. I think of my friends, especially my girlfriend Maria. 'Don't worry about the seventeen days, Steve, just finish. No one wants you to kill yourself. Take three weeks, or a month.' Maybe she's right. This is so much harder than I...

'Oh, shit!' My model fire has quietly spread through the undergrowth and is now a knee-high blanket of flames fifteen feet across. The entire copse is illuminated out of the blackness like a theatre set and the flames continue to creep in all directions.

A newspaper headline, 'Charred Remains of English Cyclist Blamed for Nantes Disaster' flashes before me. I transform into a blur of frantically stamping and beating limbs. I hurl the contents of my cooking pot and all available liquids at the inferno.

Finally the area is a smouldering wasteland. I strain as hard as I can to pee sporadically around the perimeters for good measure and fall exhausted onto my sleeping bag.

Still hungry, I roll a cigarette and chuckle myself to sleep.

Saharan Sand Between My Toes
Casablanca Airport, Morocco: 9 November

'*Dear friend*

Greetings from Morocco: Arrived Marrakech at 2.00 p.m., Saturday seventh, 16 days and 2 hours from London start. Very sore arse, cracked lips; nice tan! First nine days to central Spain one long rainstorm, high winds, nightmare. Lost a day waiting for cycling partner at Bordeaux on Day 5, left him behind with injury at Bayonne on Day 6. Fitness good on reaching mountain pass over Pyrenees to Pamplona. Sunshine finally by Valladolid, covered 210 miles racing down from Spanish plateau to Seville on Day 11. Ferry to Tangiers on Day 13, Morocco big shock: terrible roads; became target practice for stone-throwing shepherd boys. Through Rabat, Sale and Casablanca on coast road, then inland to desert and Marrakech. First celebratory beer the best! Thanks for your support, will be in touch when boat building – and the real adventure – begins!'

I finish the last postcard and wait in line at the *bureau de poste*.

'How many cards?' the clerk asks in French.

'One hundred and five, please,' I reply with a casual shrug.

He wields his ink stamp like a weapon and hammers its down upon each card in turn with unprecedented fury. I hand over my remaining Moroccan dirhams, including a generous tip for his effort. After boxing up my bicycle I board the flight back to London.

During the flight I gaze down upon the regions of Spain through which I had cycled – the green rolling hills and finger-lakes of Extremadura, the high, dry, plateau region – with a curious mixture of emotions. I delight in my achievement but feel disappointment at having to race through entire regions and cultures, missing everything. I never want to travel like that again.

The Hardest Part
Exeter, Devon: 2 August 1993

The hardest part of an expedition is over when it begins. Maybe that's wishful thinking but, right now, being ready to circle the planet by human power seems as formidable a task as when the first rocket scientists contemplated how to leave the planet altogether.

Thanks mainly to the incredible fund-raising efforts of my father, mother and a few key friends, the London-to-Sahara bike ride raised £3,250. Jason and I have since increased the total to about five thousand pounds; he through selling his carpet cleaning business, while I donated my lecturing fees from a three-day environmental course at the University of Leiden, The Netherlands. I handed in my notice at work in March in order to work full-time on the expedition.

Since becoming unemployed I have taken up my father's invitation to live with him at Queensway, and have been living on a paltry £35 per week in social security benefits. Jason, meanwhile, took his guitar and van on a busking tour of Western Europe, witnessed war in Bosnia and returned in June to London – and to £35 per week and a bed at Dad's flat.

The lowest professional estimate for building a wooden pedal boat was £25,000. By the beginning of this year we realised our only hope was to build the boat ourselves. In February, just before his busking trip, Jason introduced me to two friends, Hugo Burnham and Chris Tipper, both of whom had recently graduated from boat-building school. Hugo and Chris were bubbling with enthusiasm for their first building project and what better, they said, than the world's first two-man ocean-going pedal boat. With the generous offer of a free workshop at the Exeter Maritime Museum, Hugo and Chris' conviction that the boat could be built for 'next to nothing' suddenly became a real possibility.

In the first few weeks of April, £3,000 was spent on timber, tools and other supplies needed to begin building the boat. The other £2,000 went to Hugo and Chris. I sent countless begging letters and phone calls, which were eventually rewarded with donations of thousands of pounds worth of glue, paints, hatches, plexiglass, propellers and fittings. The Ecological Trading Company, who pay western prices directly to tribal partners in return for sustainable logging practices, donated all the hardwoods required for the boat's keel, transom and hull.

The pedal boat is, by all accounts, a simple design that ought to take two men no more than six months to complete. After five months the basic structure is barely half-built although, in fairness, what is emerging is a vessel of superb quality and strength. Each weekend I drive from London to Exeter to offer an extra pair of hands, sometimes with Maria – who is becoming an accomplished sander – and now Jason. The main problem is money, or the lack of it. Whenever I can raise extra cash selling names on the hull – at the occasional boat show or as the speaker at a club function – it goes to Hugo and Chris. The trickle of cash helps, but is insufficient and the guys are understandably disgruntled. In my obsessive passion to make this expedition a reality, I tend to overlook the obvious – that not everyone shares it.

But what shocks me is the shrewd opportunism that seems to have replaced the original enthusiasm. Chris and Hugo informed me this morning that unless I give them £16,000 for the work done to date they would both walk away, taking the contents of the boatyard, including donated supplies, with them as security. Hugo also hinted at the speed with which a chainsaw could transform a wooden boat into so much firewood.

Every penny and effort is invested in a twenty-six foot wooden hull that, as she stands, is virtually worthless. The pedal boat is what defines this expedition. She is the symbol, the soul... everything. With her, all of Jason's efforts to build media interest and my efforts to find corporate sponsorship could make the expedition happen. Without her we are, again, two penniless nobodies with a good idea.

Sometimes no amount of determination is enough. We need a saviour, and right now that saviour is my girlfriend Maria. On hearing of our dilemma over lunch she, with truly saintly generosity, offered to loan us her own savings to buy us time to complete the boat and find sponsorship. This is a great risk and burden of responsibility because there are no guarantees of ever finding sponsorship. We can either take the risk or give up.

Later this afternoon, Hugo and Chris reduced their demands to an immediate £4,000 with more to be negotiated later. Jason and I have decided to accept the responsibility of Maria's loan, pay the guys to finish the build and hope for the best.

Making A Splash In The Papers
Exeter, Devon: 11 November

'Pedal Pair Sub Sinks'

This absurd headline, hidden in the squalid depths of the equally absurd and squalid *Daily Star*, marks the expedition's launch into the world of publicity. Its redheaded weasel reporter, who claimed yesterday to be from *Yachting Monthly*, goes on to write that, 'Two students, Steven Lewis and Jason Smith, sunk their pedal-powered submarine yesterday, after it was swept out to sea by high winds and capsized.'

What actually happened was that Steven Smith and Jason Lewis almost made a monumental balls-up of their inaugural voyage into the swollen River Exe (nine miles inland) and narrowly avoided being swept over a weir.

It happened, as balls-ups often do, because we were in a dreadful hurry and, I suppose, because we don't have a clue about boating. It was a foolishly premature excursion for the vessel, but since the museum donated the space to build her for the last eight months, some publicity was the least we could do to help save it from bankruptcy

It took the strength of ten men to manhandle the twenty-six-foot-long boat weighing nine hundred pounds from the boat shed into the adjacent canal. Jason was first to clamber gingerly on board. I waited for him to sit at the pedalling end of the main compartment before I dropped down into the open hatchway. She felt as unstable as an ordinary kayak, wobbling precariously at the slightest movement.

Inside, the central cabin is a naked wooden shell, the only fittings being a pedalling mechanism and a builder's breeze block at the pedalling end that serves as a seat. The pedal mechanism is an astonishingly crude contraption based around the upturned half-frame of a rusty old ten-speed bicycle, bought at an Exeter flea market for a fiver and sawn in half. A bike chain connects the pedal cranks to a smaller cog on an industrial gearbox. An inch diameter, ten-foot-long steel shaft runs from the gearbox through sealed bearings in the hull and skeg to a specially made, eighteen-inch long, two-bladed propeller. Steerage comes from a pair of ropes running all the way forward from the rudder, along the rear deck, through the central cockpit and back to the pedal position, which are pulled in the manner of a stunt kite.

Jason sat uncomfortably on the crumbling breeze block, took hold of the steering reins and pressed his feet into the pedals. The boat jolted forward consentingly, the assembled crowd of reporters and museum staff clapped and murmured compliments, while we pretended not to be thoroughly relieved merely to remain afloat. But seconds after pedalling beyond the stagnant and enclosed canal basin into the river channel, our growing confidence quickly plummeted into outright panic. A hundred yards downstream the river dropped vertically six feet in a menacingly loud cascade of white foaming water.

'Jason, Jas, head upstream... the other way!' I spat the words furiously through a grimacing smile as I stood waving to the receding line of photographers at the quay.

'What the – I'm trying, for heaven's sake. I'm trying! It won't turn!' Jason desperately tried every combination of rudder tilt and pedalling direction – full speed ahead, rudder hard over; full speed in reverse, rudder hard over – but whatever he did, it made little difference to the boat's heading – directly downstream.

The best direction he could manage was a diagonal traverse across the river to the opposite bank, where a bemused line of office workers had already gathered, leaning against the iron railings. I crawled like a whimpering puppy along the deck to the bow and tried to hide my blushing face as we crashed with a heavy, splintering thud into the stone-walled riverbank. I lunged for an overhanging tree branch and gripped the boat's tapering deck with my thighs to keep us from being swept over the raging weir. Jason waved frantically for rescue, which eventually arrived in the shape of a local fisherman in a small black inflatable with a deafeningly loud outboard motor – just in case there was anyone left on the riverbank not yet witness to our utter humiliation.

It was with great magnanimity and suspension of professional instinct that the other newspaper reporters and a local TV crew decided to overlook the unfortunate incident and focus instead on our mission, and on the heroic struggle of the Exeter Maritime Museum to avoid closure. They even managed to keep a straight face while asking whether or not we felt confident about pedalling across the Pacific and Atlantic Oceans, which is more than I could have done in their place.

Yesterday we learned something important about boating. That three-foot-long heavy rectangle of laminated wood, called a centreboard, is not an optional accessory that can be left behind – propped up against a shed wall – if one is in a hurry. This part is about as essential as the steering wheel of a car.

The Boat Show
London: 15 January

It is the final day of the London International Boat Show. The last two months have flown by in frantic preparation for this event. All remaining funds have been spent on finishing the boat, producing a colour brochure and video and printing expedition T-shirts for sale. All the usual last minute panic and problems apply.

For example, in the rush to produce a thousand copies of our brochure I had to dictate the text over the phone to a printer in the East End of London. The result of a harried East Ender's mishearing of the word 'rations' is that our literature now declares, 'Jason and Steve will be surviving on a strict diet of dehydrated Russians for the ocean crossings.'

Cold war cannibalism aside, media interest surrounding the expedition has exploded, heightening expectations of desperately needed sponsorship as our July departure date approaches. Donations of marine equipment, bicycles, clothing and camping supplies are fairly easily won with the promise of photos of the gear in action, but corporate cash sponsors remain elusive.

Donations from individuals, however, have been pouring in over ten non-stop, twelve-hour days at the show. We have raised almost seven thousand pounds. Instrumental to our success is my father, Stuart, who is the ultimate salesman. He loved the concept of the expedition from the very beginning and has created for himself an invaluable role in what he does best – winning over the public. His enormous energy and enthusiasm attracts an endless stream of visitors to our peculiar bright orange exhibit. Spellbound by Stuart's banter, each visitor is powerless to resist climbing the wooden steps alongside the boat for a look inside, then down the steps on the far side to 'meet the guys who are going to do it'. Some help by buying an expedition T-shirt or their name on the boat for ten pounds. Others offer sound advice, contacts around the world or simply their best wishes.

Some advice is sounder than others, one of the others being the man who finally snapped my father's patience. He arrived at the busiest, most stressful peak of the weekend crowd and stood on the platform inspecting, nodding, shaking his head and re-inspecting. The line of spectators waiting to climb the steps grew longer and more impatient, but he seemed oblivious to Stuart's polite prompting to move on. When an emphatic nod of the head finally seemed to indicate a conclusion, the man took two steps forward... and stopped again. He then proceeded to lip-read the names of all one hundred and fifty six sponsors that had previously been inscribed on the pedal boat. Turning slowly round to Stuart the man declared, gravely, 'Nah mate, you ain't gonna to fit all those people in there.' It was the final straw.

'What do you think this is,' Stuart screamed, 'Noah's Ark? Now clear off!'

Moksha – *Sanskrit for 'Freedom'*
London: 27 January

Jason and I stand beside HRH the Duke of Gloucester (who kindly agreed to be a patron and to attend the naming ceremony) on a chilly grey day on the Thames near Tower Bridge. Wearing only a thin expedition T-shirt and jogging pants (to offer the impression of fitness), I try to ignore a cold blustery wind that sweeps upriver and turn to face a tight wall of press photographers with their clicking, whirring cameras, microphones and tripods.

Maria stands proudly in front of the pedal boat, which sways gently in a suspended cradle over the water's edge. She waits determinedly, pensively, holding a large bottle and an endearing frown and shivering in a billowing blue dress. She looks beautiful. I ought to have spent more time with her, I suddenly realise. The demands of the expedition seem to dictate every waking moment these days. The same is true for Jason. We used to be friends first and colleagues second, but now we spend all our time together keeping a rein on the evolving beast that is the expedition.

'I name this vessel *Moksha*. God bless all who pedal in her,' proclaims the Duke with due solemnity. Hearing her cue, Maria jigs the bottle furiously. The cork flies skyward and *Moksha*'s bright orange decks are anointed with a spluttering shower of champagne.

Everyone cheers. I smile with a delightful sense of the surreal. On any other day we might be dressed in oily rags, straining our backs to push-start a stalled Renault along Peckham High Street, surviving on bangers and mash bought with dole money. But today we're hosting a party for one hundred that includes royalty, celebrities, family, friends and the nation's press at the prestigious St Katherine's Haven Yacht Club.

A band of invited schoolchildren sing a sea shanty with sweet, piercing voices as *Moksha* is slowly lowered to the water. Beyond the lock gates, on the River Thames, a pre-arranged motor launch waits to pick up the press for photographs of us pedalling under Tower Bridge. A reporter squats at the wharf-side and calls down to me:

'Hi, I'm John Mortimer, from *The Times*. Tell me, why *Moksha*?'

In the Vedas of Hindu scripture, 'Moksha' is the fourth and final degree of liberation of the human spirit. Aldous Huxley, one of my favourite authors, studied Hinduism and other Eastern wisdom traditions over many years. In his final, utopian novel, *Island*, Huxley describes a hallucinogenic ritual performed with 'Moksha-medicine' by the island's inhabitants to help them avoid the corruptive influence of habit and ideology. *Moksha* is also the title of Huxley's account of his experiments with LSD in the 1970s, which lent him some remarkable insights into the workings of his own mind. Our pedal boat has been christened *Moksha* in the hope that she will bring similar gifts of liberation and insight.

'It's Sanskrit for "freedom",' I yell back. I doubt that *The Times* really wants more detail than that.

Why Extend The Agony?
Salcombe, Devon: 28 April

Our failure to find a money sponsor has left us with few choices. One option was to stay in England and continue hunting for sponsorship for another year or more. This was a dreadful, soul-destroying prospect: more months, possibly years of proposals, phone calls, meetings and rejections, another miserable winter of abject poverty in a damp London flat. Besides, unless we go through with our planned departure this summer all of Jason's efforts to cultivate media interest will be wasted.

However, if we do leave as planned we only have enough money to cycle east as far as Russia, maybe Central Asia at a pinch. If, by some miracle, we reached the Pacific coast of Russia or China, it is fantasy to believe we could raise the capital there to have *Moksha* and all her supplies shipped over to us when we can't even manage it in our own country.

The solution we hit upon was to leave as planned but to switch directions and go west. Having spent all this time building an ocean-going pedal boat, why let it sit in England while we struggle through Eurasia? Why not do the Atlantic first? In whatever direction we travel we will eventually find ourselves without money in a foreign country. Assuming that we survive the Atlantic we'd much rather be penniless in Florida – having become the first people ever to cross the ocean from continental Europe to America by human power (all previous attempts have either set out from the Canary Islands or finished in the Caribbean) – than merely be two destitute cyclists in Kazakhstan. The change in direction means that we'll be pedalling across the Atlantic only five months from now, which is beginning to scare me. We are both now enrolled on a navigation course and we're certainly paying attention in class.

The plan to go west makes sense but it requires us to take on more debt in order to pay outstanding bills and get the expedition, including an ocean-ready *Moksha*, down to the Atlantic coast of Portugal. Our financial saviours this time are my dear mother, Sylvia, and Jason's parents, Sebert and Gillian.

It is an enormous risk, a leap of faith, and possibly more so for our parents than for us. If we succeed in the great voyage then our chances of finding sponsorship in America and paying them back are good. If, however, we drown trying, the terrible suffering of our parents might be compounded with the guilt of having made it possible. I'm amazed and immensely grateful that our families have supported us so strongly rather than try to dissuade us. Jason's mother took to including press cuttings of disasters-at-sea into her letters to begin with, but on the whole our families have displayed a great deal of trust and confidence in our abilities.

Moksha must surely rank among the safest and strongest boats of her size ever built. As long as we avoid other ships, shipwrecking ourselves on a coast or falling overboard, there's no reason why *Moksha* shouldn't carry us safely to the other side.

Still, we focus all our energy and determination on making *Moksha* as seaworthy as possible for the 4,250 mile Atlantic voyage. During the last few days of capsize tests and sea trials on the south coast of Devon we have begun relating to *Moksha* not as a beautiful designed object, nor as a fund-raising emblem for the expedition, but as our total life-support system. We have only one chance to get it right. Once we head out into the Atlantic Ocean a pedal boat without sails or a motor has no chance of turning back again. With only VHF radio communication we have little chance of rescue or support. The next sight of land will be America after months of sweat, toil, isolation and storms.

The tension builds with every passing day. And there's a domino effect of good fortune and a contagious enthusiasm, as though this journey we created now has its own force and we are swept along in its wake. 'Whatever you can do,' wrote Goethe, 'or dream you can, begin it. Boldness has power, energy and magic in it.'

This is so true. I look back at that first burning idea in Paris and appreciate the monumental journey that has already been made. The relentless efforts of our team transform the near impossible and make it achievable, though there is a daunting amount still to be done. Jason recently discovered a superb cameraman called Kenny Brown, who is rapidly proving to be an entire support-, film- and publicity-crew rolled into one. This frees Jason to concentrate on acquiring all the food and safety equipment for the Atlantic crossing, while I deal with communications, navigation and boat fittings. Maria has talked the RAF into donating ex-fighter-jet lifejackets and life rafts. Jason's father is currently persuading the army to donate dehydrated food and Jason is negotiating with the Metropolitan Police for the loan of a boat trailer to carry *Moksha* all the way to Portugal – and presumably hoping they don't bring up the subject of unpaid parking fines. The courier company DHL are loaning a tow vehicle, which will be packed with supplies and driven by Kenny's friend, Martin Gascoigne.

This morning began as planned, with speed-testing *Moksha* in Salcombe Harbour and making notes on how her fittings and general comfort could be improved; where to situate the cooking stove, food and cooking utensils within easy reach of the passenger; how and where to stow the charts and screw-in a plastic holster for the global positioning system (GPS). Cushioning is a big issue. A ride in *Moksha* has all the comfort of a builder's barrow.

In the afternoon we pedalled out into the English Channel with the intention of spending a night at sea.

Ten miles out into the Channel, where the steep craggy cliffs of Bolt Head and the smooth lines of Bolberry Down are reduced to a low brown silhouette, Jason read my mind exactly and broke the silence.

'God it's boring, isn't it?'

We have been chuckling at his comment ever since and at the ridiculous, hideous irony that we have created for ourselves. A few months from now we'll be doing this all day, every day, for months on end. But in less than four hours in the English Channel we had had enough.

'Look,' Jason protested. 'We already know it's going to be a bloody nightmare. I can't see why we should prolong the agony by pedalling around in the English Channel when we could be in a nice warm pub getting the beers in.' He had a good point.

And so, this evening, we find ourselves sitting in front of a cosy fire at the King's Arms, drinking beer when we ought to be about to spend our first night at sea.

Jason suddenly leaps to his feet.

'Bugger! What time is it? Ten-thirty. Where's a phone? Might just catch them.'

'Catch who?'

'*Southwest News*. I told them we'd be on our second day at sea by now. They're expecting me to call on the mobile for a phone interview – live from the English Channel. Forgot all about it. Damn! Never mind, I'll call them from the telephone box outside. They'll never know the difference. Anyone got 10p?'

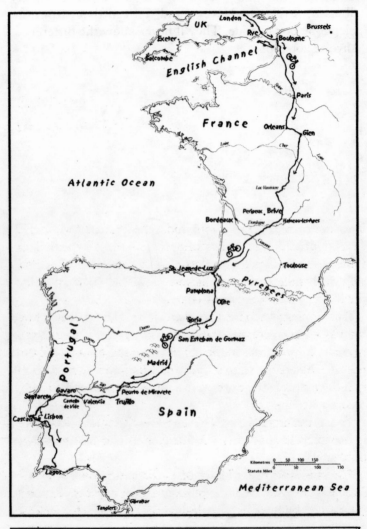

ROUTE LEGEND   PEDAL BOAT   BICYCLE

2. Europe
(July – October 1994)

The Big Ball Drops
Greenwich: 12 July

The line of zero degrees longitude, the Prime Meridian, is carved neatly into the stone courtyard of the Royal Observatory at Greenwich. Jason and I straddle this line and grip the handlebars of our bicycles nervously as we wait for the ball-clock to drop, signifying midday.

The moment is too big to capture; it overwhelms me. I hug my sister, squeezing her tightly. It may be years before I see her again. I spot faces in the crowd – friends, family – all the people who enable us to stand here. I long for entire days to spend with each one in turn, to express how I feel. But only seconds remain.

'Face the camera, Steve. This one's for Madison.' (Madison is our bicycle sponsor.) Damn Kenny and his incessant publicity!

'Christ Kenny! Can't I have one goddamn minute with my family?' I am a bottled-up, explosive mixture of expectancy and exhaustion. None of us have slept or eaten properly for the past two days in the chaos of pre-departure – loading up supplies, doing TV interviews and vacating flats. To top it all, I had to drive a fifty-foot van and boat trailer rig across London through the morning rush-hour traffic. We arrived horribly late.

The bell strikes midday. I glance across at Jason. Our eyes lock.

'This is it. Good luck!' I say, and gulp.

'Well done, mate.'

The culmination of three years of preparation is suddenly upon us. We wave back to the clapping, cheering crowd and glide between the courtyard gates. As if floating through a dream we cruise silently along Blackheath Avenue where long rays of sunshine flicker through the trees.

I remain in a daze as we bank through the roundabout at Shooters Hill. The air is so clear, the road so smooth. Kenny again invades the moment, perched on the back of an overtaking motorbike with his infernal camera. The motorbike slows and closes in on me.

'How do you feel to be finally off, Steve?' Kenny shouts while looking down his viewfinder.

'We're really doing it; we're on our way to Rye. I feel fantastic!'

'And where do you go from Rye?'

'Across the channel to France, Spain, Portugal... and then the Atlantic!' The camera swings to Jason.

'Oh man, we're lost!' Jason grins. 'Five minutes into the trip and we're lost already. A21, where the fuck's the A21?'

By mid-afternoon we are approaching a steep hill surrounded by farmland near the town of Sevenoaks. The euphoria is spent. We are both utterly shattered. Jason spots a gate, which opens onto pasture. He turns in and I follow. We barely say a word, letting our bicycles fall beside us as we collapse into a deep green swath of scented grass.

I notice the flies tickling my face, the warmth of the sun, the chirping of a sparrow then gladly surrender myself to glorious sleep.

Maiden Voyage
Rye, Kent: 14 July

5.00 a.m.: Kenny and Martin delivered *Moksha* by trailer to the coast yesterday and we spent the night camped out on the quayside ready for an early start. It was my last night with Maria. We slept together, wrapped in blankets, on the foredeck of a fishing trawler, the *Snodgrass*. I suppose I ought to be focusing on pedalling across the Channel – the world's busiest shipping lane, but I keep staring at Maria and wondering how on earth to say goodbye, how to say I love her and know that I'm leaving her at the same time. We knew this was coming, she knew it when we first met two years ago and we've talked endlessly about it, considered all the options and finally agreed to go our separate ways. For my part I know I can't be both a good partner and a good traveller. I only hope I've made the right decision.

I climb down the steps behind Jason and he pedals *Moksha* cautiously along the quay to the mouth of Rye Harbour in a breathless dawn. I stand in the open hatchway capturing final moments of England: the smell of wet grass and seaweed, cows grazing in a muddy open field beyond a freshly-clipped row of hawthorns. Two seagulls squawk and cavort over the steaming marshland and head inland, where the medieval stone heart of the old port sits ragged and pale on a low hill.

I wave goodbye to my mother and Maria, who stand at the very edge of the quay, leaning into each other for support, alternately waving and wiping their eyes. I feel immensely lucky, proud, grateful and sad, watching them fade into the distance. How must a mother feel watching her only son vanish into the vast blue unknown? And yet to this day, especially today, she has never shown me her fears, only her support.

I look around the boat, anxious for some activity to displace my tears. *Moksha*'s insides are a ruthlessly spartan composite of varnished plywood, plastic and steel with the cosiness of a cheap coffin. Home-made canvas covers are stretched over a row of storage compartments at knee height on both sides of the central cabin. Higher up, wood gives way to plastic windows in all directions, making the central cabin resemble the cuboid cockpit of a World War II Messerschmitt fighter plane. The only concessions to comfort are a large blue cushion made of PVC on the passenger's bench and a knobbly, inflatable black rubber cushion on the pedal seat. The pedaller sits facing forward in an ex-go-cart racing-seat with the pedal system immediately in front of him. He steers by grabbing hold of two short handlebars (taken from electric angle grinders), one either side of him, which are attached to pulleys running through the cabin walls and all the way back to the rudder. The all-important compass, to show the pedaller if he is steering the correct course, lies embedded in the bulkhead ahead of him, next to the passenger.

The passenger can choose to sit facing the pedaller at the opposite end of this central cabin, which is about ten feet in length and four feet wide. Otherwise, he can stand up through the open hatchway and look out to sea, clamber outside on deck, or alternatively he can swivel his legs round from the sitting position and slide himself feet first into a slim, tapering bunk cabin at the bow end of the boat, where he can only lie down. A third cabin, behind the pedaller at the stern end of the boat, is for storing supplies.

I find a video camera in the storage well to my left below the compass and point it towards Jason in the pedalling seat. His face, glistening with sweat, bobs across the screen, bulging and contorting with each laboured breath.

'This is ridiculous!' he gasps. 'It's five-thirty and I've got sweat dripping off my brow. I don't think I've ever had sweat dripping off my brow this early before.'

'How long have you been pedalling for now?' I ask from behind the camera.

'Oh, 'bout half an hour.'

'Half an hour! Is that all?' I laugh at his wheezing red face.

'Whaddya mean, is that all! It's long enough, mate, I tell you. Wait till you get in here, the laughs will be on you. How many miles do we have to go?'

'Let's see, Rye to Boulogne. Oh, about thirty five.'

'Thirty five miles at walking speed.' He mutters to himself, looking about for some interim amusement. He finds the VHF radio, switches it on and puts the microphone to his mouth.

'Hello Dover Coastguard, Dover Coastguard, this is pedal boat *Moksha*, *Moksha*. Radio check please.' He waits expectantly for a voice to burst in on the irregular crackle.

'Here we go; are they going to acknowledge our presence?'

Until now the only acknowledgement has been a letter, advising us in the sternest possible terms not to attempt a pedal-boat crossing of the English Channel. On the opposite side of the water the French Coastguard have gone further, pointing out that under French law pedal boats are classified as 'beach craft'. If we are found in French waters beyond the perimeter of the beach zone we may be arrested.

I understand the sense in dissuading people from becoming navigational hazards in the world's busiest shipping lane. And I recognise the challenge in managing this treacherous channel is compounded by the fact that the populations on either side of it happen to be the English and the French – two peoples notorious for ridiculous stunts and separated only by a tantalisingly thin strip of water.

But this is no drunken bet with a raft. Ours is a vessel built to withstand the awesome power of the Atlantic and Pacific Oceans. 'Our two nations,' I wrote in reply, 'have led the world in exploration and maritime adventures for centuries. Where has that spirit gone? Is commercial traffic now the only consideration?' Hence Jason's attempt to goad the authorities with a 'radio check' request.

'Err, Dover Coastguard. Reading you loud and clear.'

'Dover Coastguard this is *Moksha*; thank you, out.' Jason replaces the microphone, raises his fist and cries, 'Whooooay! First contact with the enemy, ha-ha!' He chuckles, takes a cold sip of beer (breakfast) then delivers his best impersonation of a German captain in a black and white war movie, 'Vee have zem in our sights, unt now... vee vill blow zem out of zee vorter. Rrrramming speed!'

At 9.00 a.m. we swap places for the third time. This is really hard work on the thighs, ankles and back. The pedalling is much stiffer than it should be – some work to be done before we take on the Atlantic. But the steering is dead easy and the overall feeling, that of slicing through the water in a very large, enclosed canoe, is a real pleasure. The surrounding sea seems unnaturally calm; the overcast sky is dull and muted. Jason takes the video camera and points it towards a large tanker appearing on the western horizon. He sits silently on the roof for a while, struggling to appreciate its enormous bulk.

The tanker drones across our bow about a mile ahead. Jason positions the camera in order to interview himself with the tanker in the background.

'We've come about fifteen miles so far,' he begins, 'and we're just entering into the heavy traffic. Err, we've seen about two or three really huge ships so far and um, I don't know what will happen if we meet one,' he adds, pointing a thumb over his shoulder. 'I guess we'll just have to take 'im out.'

The day passes uneventfully, with surprising ease, and we pedal into Boulogne harbour well before sunset and moor up alongside a fishing vessel. We covered thirty-five miles in about thirteen hours. No French Coastguard police in sight.

On The Road To Paris
19 July

We are back in the saddle again for the long haul south through France, over the Pyrenees Mountains and across Spain to the Atlantic coast of Portugal.

Four days ago, as we sat at the wharf-side nervously watching *Moksha* being scooped out of Boulogne Harbour, our strategy for this phase was settled. In view of the desperate financial situation it was agreed that we should restrict spending to basic subsistence and fuel for the tow vehicle. Enough money must be held in reserve to cover our driver Martin's return trip to London, once *Moksha* has been delivered safely. Nightly accommodation through Europe will therefore have to be free – in other words a sleeping bag in a field. We know of four offers of accommodation – three in France and one in Spain – but apart from these we'll have to rely on lakes and rivers for keeping clean.

Given the need for wild open spaces it makes sense to avoid cities altogether. If, however, we are not to concede defeat in our hunt for a sponsor before the ocean challenge then the capital cities of Paris, Madrid and Lisbon are the places we must visit, and with maximum publicity. From that point of view, to have pedalled into France without being arrested struck us as a missed opportunity.

From Boulogne we cycled a short distance to a summer school in Hardelot, where we spent the weekend with the kids, relaxing and watching the soccer World Cup final. From there we continued south on the Abbeville road as far as Poix and spent a first, idyllic night in the woods with a fire, a thirteen franc bottle of red wine, fresh bread and Camembert and some army-issue peaches-in-syrup. After the intense mayhem of the expedition build-up and launch it was bliss just to listen to a crackling fire and the sounds of the woods.

Today we have covered forty kilometres to Beauvais, gliding smoothly along well-surfaced roads in these undulating, intensively cultivated lowlands. The rolling, arable farms are a surreal green and fertilised to death. Industrial acres of wheat, cabbages, corn and barley carpet the hills at the edge of town. Plagues of greenfly fall like sticky showers of green snow. Jason's long hair resembles a clump of shimmering moss.

We coast through a quaint hamlet. I am moved by the sound of piano practice coming from an open window. Fields of wheat again, their stalks sometimes flattened by wind or rain, or perhaps by children playing den games. I glance at the map on my handlebar bag and stop to check the route.

'Aargh!' I fall sideways and disappear into a hedge. 'Damn SPD pedals!'

A condition of our bicycle sponsorship is that we must use 'the latest gear'. We managed to talk our way out of the Lycra suits but they insisted on shoes that lock onto the pedals. For the third time today, I forgot. It keeps Jason amused.

'When you've finished with that hedge, mate, let's have some lunch.' He sniggers.

It begins to rain. Jason huddles underneath a tree and opens an army ration of chicken casserole and another sachet of corn beef hash. An almost total lack of exercise in the last few months leaves me desperately needing to gain weight. Jason's paunch, which he attributes to the amount of beer consumed during farewell parties, reveals his need to lose some.

'OK, it's time to get serious and fight this flab head on. My diet regime is going to be strict and simple,' he exclaims. 'No beer, from now on I only drink red wine... and plenty of it.'

We approach Paris late in the afternoon. Farmland gives way to colossal factories, warehouses and garish billboards. The air thickens and the world becomes oily and grey, like a mechanic's rag. The hideous, concrete tower blocks of Saracelles dominate the eastern skyline, car dealerships line the road to the west. We cycle on, becoming more wary of aggressive drivers. I swerve to avoid a dead dog in the gutter. The traffic builds and diesel trucks spew dense, black clouds as they pass. We have to stop and stand more frequently at red lights, slowly making our way through the working intestines of a capital city.

Good and Evil
Orléans: 21 July

We practically fly along the road between Paris and Étampes and come to a bristling sea of bright yellow sunflowers. There follow fields of barley, cabbage and corn as we approach Orléans.

We need wine. I shout ahead for Jason to stop and veer across to a Le Clerc supermarket. It is just closed. A woman directs me to Carrefour, describing it to be 'just around the corner'.

Several kilometres later we approach the supermarket. The lengthy diversions have put Jason in a foul temper and he drags far behind. He doesn't appear to have enjoyed much of the journey so far and I'm unsure what to do about it. Maybe I'm the problem and he just wants to travel by himself. He has been hinting at this for several days, speculating on whether take a detour to visit some friends in the south of France and meet up with me in Spain. He admits to finding the whole idea of being on a team expedition a burden too. It ties him down to a route and a schedule whereas he'd rather please himself and not have to make compromises. But it's more than travelling together that appears to be eroding the strong bonds we shared as students. It is also the long months of increasingly frantic preparations that led up to it.

We walk out of the supermarket laden with bags of wine and fruit. I am busy trying to stuff my share into my pannier bags when Jason starts hurling obscenities at a group of North African men, one of whom he has caught trying to steal from his pannier bag. The largest of the four, seated on a moped, kicks Jason's bike, which topples over with a loud crash. Jason retaliates by kicking the youth's moped. He promptly launches himself at Jason.

They roll about the floor in deadlock. I look at the remaining three. They look back at me. None of us are sure whether to start another fight. For the moment we are all happy to be spectators, watching Jason and their leader writhing around in a tangle of rolling, spitting fury. I stand in front of our bicycles. Without them we are sunk.

The short, stocky one of the three becomes more agitated. He decides to don his friend's motorcycle helmet. He then lunges at me with a blood-curdling shriek and performs a flurry of wildly inaccurate high-kicks and punches at my face.

Having made no contact at all, he stops for a breather. Jason's opponent suddenly leaps to his feet, grabs the moped, does a running jump onto it and escapes in a cloud of smoke and ear-splitting noise. Jason chases him for a short time, slows and is quickly overtaken by the other three who scurry past him in pursuit of their fleeing leader.

Jason remains angry and overheated as we cycle into the centre of Orléans. He stops at an ornamental fountain to dunk his head underwater.

'Are you OK mate?' I ask, as he wipes his eyes and smoothes back his wet hair.

'Yeah. Just a bit wound up, that's all and annoyed with myself. Seven years of bloody karate and in the heat of the moment I couldn't remember any of it.'

'I think you did pretty well. He ran away. Let's find a nice camping spot and forget about it.'

We cross the square and study a large map of the city for directions to Vierzon. A man stops his car and steps out to greet us. His second sentence is to offer us a bed for the night. I sense Jason's wariness. He's thinking 'Robbery, thuggery and now what, buggery?' I make the polite excuse that we must continue. But if we could wait for him to grab his bicycle, the stranger insists, he could guide us to the road to Vierzon. We accept. Romauld reappears from his apartment with a sparkling racing bike and a large bag of fruit and biscuits, a present for our journey.

As we talk and ride together, it turns out that Romauld has toured the Himalayas and China on a bicycle. He is also a musician and practicing Tibetan Buddhist and altogether a genuinely nice guy. He repeats his offer of a place to sleep. This time we accept. We turn around and cycle back into town feeling a bit foolish. Romauld's girlfriend greets us warmly at the door, even though we must stink after a day's ride.

Alone At Last
Gien: 22 July

We cruise gently along the Loire valley, past ancient farms and riverside hamlets. An old lady leans through a flaking, sun-bleached window frame to feed leftovers to noisy geese. We pass more rippling fields of bright sunflowers on the empty road to Sully and head towards Gien.

We shelter from the searing sun under a bridge by the river. I am too exhausted from the heat to eat lunch. It would have been easier to cycle down to Portugal in the spring or autumn, but it's more sensible to plan the passage to America in reverse – and avoid the summer hurricane season in the Caribbean. We'll therefore cycle through the summer heat in order to reach the coast by September and spend the winter months crossing the Atlantic.

'You all right, Steve?' Jason asks. I am too tired to answer.

'This was the deal,' he continues. 'I need to lose weight and you have to gain some, which means I get to carry all this food and you're supposed to eat it, remember?' I respond with a weak laugh.

The conversation meanders along aimlessly, exhausting me as much as the heat. We have run out of interesting things to say to each other. If Jason still wants to cycle south to St-Tropez to visit his friends he needs to do it now, before we start climbing into the mountainous regions of Creuse and Haute Vienne.

'We'll say goodbye here then,' I say. 'I'm going to find a cool lake somewhere in the mountains and hang out there for a few days. I'll meet up with Kenny and Martin at the summer school near Brive. Where will I see you again?' Jason sits quietly studying a map before answering me.

'I'll carry on up the Loire and then head south down the Rhône valley. I should reach Saint Tropez in three days. On the way back I'll hug the coast to Perpignan and Barcelona. I'll meet you in Madrid on, let's say, the ninth of August.'

We discuss how to split up our supplies. Since Jason is adding an extra thousand miles to his journey, I offer to take the heavier items. We argue selflessly, insisting that the other should take useful tools – the can-opener, the penknife – of which we possess only one between us. I watch him ride off and wave goodbye.

I'm surprised how good it feels to be alone. I've become so used to living and working constantly with the same people, the need to be alone just didn't occur to me. There was no time.

Tiring quickly under the fierce sun, I cycled only a short distance this afternoon and came to rest under an apple tree on the banks of the River Sauldre at Argent. Unable to face food, I empty a sachet of electrolyte powders into my water bottle and sip it whilst throwing sticks into the stream. I fall into a long, restful sleep.

Puppy in the Stream
Argent: 23 July

I wake from a twelve-hour sleep feeling thoroughly rejuvenated. I pack up my things and freewheel down to the centre of the village.

At the café I order coffee and strike up a conversation with a middle-aged German lady. She has been cycle touring for the past six months. Judging by her appearance – a haphazard bundle of canvas and cotton secured with bits of twine – it might easily have been thirty years. She is not, surprisingly enough, destitute; in fact she owns a small house in Munich, but prefers to be a vagrant on wheels. Whenever she needs money she sits and begs at supermarket entrances. She has been travelling in France for three months. Under French law she must now register with the police as a 'traveller' and report to the gendarmerie at every town she comes to. She thinks she will move east instead, to Switzerland and Italy. It seems a strange and harsh path to take, but who am I to judge. She must have her reasons.

The morning's ride to Châteauneuf is pleasant and cool, but a baking heat bears down upon me towards noon. I keep searching ahead for the next line of shade trees. How unbearably hot will it be to pedal *Moksha* in the sub-tropical Atlantic Ocean? At least a bicycle provides a cooling speed. I reach down for my water bottle and, lifting my head back up to squirt water into my parched throat, notice that I'm gliding under a banner stretched high across the road, announcing tomorrow's fair. Should I stay? No, I promised myself a mountain lake. I compromise with a lunch stop at the river.

A young girl throws a stick into the River Cher near a low, crashing waterfall. Her tenacious puppy launches itself in to retrieve it. He is taken by the current and cannot paddle fast enough to swim back upstream to her. I worry that the dog might drown, since neither of them has the intelligence to see that going sideways, to the bank, is the only answer. She watches the animal's struggle, jumping up and down and shouting encouragement. His front legs chop rapidly at the water in front of his bulging eyes and he goes nowhere.

A tall boy dives in and drags the animal to the bank. They embrace, dog and boy, in a frenzy of barking, whimpering delight.

The boy ploughs back in the river above the waterfall and lets the current launch him over it. The puppy cowers and will not follow. It is time to head on.

I am lost in thought on the long climb to Guéret and full of questions. What is the expedition really for? Is it some grand objective I'm using to make my life feel more significant or worthwhile? What kind of a weirdo am I anyway, always questioning? Today I feel cursed with it. I want to be a normal, unafflicted, playing-by-the-river sort of person; a warm and comfortable family man, at peace in his place; one who leaves a respected name in stone.

I passed silently and unnoticed through the town, peering up at the softly glowing windows of its homes with a touch of envy. The town looked magical by lamplight. I continued climbing until my energy was entirely sapped.

Now, with the aid of moonlight, I unroll my sleeping bag near a huge, disfigured oak tree at the edge of a field of sheep.

The Magical Pool of Youth
Near Guéret: 24 July

I awake to the crowing of cockerels that pierce a freezing, misty dawn. I dress quickly and rummage through my food pannier for breakfast – some biscuits and an apple.

I set off at a pace to beat the chill, soon arriving at Pontalion. I buy milk, bread, fruit juice and more biscuits. I carry on through to Bourganeuf, yet another of the many picturesque villages that cling to the mountainsides of central France.

I stop for a lunch of army-ration mulligatawny soup and finish a book of poetry while languishing in the afternoon heat.

'Enjoy every minute of your life,' one poem begins, 'as if you were just on the brink of losing it.' My mind immediately turns to *Moksha* and the Atlantic Ocean, now only weeks away. I've tried and tried to imagine what it will be like, hoping to rationalise the risks and reassure myself, but I hardly know where to begin. I've nothing in my experience with which to compare it.

I pack up around five in the afternoon and continue up towards Lake Vassivière. The steep, mountain lanes wind up and up. Is there no end to this agony? I am breathless, overheated and hellishly thirsty. At last, I reach flatter ground at the lake and stop at a large-scale tourist map. My legs are wobbling uncontrollably. The virginal, lakeside paradise I have spent days dreaming about is actually a large complex of caravans and car parks packed with people. There are posted rules for visitors that prohibit fires and camping anywhere other than the main site.

I haven't exerted this much energy only to jostle among packs of screaming families with barbeques, radios and fat ladies in bikinis. I decide to skirt around the lake and find an illegal spot.

By sunset I have walked several miles along the wooded lakeside track and am very tired. This will be far enough, well out of earshot of the campsite. I dig my heels into the soft earth and drag my bicycle through thick rhododendron bushes, down the slope to the water's edge.

What a fabulous den! I leave the bicycle propped against a tree and comb the ground for firewood. The rocky shoreline will be my cooking place, where I can build a safe, undetectable fire. The lake stretches like an enormous, black marble ballroom in front of me. Behind me, the bank is littered with purple-blues dots of wild blueberries. The lake water tastes pure to drink. I strip off my clothes and dive in.

Aaaah! Magical pool of youth! I dive deeper down through the thermal bands, getting colder and colder, and pull myself deeper still, eager for the cold that makes my headache. Then I go limp and let my full lungs carry me back to the surface, where I exhale and howl with joy. Every cell of my body tingles with delight. I swim out further and further into the liquid marble, shedding every ache and pain, until I can barely see the distant glow of my fire at the shore. To the east – a huge, soft, white moon. To the north – the sky crackles furiously with a summer storm and everywhere there are stars.

56

Lac de Vassivière
25 July

I have travelled in my sleep. The foot of my sleeping bag is almost in the lake. The rest is covered in squashed blueberries. Plenty more remain intact for a delicious breakfast.

Before departing, I squat at the water's edge with remnants of bread, Camembert cheese and an inch of red wine in the bottle. The crusty bread floats, becoming a vessel for the cheese, which I anoint with wine. I push my symbol of gratitude out into the lake.

It is another cold, damp morning. I try cycling along the dirt track back towards the road, but collide with a large stone and cannot unclip my shoes from the pedals fast enough to avoid falling sideways into a gorse bush.

'Aargh! Damn SPD pedals!' I crawl out from the prickly mass, looking sheepishly around for sniggering spectators.

It is difficult to warm up on the long, freewheeling descent through the forests of Haute Vienne. I ride carefully on the wet roads muddied by logging trucks. But I feel wonderful. I have bathed by moonlight in a magical lake and slept in a bed of blueberries. Everything appears more beautiful today.

It is late afternoon before I finally arrive at the pre-arranged meeting place, a summer-school camp in the hills south of Brive. This is a rambling hamlet of stone cottages around a central green, with a large modern stable block for horses at the rear. I find Kenny and Martin rearranging boxes of supplies in the back of the DHL van. *Moksha* is parked on her trailer under a tree some distance away.

'Hey Steve,' says Kenny. 'We thought you'd both be here earlier.'

'I got lost – did three laps of that lake down there before I found the right road.'

'Where's Jason?'

'He decided to go on a bit of a detour, via St-Tropez. He said he'll meet us in Madrid in a couple of weeks.'

'St-Tropez! Ye must be jorkin'!' Kenny screams, his thick Scottish accent harsher than ever. He jumps down from the van looking very upset. 'He can't do that! How ken ah make a film documentary of you-two's journey if there's no footage of Jason between Paris an' the middle o' Spain?'

'Look, I don't know what to tell you Kenny. He needed some space. I've got a number where he's staying, give him a call.'

The road to Mont de Marsan
31 July

I continued my cycle ride alone through the Dordogne and down to the plains of Landes, heading for the coast near Biarritz and our next meeting place. Kenny managed to persuade Jason to shorten his detour and cycle due west from Montpellier to Toulouse, where Kenny is waiting with his camera. We will all cross the border to Spain together before Kenny and Martin take the van and *Moksha* on to Madrid, while Jason and I tackle the mountain pass through the Pyrenees, down to Pamplona, continue south and then west through the central Spanish plateau.

I chug along late into the night on a flat, featureless road. The night is black and so thick with flies and chirruping cicadas that my mind has ceased to register them. An oncoming car overtakes another and narrowly avoids colliding with me head-on. I feel my heart thumping and look over my shoulder to see the red tail lights slowly come together as the cars melt into the distance. Their menacing growls fade and my world shrinks once again to this heavy breath, this feeble patch of torchlight, this buzzing of rubber on a flat road.

I'm quite concerned about our group, not to the point of worrying whether we'll make it to the Atlantic, but just the spirit in which it's being done. Does a team spirit even exist? We all seem to have very different agendas: Kenny and Martin have made it plain that the sooner we get to the coast the better, so they can get back to London and Kenny can sell his documentary; Jason, on the other hand, maintains a libertarian view of travelling in which each man ought to be left to do whatever he pleases – and it should all work out fine in the end. Our teamwork, such as it is, seems to be tolerated while it furthers individual interests and not much farther. I sit somewhere in the middle, finding myself more in favour of Jason's desire to fully enjoy the journey than Kenny's urgency to finish it, but also more inclined to keep together as a unit (as Kenny needs for his film) than Jason feels is necessary. Whether that makes me a better bridge as the team leader or merely twice the target for resentments remains to be seen.

The mountain pass to Pamplona
Spanish Pyrenees: 4 August

It is a terrific, sky-shattering thunderstorm. My ears are blocked at this altitude. I hear only muffled rhythms – the heavy patter of torrential rain, water spraying from tyres, violent breathing. I crawl up the tortuously steep road, staring ahead at the grass verge and the vague, rustling shapes of leaves and branches that burst into sharp detail with each lightning strike.

Breathing harder now: in... out, in... out, I feel my lungs stretch to their limits and press flat against my rib cage; the water cascading down my face becomes a spray mist with each exhalation. The summit marker appears as I curl round the final bend. I stop to look back for Jason and feel the steam evaporating off my naked back. I am trembling and barely able to stand from the huge effort of the climb and the blinding, electric exhilaration of the storm. Jason's boiling wet face reveals the same rapture in ecstasy at the summit.

'This,' he roars above the storm, heaving to catch his breath, 'is fantastic!'

I let out a long giggling laugh. This is it! This is what the expedition is for, for moments like this: to stand on the mountaintop and feel the raindrops bursting over naked flesh and cooling the body's heat; to feel primal and pure above the wilderness on this raw angry night; to let all fears, black forest and thunder, gripped hands and surging blood, bulging eyes, breath and labour all unite in one gigantic grateful release.

We stand facing each other speechless, leaning into our bikes, heaving and laughing, almost crying.

Soon I begin to shiver and re-acknowledge my mortal limits. The magic spell dissolves into the blackness. We reach down into our panniers, wriggle into warm clothes and rain jackets and begin the long winding descent to Pamplona.

One silent mountain village after the next appears and disappears as we rip through sheets of water on the road. We come to a hamlet where a crowd is silhouetted around the headlights of a car that has crashed into a stone cottage. An old man in a dark suit is slumped against the dashboard with his hat displaced onto his cheek. There is a plenty of shouting and waving of arms among the spectators but no discernable help. The crowd finally opens to swallow a wailing police car. We remount and continue on to Pamplona more carefully.

Dead Dogs And Englishmen
Olite: 5 August

Mouth is dry, ahem, dusty. Here we are in Spain. E-vee-var-espana! Dusty, dusty, poor land, bad luck really, or maybe not! Maybe it's just the way the weather works. Yeah, clockwise in the northern hemisphere, isn't that it? Clouds come across from America, right? We get all the bloody rain don't we? Us and the Irish. Keeps us lush and green – isn't that nice! 'Looks like rain Mrs Simmons! Never mind, they give it drier for t'moro – rain again the weekend. Oo! Better get me washin' in.' That's it, no rain left when it's Spain's turn, hardly a drop, greedy Brits eh! The wind's all dry, till after it goes back over the Atlantic again to the Caribbean. And don't they get it, cor blimey! Rain? You've never seen anyfink loike it! Why am I talking to myself in a cockney accent?

This happens to me a lot. I get bored in the monotony of cycling for hours on end and my mind goes into demented idiot mode. I hope I'm not the only one.

Argh, the worst are those irritating little people in my head! The voices, and those bloody awful pop songs that keep playing, over and over again!

'Hey! You guys took one helllll of a beating! You guys, you guys took one helllll of a beating!' Who's that? Oh God not him again! It's that Danish football commentator from 1983, when England was beaten by Denmark. What are you doing back in my head again, you smug little bastard? That was eleven years ago!

'Oh, you guys took one helllll of a beating! You guys took one helllll of a beating!'

Oh go away, please!

A hill comes into view. Ah, a hill! Something interesting. Am I getting any better at this, cycling I mean, especially going up hills? I remember when I started this trip I'd go at them hell-for-leather in the highest gear possible – standing on the pedals, gripping the handlebars, almost bursting blood vessels in my neck trying to beat the gradient before it beat me. What shall I do here? I'm slowing down now as I come on to the hill. Click down a gear, yes, that's it, much more civilised behaviour. Definitely a more mature cycling technique Steve, well done sir – and again, down another gear! Feet going round like the clappers now, much easier on the knees. Not sure about the testicles though – bit too much rubbing and chafing for my liking!

From the top of the hill I spot Jason about a mile ahead. I descend into another unremarkable Spanish village. Fat, cheery-faced men sit around a bare wooden table in front of a tumbledown café, apparently content to do nothing. I stare at them, marvelling at how long they can sit there and ignore the house right beside them, that has entirely collapsed, or the dead dog that lies scattered in pieces over the road.

We return to the barren, pale colours of Spanish scrub. I smile and cast a wave at a leather-skinned herdsman with his flock. He lifts his stick in reply. It amazes me how his animals can graze enough goodness from this baked earth for any of them to last a month. And yet they've managed here – farmers and their flocks – for God only knows how long, countless generations I suppose.

Bears, Bulls and Billboards
Gavaro, Portugal: 17 August

Jason and I continued cycling together (or more accurately, within a few miles of each other) until we reached Madrid. Our final day together, which I described in my diary as 'The Perfect Day', was a turning point in our relations. Or so it seemed at the time. Now I'm not so sure. When Kenny interviewed Jason on camera the following morning to ask him 'Hoowz it all gooin'?', he replied:

'Yesterday was probably the first time things have really come together for me. Everything seemed to go well. The main reason, I think, is that I decided to get up early and really seize the day...'

Jason continued talking. I eavesdropped from the living room and smiled, remembering it all – how we rose at dawn, rode off in the silvery light, stopped for coffee as the sun broke over the hills. Then there was the two-hour mountain climb up Somosierra, the cool lake and the picnic in the afternoon and finally a beer at a roadside bar as we watched the sunset. We had done all this together and I expected him at some point to refer to my presence. But I wasn't any part of Jason's recollection. Anyone watching Kenny's interview could only assume he had spent the day alone.

Our few days in Madrid gave us some newspaper headlines (but no sponsors) and the opportunity to clean up, do laundry, go to the cinema and eat like civilised people. Kenny and I were the first to become restless. We decided to cycle on ahead. Jason said he'd catch up.

The next few hundred miles of Spanish roads were a fairly uneventful series of moderate, sweaty climbs through the region of Extremadura to the mountains bordering Portugal. I quite enjoyed riding with Kenny, who has a genuine and lifelong passion for cycling. I often had trouble keeping up with him.

And so I was surprised to see Jason's bicycle ahead of us on the morning of our third day out from Madrid. It was leaning against a tree halfway up the mountain road to Puerto de Miravete. We followed a trail through dense bushes and found Jason busily gorging on blackberries like a bear with suspicions of an early winter.

That day, the fifteenth, was Kenny's birthday. We spent the afternoon at a roadside bar in a dreary little town called Jaraicejo. Cheap Spanish beer and a lunch of crisps led inevitably to a wobbly onward journey and shocking headaches by the time we reached Trujillo.

The following morning I opened my sore eyes to a terrifying 'mirror-vision'. Two enormous, blood-streaked eyeballs were staring back at me. Between the two eyes lay a broad reach of black, matted hair and clumps of dried mud that narrowed lower down to a pink, dripping snout the size of my head.

'Heeelp.' I blew the words pathetically from the corner of my mouth, then turned slowly to face the cork tree where I remembered last seeing Kenny laying in his sleeping bag. He was still there, curled up and motionless, like an enormous dewy turd in the grass. The monster snorted and I felt the ground tremble as it thudded across the field. Sitting up, I saw Jason reading a book, still half inside his bag and resting against another cork tree.

'Jesus! It could have... Jesus! How long have you been awake?'

'About half an hour,' he replied coolly and turned the page.

'Why the hell didn't you wake me? There's a fucking enormous bull over there!'

'I know. I was a bit worried about your red sleeping bag at first. I've been keeping quite still and ignoring him... seems to work. Ah, they're pretty docile really. You want some tea?'

We changed our last pesetas for Portuguese escudos at the charming hill town of Valencia, and waited our turn behind a line of farm animals and horses to fill up our water bottles from a spring that gushes into a medieval stone trough.

I fell out with Jason because he had forgotten to bring his passport with him – it was either at a friend's house in London or with his parents, he said – but it didn't seem to matter. We sauntered unchallenged – as we've done upon entering both France and Spain – through to Portugal yesterday, where began a blissful winding descent through the forests of the Tejo valley as far as Castelo de Vide. It was here, among the medieval cobbled streets, rich mosaics and the cool gardens that I fell in love with Portugal.

Today's ride has been even more enchanting and delightful. Beginning with another long descent to Gavaro, we passed through tiny mountain communities. Jason sat watching a shoemaker at work in his medieval workshop, and there were farmers scything wheat in stone-walled fields. We stopped frequently to witness this living, largely pre-industrial community, or to reach for wild figs and grapes that dripped from the hedgerows.

Now in Gavaro, we branch off the main road to find a sheltered lunch site at the river. We each carry a hatful of food – figs, apples, walnuts and grapes scavenged from the wild, plus tomatoes, melons and apricots that have fallen from overloaded trucks.

The sun sets as we cross the mighty, glistening Tejo River at Santarém, where a band of barefooted gypsy children play buccaneers on flimsy rafts. Lisbon is another fifty-five miles south.

It is dark. Tensions rise as we re-enter the dirt, the traffic, the billboards and the ugly greys of another capital city.

At 9.30 p.m. we agree to abandon the increasingly hazardous bid to reach Martin and *Moksha* in Lisbon, settling instead on a roadside wasteland strewn with rubbish and used syringes. I ought to have backed Jason's preference to make camp earlier, in the countryside, but instead went along with Kenny's eagerness to finish. As a result, we endured hours of fear and loathing, night-riding the main shoulder-less road into Lisbon. Car drivers left us in no doubt that the only consequence to them of murdering a cyclist would be to add fractions of a second onto their journey time.

Salazar's Bridge
Lisbon: 31 August

'I still reckon we could swim the Tejo,' says Jason regretfully.
   'Ay, as long you didn'a swallow any of it,' Kenny replies. 'It's wretched. Right, we're droppin' yoo twos off here before

we get to the bridge – human power all the way, remember?' This bridge is as far as we got in Lisbon on our last day of cycling two weeks ago. Since then we have taken good advantage of the hospitality of the Yacht Club in Cascais, twenty miles to the west, in preparing for the Atlantic – antifouling the hull, remedying a stiff and noisy pedal mechanism, installing solar panels, wiring the electrical system and organising all the food into daily ration bags.

'Ah, c'mon!' I implore. 'This is a motorway bridge – no bikes allowed. If we're caught we'll have to cycle fifty miles north to the nearest legal bridge and fifty miles south again to get the other side of this river. It's only a couple of miles across the bridge. Can't we stay in the van till we get to the other side?' Kenny shakes his head and slows the van to a stop on the approach ramp. I jump out and Jason helps me unload my bike first, then his.

It is our first day of cycling in two weeks. Jason and I wobble along the hard shoulder. The van drives away with *Moksha* in tow.

'You heartless bastard!' I shout at the van as it accelerates away.

We begin the long climb onto the April Twenty-Fifth Suspension Bridge. This is a six-lane motorway that spans the mouth of the Tejo River and connects Lisbon to southern Portugal. Formerly the Salazar Bridge, before it was renamed in 1974 to commemorate the overthrow of fifty years of dictatorship, it has recently been the subject of violent demonstrations against the levying of a toll, enacted to recoup the enormous cost of renovation. Several of the drivers, assuming that we are making some kind of political stunt, clench their fists and cheer in solidarity. Many others wave their fists in anger, hurl obscenities and honk their horns.

Virtually no one passes by without expressing one passionate opinion or another – baffling behaviour to any Englishman.

'So what? Get over it!' I yell back. We continue up the ramp. A car brakes to a halt and two men jump out to grab us, but we accelerate past them. Another swerves into Jason's path. This is madness! Why would Portuguese drivers, of all people, suddenly become concerned with safety or highway law? Maybe it's more personal, a national thing, not just about cyclists illegally using the great bridge – symbol of the glorious Revolution of the Carnations – but foreign cyclists to boot! A third driver tries swinging the car door into my path. Jesus! I thought we were crazy!

We progress onto the central span of the bridge and pick up speed. We spot a motorcycle policeman ahead, who has stopped a car and stands cautioning the driver in the shoulder lane. Jason cunningly swerves out into the middle lane – I follow him – hoping to avoid being seen. Fat chance of that with all these drivers tooting their car horns and hanging halfway through their windows, hurling abuse! The policeman turns around, wondering what the pandemonium is all about, and catches sight of us as we pass him.

He leaps onto his motorcycle and in seconds has accelerated past us with all lights flashing. We are directed back to the hard shoulder and wait there, mentally preparing for that time-honoured 'I'm just a dumb tourist, didn't realise officer, honest!' vacant expression.

It's not working. The officer is mad as hell, but it takes him a while to figure out how best to punish us. The only safe option at this point, roughly halfway across the bridge, surely, is to escort us on to the next exit and off the motorway. The problem with that is that the next exit is on the south bank of the river, which is precisely where we want to go. We know that. He knows that. Unfortunately, he knows that we know that, which is why he opts for the most dangerous and disruptive manoeuvre imaginable – just to deny us the satisfaction.

One by one, he orders all three southbound lanes of traffic to stop moving. The enormous motorcade, involving hundreds of cars and trucks, comes to a halt. He crosses the central divide and repeats the process, halting all three lanes of northbound traffic. He motions for us to come forward, braving a crescendo of horns and screaming insults, before escorting us northwards and finally back down the long ramp to the first exit leading back to Lisbon.

No words are spoken. The policeman merely points a leather-gloved hand to the exit lane and he speeds triumphantly away in a volley of gear changes.

We watch him accelerate into the distance. 'We were so close,' I complain bitterly to Jason. He shakes his head and turns his bicycle around.

'Fuck this. Let's go,' he says calmly. He begins cycling back up the ramp, now heading south on the northbound shoulder of the motorway bridge.

'Oh Christ!' I find myself following him.

My heart pounds as I race up the ramp to the central span once more, this time facing oncoming traffic and a much narrower verge. Vehicles hurtle past my right shoulder. The drivers are more determined than ever to stop the infidels. Jason takes many by surprise, but they are ready for me with their doors and fists, which I relentlessly dodge and duck while trying to keep my balance. Over my left shoulder I can see the Tejo estuary glistening several hundred feet below. There is no option but to push on. I fall gradually further and further behind Jason. There seems to be no end in sight to the assault course and the tirade of abuse.

At last! I accelerate down the ramp at the southern end. There is no sign of Jason. He must already have cleared the bridge, but in doing so has activated a small army of policemen now scurrying to create a human net to catch me.

There is no hope of escape. I come to a stop in front of long line of purple-faced officers, four of whom frogmarch me into a building.

'Passport!'

'Sorry, I haven't got it with me,' I lie.

'This is very serious offence. It will cost you 7,000 escudos!'

'Well I'm terribly sorry, but I only have 500 escudos left. Isn't this the road to the Algarve? I didn't know...'

'You not go anywhere. 7,000 escudos, or you stay here!'

'Fine. I'll stay here then. But tomorrow I'll still have 500 escudos.'

After a long, pointless argument they set me free. I thank them for their leniency and cycle on for several miles in search of Jason.

'Pshht! Oi, Steve!'

I screech to a halt and, turning around, I see Jason crawling out of a hedge with a big smile on his face and an enormous cheese sandwich in one hand.

'What a rush, man! Ha-haaa! Did they catch you?'

'Yes, but they let me go. You crazy son of a bitch! That was great, though!'

'Yep, haven't felt this alive in a long time,' he declares, muttering through his mouthful.

Lagos
Algarve coast: 29 September

I sit cross-legged in *Moksha*'s cramped fore-cabin, hunched over a bundle of canvas that must be stitched into the shape of a narrow, tapering bunk. The sun's withering heat blisters

Moksha's deck paint where she stands displayed on the quay. The cabin is becoming unbearably hot to work in, but at least it is a quiet, dull place in which to suffer a hangover.

It is hard to believe we've been in Lagos for a month. The plan was to depart by mid-September, after which the weather rapidly becomes less reliable, but we seriously underestimated the amount of preparation required for the ocean voyage. Our choice of departure place doesn't make matters any easier. Lagos in September is a hotbed of fun and iniquity and very hard to leave. The prospect of pedalling out into the Atlantic, from which I might never return, adds an urgency and intensity to the many parties, pub-crawls and beach activities. I seem to have settled on the dubious reasoning that unless I appreciate now what it means to surrender completely to temptation, I might never get another chance.

I hear footsteps approaching the boat.

'Ah Papa, a boat! Can I go in?' A young girl's voice echoes through the hull.

'No dear, that's not a boat. That's just a model of a boat so you know what a boat looks like. Come on!'

I wipe the sweat dripping from my forehead and continue sewing. Another voice approaches.

'Look 'ere Bill. Says it's a pedal boat. What's it doing out of the water? Oh, ay! Says it's going across the Atlantic Ocean, Bill. Four and a half thousand miles... look Bill... around the world by human power... they're English lads 'n'all.' There is silence. 'Hey Bill, you can get your name writ on the boat for – '

'Rita! You listen to me. If you put any money in that box, you'll be pedallin' back to England.' The footsteps fade in the direction of the bar, Maia Lua.

I clamber out from the forward compartment, stand in *Moksha*'s open hatchway and enjoy a cooling breeze. Rows of sailing yachts gently rock and chime out in the marina.

Beneath me, leaning up against *Moksha*'s wooden support cradle, is a large display board illustrating our purpose and route around the world. Alongside it is a large white ammunition box chained to *Moksha*'s rudder on which 'Donations Welcome' is painted in bright red lettering.

'The cunt box must be losing its magic,' I whisper to myself.

The cunt box was a ludicrous experiment inspired by Colin Wilson's book, *Occult*, concerning the history of magic. After drilling a slit into the top of the ammunition box, I surrounded this hole with concentric circles of bright colours while focusing with great intensity upon the image of a psychedelic vagina – the magical theory being, of course, that a good proportion of passers-by (straight men and lesbians, presumably) would be overcome with an irresistible urge to penetrate the hole with hard cash, with the subliminal promise of sex. Jason and I have been surviving on the proceeds of the cunt box ever since. As daft as it would seem to give the enchanted slit any credit for this considerable sum, I fail to see the harm in trying. It is, after all, only a slightly more direct version of most commercial advertising.

I jump down onto the quayside and pull *Moksha*'s hatchway shut. I unlock the ammunition box, pick out the coins and drop them into my pocket. I begin walking along the cool, cobbled labyrinth of streets back to the apartment, stopping at the vegetable market in the town centre. Continuing on, I pass the stone square that was the slave market. As I look around, noticing the gaily-painted fishing boats jostling on the quay and the relaxed smiles of tourists, it defies belief that this place was, not so many generations before, filled with manacled, terrified, bleeding and diseased Africans bound for New World plantations.

At the apartment, Jason is slouched on the sofa reading. There is no sign of my father, who has come to Portugal to see us off.

'Where's Stu?' I ask, unloading the shopping onto the kitchen table.

'He's gone to the pharmacy for diarrhoea tablets – dodgy kebab last night.' Just as Jason finishes his sentence, Stuart bursts in, laughing. With him, instead of medicine, he brings a box of lime tea (an excellent substitute for tobacco in joints) and two German girls 'to meet the guys who're gonna do it' (Stu's favourite line). I sense the demise of yet another day's good intentions.

'By the way, Jas,' I tell him, reaching into my pocket and counting a handful of small coins. 'The cunt box is losing its magic.'

'Oh. We'd better be on our way then.'

Ready To Go
Lagos: 12 October

The cool marble of the marina office floor feels soothing on my bare feet as I stare at the posted weather-fax. At last, a stable zone of high pressure has arrived to break a fortnight of erratic, stormy weather.

Since the arrival of the autumn gales our departure has been repeatedly postponed, much to the disappointment of family and friends who couldn't extend their visits any longer. There has been no decent window of good weather, essential to avoid the danger and embarrassment of being blown straight back to Portugal or washed up on the coast of North Africa. The pressure to take a risk in order to satisfy everyone's desire to wave us goodbye was intense, just as the famous ocean rower, Peter Bird, had warned us months ago in London. 'Pressure will come from all sides,' he said. 'But for God's sake ignore it. Leave when you are absolutely ready. It's your lives at stake and there's no going back.'

I stare out at the fishermen unloading the morning catch. Are we ready now? We thought we were ready last week, before a lucky encounter with a visiting yachtsman who asked whether we had remembered to oil the gas canisters for the cooking stove. Oil the gas canisters! Whatever for? Because otherwise the salt air, apparently, would corrode through the thin metal cylinders. *Moksha* would have become a ticking time bomb ready for the spark that would blow us sky high. Another chance conversation with a Portuguese fisherman revealed a second critical omission – *Moksha* had no zinc anodes to combat electrolytic corrosion, which is a problem that affects the weakest metal in a circuit of different metals exposed to seawater. Boat owners protect the useful metal parts of their vessel – propeller shaft, propeller, engine and fastenings – by attaching a sacrificial lump of zinc, which is the weakest of all metals, and replace it regularly as it dissolves away. I'd never heard of a zinc anode. But without them, *Moksha*'s aluminium propeller, the only one we have, would dissolve to nothing in a few months. Considering the years of preparation that have brought us to this point, it is unnerving to say the least that it might all have ended disastrously for want of a cupful of oil or a golf-ball-sized chunk of cheap metal. What else have we overlooked?

Jason and Kenny enter the marina office. Like me, six weeks of hard work and harder play in Lagos has left Jason with a visibly less healthy aspect than when he arrived. But Jason carries an added burden, a souvenir of love from a Brazilian waitress that penicillin injections have yet to cure. Kenny, anticipating a decision of some import, has already begun filming as I greet Jason.

'Morning Jas. You ready to go?'

'Yeah. And finally able to go, thank God!' I give him a blank stare.

'To the loo!' he explains, theatrically.

'Oh, the old wazzoo! Yes, of course. Well, that's good. Tomorrow it is then.'

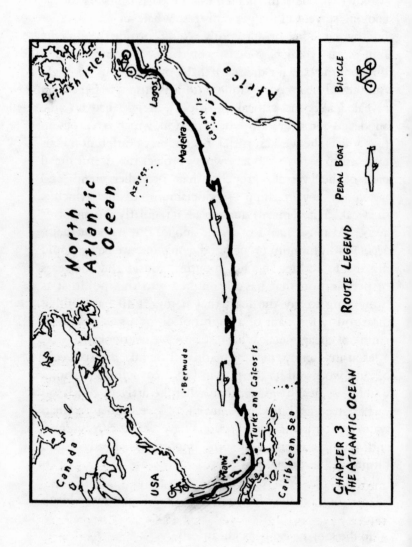

North Atlantic Ocean

British Isles

Africa

Lagos

Madeira

Azores

Canary Is

Bermuda

Canada

USA

Miami

Turks and Caicos Is

Caribbean Sea

CHAPTER 3
THE ATLANTIC OCEAN

ROUTE LEGEND   PEDAL BOAT   BICYCLE

3. The Atlantic Ocean
(October 1994 – February 1995)

Weird New World
Lagos: 13 October

9.30 a.m.: *Moksha* glides underneath the footbridge and past the marina, heading for open sea. A small crowd is gathered upon the bridge, looking down.

Someone shouts down, 'They're finally leaving!' I vaguely recognise him – a security guard at the harbour. His emphatic glee is a bit discomforting. Others clap and cheer, though some (perhaps holidaymakers, newly arrived) with a bemused look who aren't too sure what or for whom they are cheering. One of the many bearded and big-hearted, semi-alcoholic sailors in town trots awkwardly along the quay, waving and shouting something inaudible. Jason pedals and steers us around the pier. We enter the swelling, vast ocean.

Woo baby, trip... ping! I've enough nervous energy to send me to the moon. The sandstone cliffs are a luminous orange from the morning sun. Seagulls swarm above a fishing trawler returning to port. Its bow wave pummels into *Moksha*'s side and I have to steady myself as we pitch and roll violently in its wake. The former rhythms of wave and swell soon return.

I take over at the pedals after two hours and Jason mumbles a few undecipherable words through pale, dry lips – about not feeling well, perhaps – before disappearing into the sleeping compartment to get some sleep. Neither of us slept last night. We were drinking Jägermeister on the beach with Stuart and our Lagos friends until dawn. I spent a long time looking up at the sky, trying to find auspicious signs in patterns of clouds and, as the sun rose, many things came to mind that needed doing – packing spare batteries, posting things back home, rearranging stores – before we could leave.

About an hour later I feel like I've had enough of the Atlantic. I just want to be still, to relax without my whole body being thrashed around from one side of the boat to the other. My neck is sore from the effort of keeping my head upright. My knees are burning and my back aches. I feel sick and so tired that I have to keep slapping my face to stay awake, keep pedalling, keep an eye on the horizon for ships. Maybe it would help to make myself a hot brew. I lean forward, step over the pedals and almost fall onto the passenger seat as another wave tips me off balance. I look behind me to make sure I didn't wake Jason. He's flat out in his sleeping bag.

Disorganised heaps of equipment and provisions, thrown in at the last minute, are piled around me: string bags bulging with onions, carrots, cabbage and garlic and plastic shopping bags of stone fruit, apples and figs; planted among them are rolls of naval charts, bits of clothing, pots, pans and cooking utensils. Using one hand simply to hang on, I use the other hand to worm down through dense layers of stores for a pack of dry biscuits and some tea bags. Now where did I put the kettle? It's big and blue and somewhere within arms' reach. I find it under a bag of plastic clothes' pegs.

I wedge the kettle into place on the stove and unscrew the cap off the nearest freshwater tank. I then grub around for the long, plastic pipette with which to squeeze water from the tank into the kettle. Find the spark gun, turn on the gas, light the stove, find a cup; add a tea bag and powdered milk. After twenty minutes of preparation I am finally poised, biscuit in mouth, to enjoy a nice cup of tea. I carefully pour the boiling water from the kettle into the cup, which is clamped tightly between my feet on the floor. A few splashes scold my ankle. I twist round to reach for the tub of sugar. A wave crashes into the starboard side. It knocks me off balance and the cup spills over. I watch the brown liquid sloshing back and forth across the wooden floor and realise that I'm going to be sick.

I quickly stand and lean over the side, almost bent double, allowing my guts to erupt spasmodically into the ocean. No wonder we refused to do sea trials, I think to myself, groaning, staring at the sea through bulging, bloodshot eyes. It would have shattered the necessary illusions.

We cross the shipping lanes about twenty miles out from Lagos. Having just finished my pedal shift, I sit outside straddling *Moksha*'s stern deck, which tips and rolls like a rodeo machine, gripping it firmly in my thighs. Inside Jason pedals. Other than a few brief words at changeover times, and once to pass a packet of dry biscuits, we haven't felt like talking. Kenny has come aboard from the escort vessel to film our farewells. He stands in the open hatchway and points his camera at me.

'Ach, c'mon Steve,' Kenny implores. 'Gimme some emorshun! Hoo're ya feelin'?'

'I can't think of anything more to say really mate.' I'm lost for words, dog-tired and emotionally shut down. 'We've talked about this for long enough. Can't say any more... just have to do it.'

The escorting vessel *Petronella* comes alongside to retrieve Kenny before returning to Lagos. Jason and I stand and wave goodbye. My father stands waving back and wiping his eyes. I swallow the lump in my throat and suddenly feel very scared and alone. *Petronella* turns and slowly vanishes into the dim horizon, back to the familiar, safe, comfortable land. We are left in a strange expanse of shifting blues and whites.

As the daylight fades the thought suddenly occurs to me – there's no going back. The effect it has on me is unexpected: I sense enormous relief because there's no need to be brave any more. It's like parachuting: you need courage before, and only before the jump, while there's the freedom not to jump, the opportunity to be a coward. There are no such choices now, thank heavens! There is only this seemingly infinite expanse: 4,250 nautical miles of ocean to pedal across at walking speed.

Colours fade to shades of grey and finally, but for the silvery flecks of surf on breaking waves, there is only blackness. I start to feel claustrophobic. Jason turns on the cabin light to hunt for a sachet of powdered orange drink. Now I can't see anything outside, only the inside of the central cabin with its overflowing storage lockers. The side-netting on the walls is stuffed with books, charts and waterproof clothing; beads of condensation start running down the insides of windows; the rope straps for opening and closing the sliding hatch hang down from it and appear to swing from side to side – though it is everything but these that actually moves.

'This is real, isn't it?' I find it all too strange for useful adjectives.

'Very,' Jason replies and yawns, wiping one eye.

'Guess what?

'I can't. What?'

'You're never going to believe this, but... I've never spent a night at sea before in my life.'

'No, neither have I.'

Strange, I thought he had. I remember him once telling me of a father-son 'bonding' weekend of sailing when he was a boy. It had rained continually, Jason was seasick and freezing and, after the sail jammed and the engine wouldn't start, he'd been forced to leap onto a navigation buoy with a rope tied to his waist to stop them drifting onto rocks. He'd sworn never to go near the sea again. But perhaps they'd only sailed during the day.

Our first morning alone at sea brings an exquisite surprise: the deep ocean is blue! Not the tame coastal colour I've always known but a completely different, magnificently rich cobalt blue. Long shafts of sunlight dance into the depths and I'd guess that you can see quite far down, twenty or thirty feet perhaps, and every inch of it this astonishing, sparkling translucent blue. I had no idea there was such a striking difference in colour between the shallows and the deep.

I stand in the open hatchway, leaning over, and scoop up a cupped handful of the new blue to wash my face. Jason stirs, wakes and pulls himself – his hairy, mottled-brown shoulders appearing first as he heaves and grunts – out of the sleeping compartment. His legs are last out. He raises his bent knees up towards his chin, swivels round on his backside to face the main cabin (with some difficulty, as the area around him remains a chaotic mess of supplies) and plants his feet on the wet floor. Despite five hours of sleep his face looks haggard, his skin blotchy, pale, puffed and sagging, with dark smears under his eyes.

'Morning. How did you sleep?'

'Great.' He inhales, sniffing the cool salt air, and sighs heavily. 'I feel better.' He sounds surprised. 'It's nice to get away from that God-awful town, all those people I hardly know getting emotional, wishing us well.' He chuckles to himself. 'No, I didn't mean that, I'm sure they meant well, happy to see us off, well, to see the back of us maybe.' He chuckles again. 'I don't know, it was all very strange.'

'Yesterday was weird, eh?'

'Yeah, like a dream,' he continues. 'It all happened in slow motion.' He grabs a handrail and pulls himself upright to stand next to me, looking out to sea. 'This is pretty cool though, you know, like a very big swimming pool you can jump into and not worry about hitting the bottom.' He scratches his belly and surveys our new world with lordly satisfaction. 'Hmmh, it's like a big blue jelly isn't it, oozing about. Mind you, get a bit of wind on her, though,' he emits a flapping trumpet noise from his lips to emphasise the point, 'I s'pose that'll be a whole different story.'

It is odd that we've never really discussed what we think the ocean will be like. I guess it's a man-thing. We've decided to do this and prepared well for it; we are bound to find out for ourselves soon enough, therefore what's the point? Any speculation would be somehow disenchanting, spoiling the mystery and our childlike thrill of entering the great unknown.

Now into our third day and I remain quite nauseous, Jason too. He wears these funny-looking, lurid yellow anti-sickness bracelets on both wrists, a last-minute package posted to him by his mother, though he claims they don't work. I sit at the pedal seat, lolling from side to side in the swell, trying to balance an army-issue aluminium plate of food on my lap. The smell of the boil-in-the-bag bacon and beans alone is enough to make my eyes roll in disgust. I relax my neck for a moment, let my head rest against the cool plastic window on the port side and try to find a stable horizon, but my eye-line is too close to the ocean to see above the shifting ridges of waves silhouetted against the sky. Sunlight ricochets off one glistening peak and catches my eye. I squint and pull my head upright again. Back to the food. I keep my eyes closed and muster all my strength of will to take a mouthful and keep it down.

Later, Jason stands up in the open hatchway, throws most of our lunch into the sea and begins the washing-up. The boat tips – keeping my body pinned against one side of the pedal seat – as he leans over to rinse the pot and scour the plates and spoons, one at a time, with a new green kitchen pad. He grunts and puffs a lot while doing this, especially when waves slide under the boat and make it roll, since much of his body weight is pressed onto his stomach. I look ahead at the compass and continue pedalling south-west. In a few minutes I begin to feel better and push the pedals harder, counting two revolutions for every exhalation of breath.

An hour passes quickly. Jason must be feeling better now, since he has the presence of mind to look for something to do. He fidgets around on the passenger seat and eventually reaches back into the sleeping area to grab the film camera. Now that Kenny isn't around, Jason has assumed control of the camera and film stock. He checks the battery level and plugs a spare battery into its charger, making sure that the coiled lead is firmly plugged into the cigarette-lighter socket in the wall beside him. Then he checks the voltmeter and a switch on the control panel.

'Good,' he says. 'The solar panels seem to be keeping up with demand.'

Jason loves the gadgetry, the special attachments for things, the fighter-jet life-jackets with their pockets for mini-gun flares, the knives that strap on: he has that eternal schoolboy's appetite for practical gear – particularly anything that might lead to daredevil exploits – and a meticulous attention to detail. He might have enjoyed being a soldier. His father, a retired colonel, certainly thought so. But he hated following orders, especially stupid ones (Jason thought that applied to most of them) and the details of how his brief military career came to an end remain vague.

Jason leans forward with the video camera over the pedal system and holds himself upright with one hand on the emergency oars. 'Shaay shomething t' the cameraah, Steeeeyve.' He speaks like the witch from *The Wizard of Oz*. 'A pearl of wisdom maybe, my pretty?' I smile briefly then pretend to be sourly unamused.

'Don't you think this sort of commentary is going to make the tape absolutely worthless?' I look away from the camera and lift a book from the side-netting. *Moksha* steers a fairly straight course by herself, allowing me to let go of the steering toggles for much of the time and leaving my hands free to read while I pedal.

'But of course it will!' His impression is now of 'Mr Chips', the Victorian schoolteacher. 'But it keeps us sane, old boy.'

'A bit too late for that now, wouldn't you say, old boy.'

Jason sniggers mischievously and points the camera at my groin. 'Mmh, serious film-making now, let's do a close-up on those, err, bacon and beans.' The mere mention of lunch recreates a sickening image that turns my stomach.

The human mind is infinitely adaptable. Already, on only our third day at sea, this strange, wet world of constant motion is fast becoming normality. The former, stable world – where one may sit comfortably or eat without having to hold one's dinner plate – is becoming the absurd dream. I can barely recall what it was like to be still, to be silent and motionless on the solid earth, to sit among trees and hills where only the birds moved occasionally across the view.

We have established a round-the-clock pedalling routine, swapping over every two hours in the daytime and every four hours at night. It is a harsh rota but we can't see a way around it, there being only one bed to sleep in while the other pedals and keeps a lookout for ships. There have been several ships today, though not close by, passing in grim silence across the horizon. I sometimes slip into morbid fantasy, a horrifying collision – the crashing roar of its bow wave as it approached, the smashing and splintering of wood, raking and tumbling along its towering metal sides as it ploughed past, and the thunderous beat of its massive propeller – and at that point I always scurry back to reality and extra vigilance.

I land the 'graveyard shift' from midnight till 4.00 a.m. The wind has freshened to a force five and the ocean regularly spits white, foaming globs of seawater through the open hatchway. I scan the horizon for ships when *Moksha* rises to the height of the swell and wait for the next glimpse as we descend into the troughs. I have counted five ships so far, mostly heading west. The last one passed within a mile of us.

At least I think it was west. The compass light is broken – the only light we didn't think to buy spare bulbs for. On the first night we tried, at minute intervals, holding a flashlight with one hand and a pocket compass with the other to maintain a vaguely south-west heading, which was very irritating. For the last two nights I have been using the stars. Provided that Orion's Belt remains in the left-hand corner of *Moksha*'s overhead ventilation hatch, then we are heading south-west... ish. Jason has a similarly vague arrangement with the moon.

I begin fiddling with the radio, scanning the short wave channels. After a long period of crackling static I find Radio Austria: an earnest discussion of the brown bear population. No thanks. More static, then Voice of America: an evangelical game show.

'All riiight! Now blue team, your chance for a five-point lead: how many baskets of leftover food were collected after feeding the five thousand on the shores of Galilee?'

'Fifteen.'

'No, the answer is twelve. Red team, here's an easy one: the sister of Lazarus...'

It is our fourth morning at sea. Jason stands in the open hatchway with the hand-pumped water-maker, singing sea shanties loudly into the wind.

'When I was a little lad o' so me mother told me; way, haul away, we'll haul away, Joe; that if I didn' kiss the girls me lips would grow all mouldy; way, haul away, we'll haul dee-dee, dee – '

His voice is strong and resonant. I sometimes wonder whether he would have made it in the music business if he hadn't left his band to do this. He certainly had the talent and determination to stake his claim to fame, and he had the dark, lank-haired, smouldering rock star look, not to mention the petulant TV-through-the-hotel-window attitude. I used to go and listen to them, Psi Jamma, playing at The Mean Fiddler and other venues around London. They did some gigs on the continent as well, in Holland and Germany. I enjoyed it. His music was the sort of high energy, coarse grunge music now all the rage in Europe and America with the likes of Nirvana and The Smashing Pumpkins.

Jason finishes with the water pump, unlashes it carefully from the emergency oars and stows the unit with its long lengths of plastic hosing back into the storage locker beneath him. In one hour he has managed to produce almost a gallon of fresh water from seawater, roughly the amount we consume each day for cooking and drinking.

It sounded good to hear someone's voice. The radio is comforting but less personal. We say very little to each other beyond the occasional necessary questions, commands or platitudes: 'You awake?', 'Keep on this heading' and 'Is that my dinner? Thanks,' pretty much covers it. It's not that we have fallen out, but that there's nothing eventful enough worth talking about. Pedalling in two- and four-hour shifts around the clock is very tiring; all the other chores – navigating, greasing the pedal system, keeping clean, making food and water and so on – are tiring; simply keeping awake and upright on a rocking boat is tiring. Life in this bouncing bubble is sending us inside ourselves through boredom and fatigue and we are slowly drifting into parallel universes. The other person is still there but for most of the time I don't need him, I've nothing to say to him, and he ceases to exist until changeover time. I speak at mealtimes to feed us or be fed, and speak again in the cold early hours at the end of my pedal shift, when his sorry arse exists sound asleep in the bunk and is required to relocate to the pedal seat at its very earliest convenience.

My two-hour pedal shift is over at 10.00 a.m. and we change places. This is always a clumsy and painful ceremony in a small, narrow boat with no room to pass or stand except at the open hatchway. 1) Jason nods for the changeover ritual to commence; 2) I clamber forward from the pedal seat and clasp the emergency oars lashed on both sides of the cabin and used for handrails; 3) I ease myself up into the standing room of the open hatchway where Jason is already waiting.

During this process, one revolving pedal invariably claws down the length of my shinbone; the other digs into the opposing calf muscle, and my head bangs the cabin roof as a wave connects with the side of the boat. Jason's head, calf and shinbone receive exactly the same treatment in reverse until we find ourselves, once again, facing each other across the central cabin.

It is not over yet. Jason's cushion-placing ritual then commences to correct for our differences in height and length of leg. Next, he grubs under the canvas compartment cover for a book to read or an audiotape for the Walkman. Finally, the whirring of pedals and chain recommences.

Now safely onto the passenger seat, I brace myself with one hand and stir a pot of army-issue porridge with the other. Porridge, supplemented with nuts and raisins, is the meal we most look forward to, partly because it has suffered the least deterioration among our rations in the five years since Her Majesty's Army labelled them all out-of-date and inedible.

I hand Jason his bowl of steaming muck, careful to serve him what appears to be the slightly larger portion, as he does with me. We are each expending over eight thousand calories per day, which is three to four times the normal rate. I estimate that most of this is spent on the continual muscular contractions involved in simply trying to maintain balance. In this situation, in which hunger is a constant companion, the careful division of food into equal portions is very important. This sounds insanely petty, even amusing, but prolonged stress and hunger (I read this in other accounts of long and difficult sea voyages) seem to have a way, slowly and unconsciously, of reducing good-natured, civilised men to selfish and untrusting beasts, which is why we are paying unnatural attention to details as insignificant as a spoonful of porridge.

I suppose I ought to practice navigating with the sextant and attempt a midday sun-sight. If, God forbid, our GPS fails, the sextant is our back-up navigational aid. I wrestle the grey case from its storage locker and take out the peculiar-looking device that cost £25 at a second-hand sale in Greenwich. Taking the sextant in both hands I stand, leaning hard against the open hatch to steady my aim and peer through the eyepiece. The sun appears to swing back and forward across the sky like a demented UFO. Momentarily I have it, bang on the horizon.

'Mark!' I shout to Jason, who notes the exact time – 11.45 a.m. plus 15 seconds.

I take a second sun-sight at 12.15 p.m. Using the two sextant angles and times I begin to calculate our latitude and longitude.

'Right. I reckon we are thirty-five degrees fifteen minutes north, eleven degrees thirteen minutes west,' I declare boldly. Jason presses a button on the GPS.

'You're less than ten miles off, old boy. Not bad for a first effort.' He chuckles and dips his head back to his book. I feel proud and relieved, though also a bit foolish for having put it off for so long. I attended astro-navigation classes last year in London and came away, having never used a sextant in anger, with my name on a certificate but only a sketchy recollection of how it was won. It was my recent good fortune to meet a crafty old salt in Lagos, who explained a simple method requiring only a watch, a sextant and the sun and in six minutes had passed on more useful skill than a blustering, gin-perspiring ex-commodore in Hammersmith had managed in six months.

Tiny crosses in pencil, each less than a pencil's width apart, mark our daily progress across a chart of the Atlantic Ocean that is almost as wide as our boat – or would be if we could unfold it. On average we travel forty miles a day, a very respectable distance when taking into account unforeseen delays. Last night, for instance, we passed close by a stationary oil tanker, which promptly dispatched a rescue boat with a Filipino crew who spoke no English. They arrived at high speed with triumphant smiles and we proceeded to shout at each other across the muddled waters for quite some time. For every word and hand-gesture we could think of to say 'Thanks very much chaps, but we don't want to be rescued. We're here on purpose,' our increasingly anxious mariners had another phrase and hand-gesture that said, 'What are you waiting for you fools? You're saved!' Eventually they gave up on us and sped back to the mother ship, flourishing final waves and expressions employed similarly the world over to politely dismiss the insane.

Our fifth day at sea and the wind has freshened to a north-westerly force six, whipping the sea up into patterns of ragged, spitting spines. But still we manage a forty-mile day. Knees and thighs are starting to really ache as we continue to push a tonne of boat through the water with the power of two legs, stopping only to swap duties. Everything is damp – the air, our clothes, the 'rat-hole' sleeping compartment. The first sensation as I wake is my burning, swollen knees. I dip them into the cooling ocean before each pedal shift.

The wind strengthens and another curtain of rain drags across our blue-white world. Normally the hatch stays wide open for ventilation, even when it rains or when a choppy sea sends torpedo-like waves that burst against the hull and throw a bucketful into the cabin. But now I slide the hatch shut with both hands.

It is strangely reassuring to be enclosed in this box. It takes me back to the caravan in Wales where I spent my summer holidays as a child. When it rained we, my sister and brother and I, would play cards or layout board games and jigsaw puzzles on a foldout table, and giggle with wide-eyed excitement if the rain drummed really hard on the roof. Our mother would light the gas fire and bring mugs of hot chocolate as we sat in a circle with the other kids from the site, arguing what to run out and play next – rounders, tag, cricket, bulldog, mini-marathon, desert island (in the sandpit) – whenever the rain stopped. There was something special about being all together, safe 'in here' and not 'out there', holed up like a family of badgers in a set and mesmerised at the patterns and rivulets of rain on a windowpane.

My brother died of meningitis when he was four years old. I was eight and my sister almost ten. No family fully recovers from losing a child but looking back on it I'm surprised how well we coped. Children adjust more quickly, don't they, or at least appear to. My parents were devastated, particularly my mother, who for a long time struggled to function, let alone smile. I'm wondering if that helps explain why I'm more cautious than Jason, not because I value my own life any more but because I'm more sensitive to the scale of grieving that our deaths would cause. I like the hatch more closed than open in really bad weather because *Moksha* is supposed to self-right after capsizing only if the hatch is shut. Jason wants the hatch always to remain wide open. Otherwise, he says, it gets a bit too stuffy.

After several days of strong north-westerlies the wind has backed to southerly and increased to force seven, much stronger than we can pedal against. In order to arrest our backward drift and keep perpendicular to the waves we deploy our improvised drogue or sea anchor – two bald tyres from the DHL van tied to a hundred metre-long length of rope. We couldn't afford a proper sea anchor, which looks like a small parachute, but anything that creates drag will apparently do.

Midday: a large cargo vessel passes within half a mile. Our sea anchor is still deployed and the thin recovery-line is wrapped around the propeller, leaving us immobile and vulnerable.

'I think the wind has dropped. Maybe we should get going,' Jason suggests between sips of rehydrated soup.

He stands watching the rise and collapse of several large, white-crested waves and his face brightens with the prospect of diving headlong, knife-between-teeth, into the ocean to untangle the propeller. The excitement infects me also. After a week of monotonous confinement any novelty, particularly the dangerous kind, demands to be taken advantage of. In the absence of money I think of alternative ways to toss a coin for the privilege.

'How about...'

'Right, I'll need to get harnessed up then.' Jason is not prepared to risk losing this chance.

'The name'ssh Bond, Jashon Bond,' he purrs in his best Sean Connery and jumps over the side.

The mission is accomplished in seconds, simply a matter of pulling the recovery-line off the propeller. Jason clambers back on board. The ocean is still numbingly cold at this latitude, even for Jason Bond. He takes the first pedal shift to warm up.

I take the logbook from the side-netting near the compass and begin to write in it. 'Your heroism will be duly noted in dispatches to Lewis family HQ.' To carry on the joke I add, 'And if you're lucky, my friend, your folks might even see fit to reinstate your picture in the family album, instead of that picture of what's-his-name, England rugby captain, Will Carling.' We laugh in unison.

'Questions is,' Jason sniggers, 'what heroism are you going to have to perform before your mom is willing to replace that picture of Sting on her mantelpiece?'

'Nothing Jason: it can stay where it is – picked that one myself.' More laughter.

It is the tenth day of our voyage and the storm system has passed, leaving only a heavy, rhythmic swell on an otherwise smooth ocean. Marshmallow clouds drift past in blue skies. We carry on with our pedalling-eating-sleeping routine.

Last night's pedalling shift was other-worldly. It felt as though the ocean was leading us by the hand in a delightful waltz. Instead of the usual violent pitching and rolling we were smoothly cradled and swung from one wave to the next, accompanied by gentle gurgling and slapping sounds that echoed through the hull. Just after 3.00 a.m. a black, oily fin broke the surface. I scrambled from the pedal seat and stood in the open hatchway as a small pod of dolphins encircled us. I stood there long after they were gone.

We rolled gently over an undulating swell in the darkness while I consulted a book of stars by moonlight and gazed up at the vivid canopy above me. There was Orion the Hunter and Sirius his hunting dog, close to heel and rising in the east. The smaller Dog Star, Procyon, was the next brightest, followed by the Twins, Castor and Pollux. I knew almost nothing at all about the constellations before this voyage. My father gave me a book on the subject before we left, with maps of the heavens and the name of each star written alongside it. I try to learn a little more every night during my graveyard shift.

With our four-hourly watches I am witnessing, for the first time in my life, all stages in the daily transits of sun, moon, planets and stars. This is of interest in itself in helping to envision through direct experience how the universe works, what moves and spins and orbits, but also stirs within me a sense of the infinite. I am not humbled by my own insignificance, as some people profess to be in similar situations, It just makes me feel glad to be alive, to be a witness and no more or less a part of the cosmic miracle than anything else.

I'm having a really hard time coming to terms with a sudden decision to make landfall at Funchal, on the island of Madeira, just as I've finally begun to accept and adapt to a life at sea. Jason was filming out on deck this morning when a wave broke over him and soaked the camera, which is now beyond our basic skills to repair. Neither of us wants to break up our journey now or risk wrecking our boat on the coast of Madeira, but we have no choice. Madeira is the only island within reach on this side of the Atlantic and therefore our only hope for fixing the camera. All the time and effort that Kenny has invested in the project will be for nothing without ocean footage.

We alter course to due west, relying on the Portuguese Current and a northerly wind to take us south-west to Madeira. If this weather holds we should arrive at the island in three days, after 14 days of pedalling.

Funchal is about 500 miles from Lagos. Miami, Florida, our destination, is 3,750 miles beyond that. If we continue our current speed of about 40 miles per day this should take another 94 days of pedalling. I'd be surprised if we can keep up this pace for that length of time though, pedalling around-the-clock and sleeping only four hours at a stretch.

The first objective after Madeira is to keep pedalling south-west until we hit the trade winds, which is a reliable belt of winds blowing south-west towards the Caribbean. Sailors tend to steer as far south as the Cape Verde Islands (latitude 15°N) – to ensure they are deep inside this belt – before heading west. The difficulty for us is that it's much harder for a pedal boat to avoid being blown too far south by these winds, and every unnecessary mile south has to be clawed back with muscle power and sweat. The winds down at 15°N may be more consistent but the United States – which we must reach in order to cycle across the continent to the Pacific – is all the way up at latitude 26°N. Taking the sailing route would add a month or more to the voyage and run the constant risk of a storm wrecking us on a Caribbean shore as we made our way back up north to mainland USA. The best solution for us might therefore be to enter the trade winds (latitude 25°N) as far across the ocean as possible and try to stay high – above latitude 20°N – the whole way across.

This strategy also has its risks. Sailboat skippers steer well down into the trade-wind belt because they know how fickle and contrary it can be at its northern edge. In flirting at these margins, in order to maintain latitude and save time later, we could get caught in cyclonic westerlies and blown all the way back to North Africa.

It is 4.30 a.m. and the climax of a three-day battle against strong headwinds. The hardest thing is that the great volcanic dome of Madeira has been clearly visible, right in front of us, for two whole days. But, even pedalling flat out and around-the-clock, we couldn't make that damn rock on the horizon look any bigger. I hope Kenny appreciates the lengths we'll go to find a bloody camera repair shop!

Large rumbling waves rebound off the island and collide with others still rolling in, creating an angry confusion of steep-sided beasts that writhe and silhouette their spitting fury on the night sky before battering into *Moksha*'s side. For a second all I see is the starry night sky, and the next is a close-up of the sucking depths at the base of another passing wave. I pedal on past the point of exhaustion, willing on my aching thighs. Half an hour to go before Jason's shift. Several inches of seawater slosh about on the cabin floor. At least we are making some headway, now close to the southern tip of the island.

The change happens quickly: we're in a tumult of waves and wind and spray; a few minutes later we're safely in the lee of Madeira, the wind has gone, and I'm pedalling in a relatively placid world of rounded swells. I am dizzy, breathless and finding it hard to focus, as though I had staggered over the finishing line of a marathon race and promptly run into a lamp-post.

I wake Jason for his shift and we make the changeover. I am tired beyond description and aching for sleep, but stand for a few moments in the open hatchway as we pedal gently towards the lights of Funchal in a blue dawn.

Four hours later I am woken again for my shift. The morning is bright and sparkling. The coastline of Madeira gradually envelops us as we creep towards Funchal, now only a few miles distant.

We have known only a bleak water-world of shifting blues and greys for the past two weeks, a world not only poor in its spectrum of colours but also of smells, sights, sounds and textures. A slight breeze coming off the land carries with it a scent that triggers my memory: it is the smell of a city, of damp, steaming pavements and vehicle exhausts. Soon, the uniform greens of land around the city become distinct shapes of trees, farm buildings, roads and pylons, their colours clear and vibrant. It is as if I were seeing certain colours – the terracotta reds of roof tiles, the pinks of apartment buildings, the rich greens and browns of the countryside – for the very first time. Nearer still we re-enter the world of municipal sounds – the clanking of cranes unloading containers at the port, the low droning of buses and the tooting of horns. What a great surprise this is, to rejoin civilisation and be overwhelmed and delighted by so much that might otherwise have remained too familiar for acknowledgement.

We head for the end of a white stone seawall that protects the harbour and come around it, then weave our way slowly between anchored sailboats until we reach the marina. We tie up at a space halfway along the pontoon.

I suddenly become nervous at the thought of meeting and speaking to people and looking into their eyes. Even the thought of walking along the street, of catching a bus, of going into a café and ordering food, leaves me slightly panicked. Not that we have the money to buy anything. Our combined wealth amounts to 500 escudos, equivalent to about two British pounds.

Our best hope of fixing the camera, Jason believes, is to approach the local television news channel with our story and hope that someone there will be willing to assist. He wastes no time in stuffing the broken camera into his rucksack and walks shakily along the wharf. I slide the hatch closed and walk in the opposite direction to the marina office. I enter the building. A tall middle-aged man with greying hair looks up at me from behind a counter. I explain our situation: that we've pedalled in from Portugal, bound for Miami, and would like to berth here for a few days, but can't afford to pay anything. He doesn't question me further or look surprised. Sorry, all our berths are taken, he insists. Maybe I should try the yacht club.

The yacht club manager tells me the same thing – no space available. Try anchoring offshore. He does, however, allow me to use the club members' shower and agrees to send a one-page fax to England, to give the news that we are safe, well and here on Madeira.

I find the shower room and undress. There's a mirror above the sink. Looking into it, I see a pair of wild eyes deeply set in dark, bony sockets. The skin on the man's face is leathery and stretched taut as a salted carcass across his cheeks and he wears a reddish-blond scraggy beard. Christ! No wonder people stop to stare and shrink away as I introduce myself. I've turned into the Ancient Mariner.

Milking The Media
Funchal: 28 October

Jason returned in triumph from his excursion with an attractive brunette reporter and a television crew. The camera had been left with the channel's technical department and would be returned in two days, good as new. It was that simple.

A three-minute feature on yesterday evening's news, followed by an article and a picture in this morning's paper, was all it took to transform our fortunes. Madeiran hospitality has been awakened. Today there is a space for *Moksha* at the marina for as long as we need to stay. A nearby fish restaurant has invited us to eat with the staff for free every night. Many curious locals and visiting yachtsmen have come by the boat today to see for themselves and offer help with minor repairs.

I am constantly hungry. As difficult as it is, at first, for people to believe that we came all the way here from mainland Europe on a pedal boat it is, evidently, even harder to believe that we arrived penniless. After trying unsuccessfully to explain this to a stream of journalists throughout the morning, hunger finally compelled me to begin charging a large coffee per photograph and a plate of sardines for an interview. A late donation of one thousand escudos (£4) from an intrigued German tourist enabled us to fill our rucksacks with fresh fruit from the street market.

I retire, exhausted, to *Moksha*'s rat-hole with a book of poems by Charles Bukowski and Jason wanders away to his newly found accommodations – an abandoned swan house at the Zoological Gardens.

A Funfair Ride in The Twilight Zone
10 November

Day 21 of the voyage: I'm dreaming. I post a sardine wrapped in newspaper through the letterbox in the front door of someone's house. My hand gets stuck in the letterbox flap. A large woman in a patterned nightdress opens the door and I'm pulled forward, tripping face-first into her breasts. I'm suffocating. There are gurgling sounds coming from deep inside her cleavage. What is that, water, an underground stream? No, it's the lapping of a boat hull going through water... the sea... this boat...

Whir, whir, whir, pause, click, donk, silence. Jason stops pedalling. It is always the silence that wakes me. Please let the silence signal only a break for him to make a cup of tea, go to the toilet, change the tape on his Walkman. He must have at least another hour left of his shift. The dead weight of my body feels damp but warm under a fleece-lined sleeping bag. Oh, this body was made to fit this bed – this bed to fit this body. I could so easily fall back now... please, please keep pedalling.

'Steve, three o'clock, time to get up.' I can't believe it's been four hours already. This is it: the dreaded low voice, the call to action.

I wipe my eyes, reach for the handrail and let my head hang loose as I haul myself into the cold wet night. I swivel round on the passenger seat and plant both feet into four inches of cold water that sloshes about the floor. There must have been a rainsquall. My bleary half-closed eyes peer out at the dark swirling shapes of waves. The wind is fresh but not strong.

I stand in the open hatchway and fumble for my cycling shoes, which are strapped to the roof beyond smelling range. I force my feet into them while snorting and puffing in that semi-paralysed, feverish state that always follows the interruption of bliss. I give Jason a nod to begin the ritual changeover.

'Evithin' orright?' I mumble, falling into the pedal seat.

'Just had a really close call,' he replies with untypical gravitas. 'It was close, man. Look, I'm still shaking.' He inspects his own hands.

'Whaa... what happnin'?' I ask, looking hurriedly around.

'I saw the lights way off, man,' he begins with a faintly American accent cultivated for just such visceral moments. 'White light in the middle, red and green lights either side –

thought it was miles away. And then,' he pauses and shakes his head, clearly upset by the experience, 'I saw a sail glisten, seemed like, you know, caught in moonlight. But it was all a trick of the light, man, seriously. The sail turned out to be a stack of steel containers on this huge fucking cargo ship, I'm talking like...' he gulps while staring up at his own raised hand, 'massive thing. And it was heading straight for us!'

'For chrissake you could've...' but he doesn't let me finish.

'I tried, man; I tried hailing them on the VHF – no reply, nothing. Then I started panicking a bit – what to do for the best? A flare, flashlight, pedal like fucking fury?' He relaxes a little now and smiles in some perverse amusement. 'And then it missed, just ploughed past, ha, see ya later!'

'I was going to say you could have woke me up. How much did we miss by?'

'I dunno, fifty feet, maybe,' he replies, scratching his head. I shudder to imagine how I might have woken into my worst nightmare.

'If it happens again, please, wake me up. That way one of us can pedal and the other can signal, do the flares, whatever. I'd rather lose out on a bit of sleep than die a horrible death. OK?'

Jason looks disappointed with my reaction, slips into the rat-hole without replying and is asleep in seconds. I sit immobile for a while in the pedal seat, still warm from his body, and think – that was our longest conversation in a week!

A short time later I stop pedalling to write 'I am still alive' in my diary.

It has been a strange and uncommunicative week of pedalling since we left Madeira. For the first couple of days we barely spoke because we were both feeling seasick, a condition made worse by Jason's foul-smelling feet and my even fouler flatulence, which I blamed on all the sardines. The camera broke again on the fourth day, for no apparent reason. That didn't help our mood either. This time there is no remedy to act upon. All we have for Kenny is a meagre few hours of film footage.

Jason has readjusted back to life on *Moksha* more easily than I. He takes each day as it comes and focuses on the daily tasks at hand. As I write, Jason is in the pedal seat patiently working his way through a book on knots. He tests himself with two lengths of rope that rest in his lap. Occasionally, he lifts his head to check the compass and gives the steering line a quick tug. He seems to be enjoying a childlike contentment – oblivious and indifferent to progress. Once every few days he'll inspect the chart to see how far we've come but it doesn't hold his interest for long. I do all the navigating, as we've long agreed. I envy, or rather admire his attitude, because this change in him is part of a deliberate, long-cherished plan to 'live in the present', as he calls it. Where better to attempt it than here, I suppose: no telephone, no job, no food to buy, no television, no family, no friends, no appointments to make or miss and no question of where you're supposed to be next – where else but here, of course!

But with me it's a different story. My head is an unrelenting parade, a never-ending street carnival of thoughts. No childhood memory seems too inane to be revisited – when standing in line at the school canteen in my charcoal grey uniform, should I have asked for the chicken and chips, or maybe the fish and chips? Or – I should have allowed my sister to ride my bike when I was seven. It was wrong to make her sweep the driveway first because there wasn't really any broken glass to puncture the tyres. And no future plans and scenarios are too insignificant for my mind to relish conjuring up, in every absurd detail and permutation, all to compensate for the maddening lack of stimulus. I don't know how long my mind can keep itself entertained in this way without fresh input. But I wonder, no, I fear, what happens at the end, when it has thoroughly exhausted itself of all rational combinations? Will my mind prefer to carry on into the realms of madness rather than be silent? I don't think I have any say in the matter. I can evidently harness my mind to perform useful tasks but beneath that it tends to carry on of its own accord, with moods and urges and obsessive, banal trains of thought that bubble to the surface and just as quickly and inexplicably vanish.

A funfair ride in *The Twilight Zone* is the best analogy I can think of to describe this life. Imagine being at the fair and saying to yourself, 'This is so much fun I wish it would never stop!' Now imagine if it didn't: your world keeps shaking and rolling when you step from the roller-coaster; it continues as you drive home in your car, throwing your head and shoulders from side to side every few seconds; you can never stand without holding onto something; you must strap yourself into bed in order to sleep and wedge pillows in around your head. For how long do you think this would be fun? Five minutes, ten, fifteen minutes? And how long can you stand it without screaming for escape? An entire day, a day and a night, two days, three? But this is reality now, the reality of the twilight zone, how can you not stand it? You must learn to live with it. But how do you live with a reality that is so fucking annoying?

Today, approaching the end of our first month at sea, we are now west of the Canary Islands, the last scrap of land this side of the Atlantic. It means that there is no escape, no option but to live in the twilight zone for another three months, or longer.

Jason can't face another night of pedalling. He has what he calls 'long-term fatigue'. Since we have only one bunk in the forward rat-hole he offers to climb into the rear compartment and nestle down among the stores and bags of garbage. Not in any state to resist, I enjoy a glorious, uninterrupted eight-hour sleep in the bunk while *Moksha* is left to drift. Jason, on the other hand, hardly sleeps a wink. Unlike the narrow canvas bunk with its cradle-like grip and high sides, the rear compartment has no 'wedging quality', no way to avoid the constant rolling of head and shoulders. It must have been horrendous.

A few days later it is my turn to try sleeping in the rear compartment behind the pedal seat. The pedalling has been hard, three days into the wind and going nowhere, and tonight we've decided to throw in the towel, or rather throw out the tyres (our sea anchor), and let ourselves be blown slowly backwards. We say goodnight and I crawl feet first in through the bulkhead hatch and settle on top of the food stores. There is no possible way to find comfort among these boxes and sacks of stinking garbage, still less a chance of actual sleep. Underneath me I can hear *Moksha*'s hull making loud, booming belly flop sounds that reverberate through the rear compartment with each passing wave. Above me I can hear distant whip-cracks of thunder and lightning and the rain drumming hard on the roof.

Hour after hideous hour I lie there, until the first light of dawn. I haul my body out into the main cabin and stand in the open hatchway, noting that the wind has slackened and veered north. It takes a few minutes to pull in the sea anchor and wrap heavy, wet lengths of rope around the hatch entrance and cabin roof. I switch on the GPS and mark our position on the chart. My heart sinks to discover we are roughly at the same place as we were four days ago. I decide to pedal for a few hours until it's time to wake Jason for breakfast. I've never been so tired.

Today is 24 November and our thirty-fifth day at sea. The weather has been playing a cruel game of cat-and-mouse for much of the last week, letting us inch forward one day and blowing us back the next. There is fresh optimism in the air this morning, with a gentler wind from the north-west and blue skies.

I pedal and stare out of a side window at the sea. Jason, who is perched on the hatch roof, is out of sight except for his left leg, which dangles down into the cabin. A taut length of fishing line crosses my view outside the window. It makes me smile.

'Is this the day, Jas?' I shout. 'You ready to haul in that whopper, eh?'

'Yep, today's the day, man. No more Mister Nice Guy,' he shouts back. 'It's fresh fish for tea, no doubt about it. Got a good feeling about this one.'

Jason is using a new lure – Lolita the Lure is her name. His fishing record so far is not good, terrible in fact. He has cast his line and lure into the ocean every morning, experimenting each time with a different lure, new weights or a different pay-out of line, and every afternoon has retrieved that line and stared at the empty hook with a complex look of betrayal and disbelief.

A box of six wooden handcrafted fishing lures was presented as a gift for our voyage by a very old German called Hans, who was the skipper of a U-boat submarine in the war and is now retired in Funchal. Hans swore to us that his lures – fairly crude wooden carvings with brightly coloured, shredded leather skirts that trail behind and conceal a steel barbed hook – would land us more fish than we could eat. What they didn't have, Jason finally announced this morning in a wild-eyed flourish of excitement, was sex appeal. They were too plain.

Sex appeal? Surely, I tried to argue, fish attack lures because they want to eat them, not have sex with them. But it didn't do any good. Jason was convinced. He spent a long time rummaging through various bags to locate a wallet of felt-tip colouring pens. Then he picked one lure with a purple leather skirt and proceeded to carefully draw a sparkling pair of eyes at the head, Betty Boop eyelashes and an equally cartoonish smile.

Minutes later, Lolita is passionately embroiled in a kiss-of-death with a monstrous twenty-five pound dorado. Jason is beyond ecstatic. 'Dynamite!' He cheers, and slips on a pair of gloves before grappling with the throbbing line.

The fish is now within feet of the boat and darting furiously back and forth. I jump out on deck and clamber along astern. I reach into the water and grab the line. Jason is soon lying stomach-down beside me. In his hands is a large sail bag with the zip wide open, which he puts into the water to try to scoop the fish up and out. The dorado has other ideas. It darts under the hull and manages to wrap the fishing line around our propeller. Jason grabs its tail and pulls it halfway out of the water. I get a firm hold near the gills and bring it aboard. The dorado, a flat-headed fish with brightly coloured yellow and blue flanks and a long split tail, is at least four feet long and all muscle. It thrashes violently in my hands. I fumble, nearly lose it, and finally retake control by hugging the slippery beast tightly to my chest. We proceed to wrestle on the rear deck. The unused sail bag, meanwhile, has gone overboard and is steadily drifting out of sight.

We begin to laugh, heartily and uncontrollably. Jason is still laughing as he dives into the ocean to retrieve the errant sail bag. I watch him swim to the bag, grab it, and start swimming back. Now about thirty yards behind the boat, his head and arms are barely visible.

Jason's return swim is slow. The swing of his arms becomes low and erratic. He has been in the water for ten minutes and doesn't seem to be getting much closer. The boat must be drifting as fast as he can swim. He must be getting very tired now. Let go of the bag, you idiot! I continue to watch and wait and hug the fish.

Oh Christ! I remember what happened to the fishing line. It is wrapped around the propeller. If I make the decision now to drop the fish, dive overboard with a knife and cut the line, then get back into the pedal seat and find Jason, it might be too late to reach him. I might not be able to relocate his small bobbing head amongst the waves. And so I continue to wait. The dorado continues to struggle in my arms. Jason continues to swim with the bag.

Jason eventually reaches *Moksha* and hauls his exhausted body onto the rear deck. He cannot talk for a few minutes. He and the big dorado lie side-by-side, gasping together – the fish for water and the man for air. Eventually he sits up, wipes his nose, and begins to speak.

'I was starting to give up,' he says, looking down at the sea. 'At one point I started to sink. And then it was, like, alarm bells in my head,' he explains, lifting both hands onto his head. Talking louder now, he adds, 'Suddenly, from nowhere, I found this huge surge of, like, energy, will-power, whatever, to swim harder.'

'Why the fuck didn't you leave the bag, Jason?'

'Didn't want to lose it.' He answers straightforwardly. 'Might come in handy.' I laugh out loud, partly at his stubbornness and partly in sheer relief. He stands up and clambers shakily back inside the main cabin to fetch the gutting knife.

I return to my seat and pedal onward. When will we ever reach the trades? All the charts, all the sailors and all the weather guides gave every indication that we would find helpful winds eighty per cent of the time. But in thirty five days there have been only two or three days of winds from the north-east, supposedly the 'prevailing' ones.

Another concern I have is the noisy clanking and grinding sound the gearbox makes. This vital piece of the pedal system, which connects the pedal chain to the propeller shaft, is starting to fall apart. Its seals have broken and the internal lubricant has leaked out, leaving the bearings to grind and wear themselves down – metal on metal. The increased friction puts more strain on our swollen knees with each turn of the pedals.

Two days later my prayers for helpful winds are more than answered with the sudden arrival of near gale-force north-easterlies that stoke up big following seas. We leave the hatch open for ventilation, which leaves us regularly drenched inside the main cabin in the aftermath of breaking waves. We have been near to capsizing several times and I suggest to Jason a few precautions; we should think about closing the hatch and using a harness on deck when going to the toilet. He doesn't think either of those things will be necessary.

The roller-coaster ride continues for several days giving us excellent, albeit heart-pounding progress. In the last three hours we have covered seventeen miles, which is faster than the speed at which *Moksha*'s hull is designed to travel.

Riding the storm involves some very strange experiences. As a huge swell approaches from behind, the pedal system completely seizes up due to the build-up of pressure. We soar gloriously to the crest, and then immediately all hell breaks loose – furious surf all around; legs and pedals revolve at breakneck speed as one grips the steering toggles and we hurtle down the wave to the trough.

The cycle repeats every twenty seconds for hours on end, in fact for days on end. The pedaller must remain focused on steering *Moksha* diagonally down the face of each wave. If one were to let her accelerate directly downhill she might bury herself at the bottom and pitch-pole (forward somersault). Steering across the wave too parallel to it, on the other hand, risks broaching (sideways capsize). At first I was genuinely terrified to be among such massive and powerful elements as these waves, but my confidence is building all the time. *Moksha* is an incredibly seaworthy boat.

Our situation is more dangerous at night when the waves are invisible. Tonight, for the third night running, we deploy the sea anchor. It would be an opportunity to catch up on sleep but for the deafening noise and violent motion.

Two days later, I am woken at 8.00 a.m. to make breakfast. The air feels warmer this morning. I look across at Jason in the pedal seat and notice how easily he turns the pedals. The sounds of the whirring chain and grinding gearbox are higher in pitch, denoting a faster speed. The sea sparkles and a drying T-shirt flaps intermittently in a following breeze. I stand up to survey the sky. Look for puffball clouds, the old men of the sea had told us back in Portugal, to tell you when you have reached the trades. And there they are, sure enough, lines of little clouds, white and fluffy as marshmallows trailing across a blue sky as far as I can see. The trades, at last!

Large septic boils, known in sailing circles as salt-sores, are causing us both a lot of pain. This is a condition familiar to any mariner who spends a long time at sea and is unable to wash away the film of crystallised salt covering his skin. Salt is an abrasive. Eventually, and particularly on areas of the body prone to brushing or rubbing against other surfaces, like the buttocks and back and arms, salt will tear and puncture the skin and cause infection. Jason has a huge sore on his forearm the size of half a golf ball. A new daily ritual can be added to our list; that of lancing salt-sores with a needle to relieve the pressure of pus.

The only other significant physical ailment is chronic fatigue, which slowly creeps up over many days of inadequate sleep until it wraps you in its dark cloak and turns you into the walking dead. One pleasant surprise, however, is that the pedalling itself is generally easier than we had expected. The biggest battle is mental. It is the battle with monotony, confinement and constant motion. If only I could surrender to the present situation, as Jason appears able to do, I'm sure I would enjoy this experience so much more. I just can't let go of wanting to be at the other side. Deprived of variety and stimulus, my mind goes wild visualising exciting ideas for the future – places to go, money-making schemes, what I might say to people I love, sensual fantasies, what I might say to people I dislike – all to compensate for the eventless, senseless present. I spend hours at a time fantasising about our arrival in Miami – encircling helicopters with television news crews, a feast in our honour, going on talk shows, corporate executives waving cheques, fighting among themselves to sponsor us, repaying our parents and Maria and being free of debt. Another daydream took me back to the fight with the North Africans in the supermarket car park at Orléans. I reconstructed the incident again and again, casting myself as a martial arts hero who left them all cowering and begging for mercy. In another fantasy I meet Winona Ryder at one of my television talk show appearances. Naturally, we fall instantly in lust, but as we leave the studios and run cross the street to find the nearest hotel room she is bundled into a car by kidnappers. Things rarely go according to plan in my daydreams. There is always some ludicrously improbable twist before I get the girl or save the day, which is why they take so long. No sooner have I pulled Winona from the burning car wreckage – having smashed feet-first through the windscreen to deny the villains their high-speed escape – than she promptly rips off her face to reveal a cross-eyed goat-creature from a distant galaxy and bleats, 'I tried to tell you, but you wouldn't listen.'

Sometimes I despair that my whole existence is just a means for employing my brain in its incessant production of strange ideas. It's like a permanently hungry baby crying out to be fed. Why am I forever dreaming of the next thing, what life could be like? For three years I've dreamed of nothing else but being here. Now I'm here and I spend most of my time dreaming I was somewhere else.

It is the forty-fifth day of the voyage and the good weather continues; we expect to reach the halfway point in a week. Maybe we'll reward ourselves with some fruitcake or alcohol. Tonight I'm going to cook our favourite meal, meatballs and pasta in tomato sauce. After that we're going to let the boat drift and have a proper night's sleep, the first in ten days. I'm so terribly tired.

In the meantime there's work to be done. Today it is my turn to make the fresh water. I lift the water-maker from its stowage place, stand in the open hatchway and take two lengths of rope to lash the pumping device securely to the boat. I throw the saltwater-intake tube and the excess brine tube into the ocean and feed the fresh water tube into the container below me. After a dozen strokes of the pump lever the fresh water begins to trickle out. I relax into a steady rhythm.

Making water can be a wonderful meditation involving a close attention to the breath and to a smooth, regular pumping action. The relentless dance of sea and sky spreads before me and I watch a squadron of flying fish leap out... long glide... and vanish again. It is a rare, tantalising and all too brief connection with other forms of life.

I feel like a visiting alien forced to remain at altitude above the clouds, occasionally rewarded with the sight of a jet plane or, when the clouds part, a fleeting glance of verdant life below. We are floating above the ocean rather than the clouds but the sense of exclusion is the same. We are hopelessly unadapted to this world. This visiting 'spaceship' and her supplies keep us alive.

Steady trade winds continue to push us westwards. We have exceeded fifty miles per day for the past ten days, enjoying easy pedalling and long, lazy spells in the sun. The place to be alone is out on the bow deck. Jason often plays the guitar or harmonica out there or meticulously washes his long hair. I sometimes just sit and whistle or sing to myself and watch our colourful company of Dorado fish circling the boat.

The washing of what little clothing we possess – a few pairs of cycling shorts, some ragged cotton shirts, two fleece-lined jackets and one pair each of smarter, heavy-cotton shorts with pleats and upturned hems (reserved for formal dinners and Sunday outings) – involves the rubbing of generous squirts of kitchen detergent into each item, then tying the soapy bundle together with a line fastened to the boat, which we throw overboard and leave to drag through the water.

'I pulled in your washing this morning, Jason.' I try not to make the words sound accusatorial, but I can feel my eyes start to tighten and my lips wobble in anticipation of conflict.

'I noticed. Thanks.' He keeps on pedalling but drops the book he is reading onto his lap and draws his eyes up to mine. His face is firm, expressing nothing, his eyes black and ready for battle. He's deliberately leaving me to stew, goading, daring me to try something. I know it. I feel my blood boil, as though the whistle has already been blown, sending soldiers scrambling over the parapet into no-man's-land; there is no going back.

'So you must have left it out yesterday and all last night, then?'

'I suppose I must have. What's your point?'

Ha! As if he doesn't know!

'The point, Jason, is that some of us spent fucking months sanding this hull down, time and time again, to make it as smooth as possible – '

'What's that got to do with my bloody washing?' he cries in a high, exasperated tone.

'Your bloody washing always seems to be out there, dragging along, don't you see? We needn't have bothered sacrificing the skin off our hands and all that sandpaper if we'd known! I'm sure it didn't even occur to you... it could add days onto our voyage – '

'Oh, bollocks man!'

'It's not bollocks! I bet if you knew the drag coefficient of a pile of clothes and the difference between a smooth and a rough hull they'd work out about the same – '

'Yeah, well I've worked out that it takes at least eight hours for salt water at this speed to properly rinse the dirt out of cotton.'

'Now that really is bollocks!'

The argument slowly unwinds to an unsatisfactory stalemate, both of us clinging doggedly to our wholly 'scientific' and indisputable claims. Jason returns to his book, hiding his face from view with it, while I smoulder on the passenger seat and boil the kettle for tea. Just now I thought I detected a slight smirk on Jason's murderous scowl, as though the absurdity of the argument had begun to register in him as it has in me. Somewhere, deep down, a calm voice urges me not to allow such trivial irritations to destroy all tolerance and sense of perspective. What does it really matter how long he lets his washing drag, even if we do arrive a day or two later because of it? Why should the sloppy way he shuffles his feet into his shoes each morning, or the way he casually wipes his nose with a pinch of two fingers, fill me with disgust?

But for much of the time there is no perspective, no change from this maddeningly monotonous regime or from him, no way to measure or correct the swirling, fermenting distortions of my isolation. Ludicrous banalities and petty resentments gestate and grow unchecked in my head for no other reason than because they can, and what's more, because they have to. The mind insists upon doing something, analysing and turning things over. I don't want to, but I can't help myself.

Jason clambers out from the rear compartment, red-faced and sweating, holding aloft a parcel covered in Christmas wrapping and topped with a yellow bow.

'Yeah, found the fruitcake!' he cries. 'My auntie baked it for our Christmas treat but what the hell. Happy Halfway Line!' He shuts the compartment hatch, swings the pedal seat back upright and flops down into it.

'I've found the scotch too,' I say, and proceed to break the seal on a bottle of single malt whisky. 'May as well swig straight from the bottle. Happy halfway, oh and happy fifty days at sea!' I toast the double milestone, shuddering at the sharp burning of alcohol as it slips down my throat, and pass the bottle over to Jason.

The first bite of cake is a heavenly mouthful of rich fruity flavours. Bits of cherry and whole sultanas burst with erotic intensity onto my taste buds. Food has become the most important thing in my life, which surprises me. I don't normally care for food. I thought I might go mad for the soft, silken feel of a woman's skin, or for the space to walk and run. But I haven't fantasised much about the joys of dry land or sex or any such thing. What really turns me on is the image of a leg of lamb with roast potatoes and steamed vegetables drowned in gravy; sponge cake, egg custard pie and creamy rice pudding.

Ideal weather cannot lift me from my deep 'funk' tonight. I'm so tired of pedalling and being cooped up in this tiny rocking space. I have nothing to think about. There are books to read during daylight but at night, except for the red compass light, we need to maintain a blackout to spot the lights of other ships. I had some romantic notion that emptying the mind would be a wonderfully liberating experience, but instead it is sending me into a mild panic.

Nothing to think about – nothing! I've exhausted memories and run out of new ideas and plans and it scares me. Occasionally my mind latches on to something new and grapples with it for a while, maybe an hour if I'm lucky. I contemplate family, how lucky I am for mine. Do I take it for granted? Will I ever settle down and start a family of my own? Or will I remain a nomad? What would it be like to be sedentary and stable, married with children? I imagine my dream woman – a tall, elegantly dressed, fragrant beauty with long brown hair. I envisage a warm country house, with a garden, near a river. I think about long dinners with friends, laughter and log fires, children and their pet animals. The image exhausts itself and a bored, empty brain bobs up to the surface again screaming, 'Feed me!'

A strange noise fills my head. I stop pedalling and keep entirely still. What is that? The waves slap and slurp under the hull as normal. But this new sound is different altogether. It isn't really from the outside coming in. It is everywhere and directionless. What is it? People. People are having conversations, getting louder. It's a party, like a house party in a new house that echoes, or maybe it's a gallery opening, it doesn't matter. My head feels like an antenna that is picking up the muffled conversations of an unknown party. What was that, glasses touching, like a toast, or a chandelier in a breeze?

The sound of the party fades, thankfully. I was starting to worry. It was going on far too long. Now I have an interesting new idea to analyse.

What am I doing here? Why do people do extraordinary things? Aha! Yes, that's a good weighty question. That could keep me going for a while.

'Because it's there?' No, Mallory's famous reply never did much for me.

'Because it's good for pulling chicks at parties?' Robert Swann's answer was funny but not credible. There must be easier and better ways of pulling chicks than walking to the South Pole.

'It is as well for those who ask such questions that there are others who feel the answer and never need to ask.' Yes, I can see where Sir Ranulph Fiennes was going with that one but people might mistake it for elitist condescension.

'Because I've got an enormous ego and suffer from a compulsive need to keep proving myself with pointless acts of endeavour?' No one has ever said that. That would be far too honest.

My favourite explanation is one offered by an American 'hobo' in a television documentary about alternative lifestyles. The homeless drifter sat in the open boxcar doorway of a train as it rattled through the Wyoming wilderness. He silently digested the interviewer's question ('Why are you living like this?') as he stared out across an undulating forest of pine and birch, while a Bob Dylan folk song played in the background. Finally he said 'Why? Hell, I don' know why! It ain't for everybody. But hey, I like it. It keeps yer shit hard.'

As for me, there must be more to it than a desire for simplicity, otherwise I would be wandering anonymously with no destination like the hobo, or maybe I'd be building myself a wooden shack in a forest somewhere. There must also be a strong element of vanity in choosing this great goal, to be first around the world by human power. And there are certainly practical advantages in doing something so audacious that it merits media attention and public sympathy, as we have discovered in fund-raising and equipment donations, and most recently in Madeira when we needed help.

I clamber over the pedals to the passenger seat and light the stove for a hot drink, still struggling to stay awake.

Clunk! Bang, bang, clunk! Fuck, that woke me up! What is that?

Bang! There it is again. It feels like the entire boat is being hammered from below.

Bang... bang! Oh Lord! I jump up from the passenger seat and stare in panic at the centreboard. The heavy straps that hold the centreboard down begin to tear under the heavy blows.

Bang... bang... bang! Jason wakes and looks up at me.

'What the fuck's going on? What's that noise?'

'Boom! Bang... bang!' The rudder and centreboard, though eighteen feet apart, are being hammered with the same blow. There is something enormous underneath; something as solid as rock. But that's impossible. We are in water more than two miles deep.

Should I look over the side? No way! People only do that in horror movies, just before a huge slimy tentacle wraps around their necks and hooks them screaming and flailing into the abyss.

'I dunno,' I reply shakily. 'Maybe a semi-submerged container lost from a cargo ship. We'll soon find out.' I scramble back into the pedal seat and cautiously pedal forwards.

A few minutes later I stop pedalling. We wait in silence.

Bang... bang! Jason and I stare at each other in disbelief.

'Just keep pedalling,' he says. I do, but now without the caution; I'm pedalling as fast as I can.

I stop pedalling after five minutes. Again we wait and listen... nothing; just the familiar lapping of wave against hull and the slow whirring of the pedal chain.

I push on in the darkness trying not to create too lively an image of whatever monster it was. Perhaps the rhythmic drone of our grating pedal system echoes a long way down into the void, attracting the curiosity of all kinds of creatures. Maybe it was a whale with an itch to scratch?

Last night we both slept for eight hours while *Moksha* bobbed and drifted aimlessly. Today I feel like a new person. Chronic fatigue is an evil, creeping thing that imperceptibly shrouds the mind like a fog, whispering negative thoughts, black emotion, paranoia and resentment.

We both try to recognise the symptoms of stress and fatigue and be tolerant of each other, but out here there are none of the usual stress releases or a network of other people upon which to gauge one's emotional balance. The challenge of keeping two confined people tolerant of each other is the hardest part of the voyage.

Our most recent clash began several days ago with my idea to make a pit stop at the British Virgin Islands (BVIs). Jason, instantly suspicious, wanted to know why.

'Well, think what would happen if we just turned up in Florida unannounced,' I argued. 'Nothing, right? We've got no money, none; we've got no sponsorship; no reporters or news cameras would be there to see it.' He raised his eyebrows and pursed his lips; he nodded; only fractionally, but he nodded. Encouraged, I pressed on. 'It could be our last chance to line up a sponsor and organise some publicity. And we could get the video camera fixed.'

'No, I don't think we should change our route,' he concluded after much thought.

Twenty-four hours later he changed his mind. 'OK, I'll agree, but only if we pick an island in the Bahamas. The BVIs are too far south.'

I pored over our charts and guidebooks looking for a suitable island in the southern Bahamas, one with safe harbour and the necessary facilities. I found only islands with primitive settlements, surrounded by formidable barrier reefs and precarious anchorage. Jason refused to believe me.

'There must be somewhere.'

'Look for yourself, Jason. I can't find anything. And don't forget, once we start pissing about in those narrow channels and shallows, surrounded by reefs, all it takes is one stiff wind to blow us off-course – end of story.'

Hours later, I made the mistake of drawing a line in pencil on our chart, which ran south-west from our current (mid-Atlantic) position straight to the Sombrero Passage, gateway to the Caribbean Sea and nearby Virgin Gorda, BVIs. It was intended as a helpful and potentially persuasive marker, such that if our daily progress on the chart continued, inch by inch, to show that we were going south-west anyway, as in fact we have been for the past week despite our best efforts on a compass heading of due west, then it might put the idea of an eventual landing at Virgin Gorda in a more credible and acceptable light. Many experienced sailors and ocean-rowers had confidently predicted that we would end up in Barbados, much further south even than the BVIs; the north-easterly trades would take us there, they said, whatever plans we made. I contented myself to let the prevailing wind settle the argument. Our actual progress on the chart, in its relative proximity either to the old route line, which ends at the Caicos Passage at the southern end of the Bahamas, or to this new, more steeply descending line to the BVIs, would eventually make a clear decision for both of us.

'You seem a lot happier today,' Jason said at breakfast this morning. It was the first we had spoken since yesterday afternoon.

'Yeah. It's amazing what a good sleep can do.' It is true. I had an eight-hour sleep in the rat-hole instead of the usual four and feel transformed by it.

'You're going south-west aren't you?' He looked over his left shoulder at the compass, then turned back to face me, his eyes burning with a sense of betrayal.

'No I... that last wave shunted me round... look, I'm trying to pedal and eat my porridge at the same – '

'That's why you're happy. You want to get off this boat and the Virgin Islands are nearest. You already made the decision on your own, didn't you? You even drew the line on the chart!' He was furious. Bits of porridge flew at unexpected angles from his mouth.

'It's just a line Jason! I'm not making decisions. I'm not hiding anything. Of course you're going to see that line! I want you to see it. It's to help us – '

'If you've changed course without consulting me... if you... right, there's no fucking way I'm going to the Virgin Islands now.'

'Look, I swear to you I haven't changed course.'

'Be honest now. You absolutely swear to me on your life that – '

'On mine and anyone else's life you like. I wouldn't make a decision like that without you.' There followed a long silence.

'All right then, I'll believe you. So, we keep heading west.'

'West, yes. And we wait and see which islands we come nearest.'

A dense fog of seething silence and mistrust seems now to have lifted, though it is impossible for me to know whether Jason entirely believes me. Perhaps he will take an interest in navigation from now on, to keep an eye on me. Jason is incredibly perceptive and can read inconsistency and deceit in body language and in the subtle variances of speech.

Maybe I wasn't being entirely honest. It's hard to know anymore. I do want this voyage to end. I feel responsible for our safe return to terra firma and I want that burden to be lifted. There are wonderful times – alone at night looking at the stars, and on clear sunny days, happily pedalling away while reading or listening to music – but I find the ocean to be a largely barren and hostile place and this boat is cramped and uncomfortable. I miss other company, variety, walks in the woods, showers, good food – life, really! And I hate how this confinement is turning me against my friend, especially when I'm really tired and start to get depressed. I find myself thinking 'Look at him sitting there, God he's ugly!' Or I'll watch from the pedal seat as he draws strange little icons into his 'Self-Analysis In Isolation' tables, which record everything he thinks and does – his hours of sleep, his diet, his bowel movements, when he pedals, when he rests, his thoughts, what phase of the moon we're in, the state of the weather, and so on – and I'll think to myself, 'What a vain and self-absorbed stranger you've become!' I dread to imagine what he thinks about me when he's really tired and fed up.

The truth is that I'm immensely fond of Jason and proud of what we have achieved. It is a great pity that we haven't enjoyed travelling together as much as I would have liked but perhaps things will improve over time. We have much in common. We are outsiders, misfits, two people who feel very restless and unable to settle for the comfortable, middle-class life that our education and upbringing made available to us. And we share a special aim to use this adventure to peel back the layers of our complex selves, to seek answers to that essential question – who am I really and how should I live?

I recall the little speech Jason gave at *Moksha*'s launch party last January. It touched me deeply, not only for the words, but also in the emotion he displayed as he tried to explain to the assembled crowd, including his entire family, why he wanted to pursue this adventure. It included a beautiful passage by one of our favourite writers, Hermann Hesse, which spoke for both of us in saying, essentially, good luck to all of you farmers, homeowners, business people, family and friends. I love you, I even envy you, and one day I may return to join you. But I've already spent half my life trying to be two things at once – both a poet and a farmer, a wanderer and a man at home, a man who searches as well as a man who keeps. I suffered great pain and anguish before realising that you can't do both and have both. And so, for now, I choose to search, to learn and hopefully to acquire a degree of self-possession and peace of mind that will make me a happier, more helpful person than you see today.

Today is 18 December and we've made another excellent day's progress. We covered sixty miles in the last twenty-six hours, almost due west. It has been a hot afternoon, with the sun beating down on *Moksha*'s roof and through the windows. We sweat through the heat, wading through lethargy like cold molasses. The overhead hatch is the only source of cooling breeze and only when the wind is following from the east.

Salt-sores have returned with a vengeance. They are erupting all over our bodies. We puncture each boil to remove the pus and cover it with a plaster. We look like a couple of tired, over-repaired inner tubes.

An ugly minerals freighter passes us to our north. It is the first vessel we have seen in weeks. Jason switches on the VHF radio and alters course to avoid it. Strangely, neither of us wanted to communicate with the ship. We've been isolated for so long that the idea of talking to strangers is unnerving.

We barely talk to each other. 'Pass the salt' might be the only spoken words of an entire day.

I lie naked on my stomach in the rat-hole, trying to ignore the pain of a huge, ripe, red, shiny boil on my arse. The constant slapping and gurgling of water echoes through *Moksha*'s hull.

What's that? The mysterious sounds have returned. I seem to have tuned into a police car chase this time, English panda cars, the old kind with the 'nee-nar' sirens. The noise continues for several minutes. Oh God! This one is more annoying than the house party. OK, that's quite enough. That's enough, I said. Enough!

'Nee-nar-nee-nar-nee-nar-nee-nar-nee-nar...'

Day 61, 20 December: chronic fatigue will soon force another full night of sleep while we let the boat drift, but the risks of us both sleeping at the same time are now greater with regular ship sightings. When the rear compartment is used for a second bed, supplies must be tossed into the pedalling area. The time taken to clear the way and resume pedalling, if, for example, a ship was heading straight for us, is an added worry. We are so low to the water that even without large waves to obscure the view, ships can be upon us within five minutes of our horizon. If we were both asleep the only sign of approaching danger might be the vibrating drone of a huge propeller, leaving us seconds to climb out of the compartment, clear the gear and replace the pedal seat before we could take evasive action. Hopefully, we will be through the shipping lanes in three or four days. By then we will be so tired that we'll just have to sleep and take our chances.

I am constantly hungry these days. I finished my daily treats of chocolate, nuts and raisins by 1.30 this morning. An enormous plate of mutton granules with mashed potato has just been licked clean and Jason now adds boiling water to our favourite army dessert – apple and apricot flakes, which comes in an aluminium sachet.

Jason hands me my steaming sachet. I balance it on the pedal seat between my bare legs. Jason, who like me is naked and hasn't worn clothes for weeks – ever since we entered subtropical waters and developed salt-sores – sprinkles some sugar into his sachet before handing the sugar container over to me. At first I fail to see his outstretched hand. The cabin is dark, the only light coming from the blue glow of our gas stove and the soft red of the compass light. 'Here you go,' he says. I begin to reach forward to take it, my mouth watering at the smell of hot apples and apricots rising up in the steam. At the same moment, a wave breaks and slips under *Moksha*'s hull. The boat rocks hard over and I feel the sachet slip from my fingers. Boiling water and soft cubes of apple and apricots spill over my groin and down my legs.

My mouth is wide-open but I cannot scream. The shock of the pain is too great for speech or action. I am launched instantly beyond this world into a new universe of white-hot agony. I begin to shake violently as if in an epileptic fit.

'Cut the pain out; divorce yourself from the pain!' It must be Jason's voice.

'Aeaaaaaah! Fuuuuuuuck! Aaaaaaaah!' I jump up from the pedal seat, climb through the hatchway and plunge awkwardly into the ocean.

'Waaaaaaah!' This is worse! Salt water only seems to magnify the pain. I clamber back on board and continue to shake and scream. I return to the pedal seat. 'Water,' I gasp, between laboured breaths. 'Give me the fresh water.' I point to the five-gallon plastic container at Jason's feet, which he lifts and carries over to me. I unscrew the cap and slowly pour the entire contents in a steady stream upon my blistering genitalia.

The precious liquid covers the cabin floor, sloshing about, while steam rises from between my legs.

'Cor! It's like a bloody nuclear power station down there!' Jason laughs. I ignore him. Humour fails me.

I spend the rest of the night lying on the hatch roof, tied down with bungee cord to stop myself from falling overboard if I should doze off, with my poor burning genitals facing a cooling breeze.

24 December: the world of motion returns, a fresh north-easterly having arrived overnight to shape the lazy-blue into sharp, white-sprayed ridges. The day passes, like so many others, with the incessant raking of cogs and chain and ends splendidly with a full pink sunset. I gaze into the painted west and pump for fresh water.

Normal people will be curled up on the sofa watching Christmas Eve specials – *It's A Wonderful Life*, perhaps, or *Dr Zhivago*. I'm struggling to produce a cupful of water on a windy ocean. Christmas dinner will be beef granules and instant mashed potato. We did, however, remember to pack Christmas crackers, silly hats and a plum pudding and will enjoy them with something no one back home will have – sunshine.

Jason wins the toss-up for the luxury of sleeping in the rat-hole. I try a novel sleeping arrangement, by lining the central cabin floor with the passenger seat cushion and sleeping there at the lowest, least rocking point in the boat. It is a vastly superior bed to the rear compartment, but because we leave the hatch open for ventilation, intermittent rain keeps waking me up. A strange set of red and white lights on the south-west horizon also bothers me.

Throughout the night I periodically sit up and scan the horizon for this beacon, a vertical line of red-white-red lights.

I consult my navigation book for its meaning – 'vessel restricted in its ability to manoeuvre'. It has no additional lights or gantries to signify a fishing vessel. In fact it appears more military.

The vessel is now silhouetted against the morning sky about four miles to the south-east, which means we must have drifted past north of it during our sleep.

I begin to service the pedal system, changing the chain and cogs, but cannot help staring back to the stationary ship. How strange! We are two thousand miles from land on top of three miles of water. How could any vessel be restricted?

I bring out our carefully wrapped Christmas package from a locker as Jason wakes and crawls out of the rat-hole with a sleepy 'good morning'. We briefly acknowledge Christmas and begin to giggle at the absurdity of the usual Christmas Day accessories in this most un-seasonal of situations. Jason begins on breakfast and we both stare back at the vessel again.

'It's bizarre, isn't it?' I remark.

'Yeah. I wonder if they've stopped working for Christmas or something?' We look at each other with identical grins and ideas in mind. Several minutes of thoughtful silence follow before Jason speaks.

'Maybe it's American – stacks of goodies on board!'

'Mmmh', I reply. 'Turkey and roast potatoes, ice-cream, apple pie...'

'Better not be Russian. They'd all be climbing on here for dinner.'

'Well, shall we?' I ask Jason, knowing there can only be one answer. The thought of pedalling up to a strange ship in the middle of the ocean, not having spoken to another soul in more than fifty days is exhilarating and terrifying. Our isolation, our routine, our whole world would be turned upside down. We may be unwelcome. Maybe we have both gone insane at sea and would expose our lunacy the moment we opened our mouths.

Why do I even doubt it? Of course they'll think we're nuts! What other reaction could there be to two people sidling up to a ship with a pedal boat in the middle of the Atlantic Ocean, waving and demanding Christmas lunch?

'Why not, let's do it.' Jason abandons the porridge and releases a shriek of laughter as I turn *Moksha* into the wind and pedal towards the unknown ship. We are both grinning madly.

We take turns to pedal hard into the wind. Two hours later the vessel can now be seen in detail. She is silent and motionless, as if at anchor. I turn on the VHF radio and prepare to alert the ship to our presence but am unsure what to say. 'Are you open for lunch?' is the question foremost in our minds as we slice into the oncoming swell, gradually closing on the ship.

'Attention all shipping,' blares from the VHF radio. 'This is the US Cable Ship *Charles L. Brown*. Please be advised we are undergoing submarine cable operations and are restricted in our ability to manoeuvre. All vessels are instructed to stay clear.'

We are now within half a mile of the vessel. I take the VHF microphone in my right hand and try to make contact.

'USCS *Charles Brown*, this is pedal boat *Moksha*, *Moksha*. Over.'

Silence.

I repeat our signal several times.

'This is USCS *Charles L. Brown*. Please identify yourself.'

'This is pedal boat *Moksha* requesting permission to come alongside.'

Silence.

'You're a what? Where are you exactly?'

'We're a pedal boat crossing the Atlantic Ocean.' I hear a voice quietly muttering to a colleague, something about a Christmas prank – must be those galley boys again.

'Very funny. Who is this?'

'Look for a little white boat on your starboard beam.' Silence again.

'Err, roger that *Moksha*, we have you now. You're a paddle boat?' I agree, not wishing to be pedantic. He asks for us to stand by for the captain.

'You're in luck fellas,' says the captain. 'If you'd arrived a few hours ago we'd have had to turn you away. We've been very busy on-deck, hauling up fibre-optic cable from the seabed and re-splicing it. Lucky for you we're just about done now. We'd be delighted to have you aboard. Just be careful to stay clear of the bow and stern thrusters.'

I scurry around the deck making sure everything is secure while Jason pedals on. I detach our sea anchor line from the tyre and secure it to the eyebolt at *Moksha*'s bow.

We come alongside. The size of the ship is staggering – a wall of steel thirty feet high and several hundred feet long. I throw up the anchor line at some smiling faces. A rope ladder is thrown down. I try to grab it, but suddenly we drop fifteen feet in the swell. Jason lashes our two small fenders to *Moksha*'s gunwale to lessen the damage as we rise and plummet against the ship's side. Other, much larger fenders are offered down on a rope, one almost the size of *Moksha* herself.

At the peak of swell I leap onto the rope ladder and begin to climb. I've never been so nervous. Every cell of my body shakes. With my long scraggly beard, emaciated face, crazed eyes and rags for clothes, I imagine the crew must be wondering who asked Santa for Ben Gun from *Treasure Island*.

I climb on deck. Semi-paralysed at the thought of meeting another human being, I go into automatic greeting mode. I shake hands, grin wildly and nod my head a lot. It feels like a dream. The deck is solid, hardly moving at all. It feels almost impossible to walk on it. I look round for Jason, who is smiling and shaking hands and nodding a lot.

Someone offers me a can of fizzy drink. I thank him and flip the ring-pull. I haven't tasted anything cold in over fifty days. I can feel the liquid running down my throat and now cascading around the lining of my stomach The sharp bubbles sting the top of my mouth and send a tickling pain shooting up my nose, making my eyes water. We are led through to the heart of the ship and into the Officer's Mess.

We sit on heavy, wooden, cushioned chairs. They don't move. They are still. My God, I don't have to hang on to anything! We survey with incredulous, jaw-dropping attention the cloth-covered dining table in front of us. There are fresh bread rolls; a jug of iced-water; bowls of fruit; a bottle of white wine.

'Please, help yourselves. We've already eaten but the cook has a few extra plates of turkey warming up for you. Bet you're hungry, huh?'

'You have no idea.' I say it slowly for full effect.

'Thank you so much,' Jason says, shaking his head. 'This is unbelievable.'

A waitress brings in two enormous plates piled high with steaming, succulent slices of roast turkey, broccoli, cabbage, roast potatoes and cranberry sauce. I marvel at each distinctive colour of food, the divine cocktail of smells, each texture in the mouth, the way a thing melts or crumbles or squashes down and surrenders its flavour.

Multiple orgasms and three desserts later, a steward comes to clear away the table. I stuff the remaining bread rolls into the pocket of my shorts.

'Now what would you like, gentlemen? A hot shower perhaps?'

'Oh Yes! Oh god, Yes!'

We find our way back up to the bridge about an hour later.

'When did you last speak to your families?' the captain asks.

'In Madeira a few months ago,' Jason replies.

'Would you like to telephone them now – a Christmas present from AT&T?'

It is the best present we could think of. The captain leads us up to the communications room. After a call to each of our families I make a third call to Kenny in London and give him the bad news about the video camera breaking again only a few days out of Madeira. It is hard to decipher the rapid-fire Scottish accent spluttering through the earpiece. He sounds very agitated.

'What's the first island you come to?' he asks.

'Um, there's one called err, Mora... Moya... Mayaguana, I think, just on the north side of the Caicos Passage. But Kenny, there's no guarantee we can make the Caicos Passage. I don't even know if there's an airstrip on Mayaguana; could be a right bugger to get to – '

'Try to make it. I'll be tracking you on Argos. Keep your radio on when you get to the passage. I'll try to pinch a boat from somewhere and bring you another camera.'

One of the crew has run up from deck level to report that *Moksha*'s bow is slightly damaged after repeated collisions with the side of the ship. We must leave now while we still can.

It is New Year's Day, 1995. There is an unexpected downside to the luxury foods pillaged from the 'Charlie Brown'. In the Pre-'Charlie Brown' era we used to savour a daily army-issue fruit biscuit (squashed fly-bricks, Jason calls them). We would drink half-sachets of hot chocolate to stretch our supply. Unwrapping the daily Mars bar could take several minutes: first, an inspection to ascertain structural stability; next, particularly if the bar is a crumbling ruin, carefully make the opening tear and apply lip suction to harvest loose crumbs; step three, expand the tear to mid-bar and inspect for casing fractures that could result in the nightmare scenario – premature-choc-slab-fall-off; all clear? Finally, a deep breath and a final look at the intact bar. Now, who's the daddy!

Post-'Charlie Brown' there is an almost limitless supply of fruitcake and American Oreo cookies – soft round muddy-brown sandwiches, boringly reliable in their uncrumbling cohesion, with a sickeningly sweet cream filling. After the initial splendid indulgence we rather miss the days of scarcity and that single rancid fly-brick biscuit.

The ocean is as calm as a village pond. I lean over the side and watch our dorado family darting around under *Moksha*'s hull, which is no longer smooth and red but a dense living carpet of green weed and gooseneck barnacles. Dancing curtains of light reflect shimmering specks of plankton and fade into the depths.

The afternoon is searing hot without a breath of wind. It is the perfect day for an untethered 'space walk'.

'We really need some photos of *Moksha* from a distance,' Jason insists. 'I think it's time we put Derek the Dragon into commission.' He reaches into the rat-hole and pulls out a package of folded rubber, which he unfolds and soon inflates into a small raft the shape of a green, fire-breathing dragon.

Wisely, Jason's first attempts to mount the dragon are done without camera equipment as he suffers one humiliating capsize after another.

'I think it's a bit out of its depth,' he giggles and disappears underwater again.

'Out of its weight range is more the problem,' I shout from the hatchway.

'I'll just have to rest the camera on its back instead. I'll swim alongside.'

This is all Peter Bird's idea. We met Peter, who is the most experienced ocean rower in the world, several times in London before the expedition began. He advised us to carry an inflatable dinghy from which to take photographs at some distance from *Moksha*, thus giving sorely needed variety to our visual record. Unfortunately, the range of inflatable vessels available in Lagos was limited to dragons or ducks. A dragon somehow seemed more adventurous.

Jason treads water and aims his camera, now perched on Derek, at me as I act out the daily routines of water making, washing, navigating and going to the toilet. At the end of the washing sequence, covered in soap, I dive in and swim out to Jason.

'Ooh! Strange feeling, both of us out here looking at an empty boat.' *Moksha* is now a hundred feet away.

'Yeah,' Jason agrees. 'Amazing to look back at our spaceship. Aside from that little wooden boat there's only ocean for thousands of miles in any direction and for miles underneath.' I remain treading water with Jason and Derek as *Moksha* drifts further away. I enjoy the surge of adrenalin and a quickening heartbeat.

We swim back together. I grab on to *Moksha*'s solid bulk with great relief.

We have been at sea for almost two months. Yesterday's calm transformed overnight to a blustery force six from the north. What little sleep I managed was punctuated with recurring, vivid nightmares – of Jason, up to his neck in water, his terrified eyes and twisted face glaring at me from the rat-hole of our sinking boat.

I lay awake during Jason's graveyard shift, listening to the roar of the sea and to Jason's movements. He spent much of the time capturing sounds onto audiotape, shouting narrative into the microphone above a howling wind and recording the slurping sound of the bilge pump in use.

The majority of *Moksha*'s ballast was food and therefore she is considerably lighter than when we left Portugal, which causes her to roll more. My concern is that a rogue wave could capsize her, or at least tip her enough to scoop a dangerous volume of water through the open hatchway.

Moksha is designed to be self-righting, but during tests at the Exeter Maritime Museum we proved this to be dependent upon the cockpit hatch being closed. At sea we have found a closed hatch to be stiflingly hot. It has therefore remained almost permanently wide open.

Internal watertight hatchways isolate the central cabin from the forward (sleeping) and aft (storage) compartments but again, in practice, the need for ventilation leaves the sleeping area permanently open at night. We never tested this capsize scenario – main hatch open and forward compartment hatch open – because it was a foregone conclusion. Flooding two thirds of the boat would definitely cause her to sink.

The only workable solution I can think of is to sacrifice some ventilation in bad weather by keeping the main hatch mostly closed. In the event of capsizing this might restrict flooding for the crucial few seconds for *Moksha* to flip right-side-up again. Jason disagrees. He prefers the ventilation. This is causing a lot of friction between us. Whenever I reduce the opening during my pedal shift he will invariably push it wide open again the moment he takes over. I explained my reasoning. He replied that he remembers the capsize tests as well as I do; he agreed there are times we seem close to capsizing. But, he argued, we haven't yet. He wants the ventilation.

11 January: it's now 6.00 a.m. and I have another two hours of solitude in which to pedal and enjoy the yellow dawn. The previous pre-dawn hours are always the hardest, when I long for the new sun.

I just tried the radio and discovered a miracle on medium wave. For months the radio has only spluttered the same short wave channels – BBC World Service, Voice of America and the French weather channel – but now, suddenly, a disc jockey from Virgin Islands Radio is yakking on about fashions and the price of gasoline in St. Thomas. It is fabulous, almost tangible proof of our proximity to the Americas, somehow more real than any GPS position on a chart.

The thrill of local radio doesn't last long. I am bored again. The familiar 'nothing-to-think-about' paranoia takes hold. There must be something, anything! I stand up and turn around, swing the pedal seat forward on its hinge and dive into the rear compartment on a desperate hunt for stimulus.

Bingo! Beneath stinking piles of garbage and mildewed canvas I uncover *The Mind of God*, a book by scientist Paul Davies. An endorsement by the *Washington Post* calls it 'the most powerful mind-bending experience you can have without violating the Controlled Substances Act'. Where did this book come from? It must be Jason's. He must have forgotten about it. Yes, this will do nicely.

It is late afternoon and the wind shifts to the north, force five. Bold formations of cloud and plenty of water slopping aboard create an air of tension. The shipping news tells of the storm that passed north of us several days ago, and from which a heavy swell remains; it sunk a Portuguese fishing vessel off Morocco and claimed the lives of the entire crew.

The easterly winds gather in strength for two more days. I keep having premonitions of disaster similar to my nightmare of last week and continually look over my shoulder at the next dreaded wave. It doesn't help to be superstitious of today's date, Friday the thirteenth, or the fact that it's Day 85 of our voyage: $8+5=13$.

Jason appears unmoved by the gathering storm. Calmed by his example I force myself to action, standing up in the open hatchway to pump for fresh water. A bad presence remains within, a gripping dread that cannot be shaken. A dark voice in my head whispers repeatedly, with slow conviction:

'You are going to die. You are going to die.' Is it tiredness?

When pedalling, my eyes are only a few feet above the waterline and the waves rise and tower above with their hideous slow sucking. If a wave passes before it breaks, then my stomach senses the rapid elevation and the lingering moment of the summit, before we slip down the back-face and the wave explodes ahead in a wall of white tumbling fury. At other times it breaks behind or on top of us. Then we hear the crash and the roar and we are swept along in the avalanche.

I feel less afraid standing up. I continue pumping for water at the open hatchway and gaze across in awe of the huge u-shaped blue valley we are in and of the towering white-capped peak thirty feet above and behind us. *Moksha* rides up and over it superbly with the ease of a resting seabird.

By the following afternoon we are both desperately tired. I struggle to maintain focus and steer *Moksha*, checking her speed by traversing obliquely down each wave. I don't think I can do this for another day. It is time to throw out the sea anchor and batten down. The ugly voice whispers again.

'You... are... going... to... die.'

No! No.

I must sleep soon.

Jason, on the other hand, comes alive. He grips the cabin roof with one hand and takes photographs with the other. He stuffs the camera quickly under his jacket when the surf closes in. He captures one huge wave and jumps back into the cabin just before it explodes around us. He gives a piercing shriek of approval.

'D'ya... d'ya see that bastard? Yihaa! I got some good ones.' He is revelling like a deranged man in these awesome, mountainous seas.

We swap places for Jason's pedal shift. I decide to stand and fight my fatigue by making fresh water. The positive action of standing and facing up to the waves, and watching how well *Moksha* rides them, seemed to give me confidence yesterday.

I stand in the open hatchway and cast the intake and excess brine hoses overboard. I begin lashing the pump cylinder to the emergency oars.

I feel a stomach-churning lifting surge. Turning my head over my right shoulder I see two white-capped waves come together to create one enormous peak. Their combined energies burst onto *Moksha*'s port side. We capsize in a flash.

I am submerged in a world of deafening noise; I am being dragged underwater at high speed. My arms flay about and I am limp. There is nothing to fight against. I don't know where I am or which way is up. My ankle is caught, somehow. I am being reeled along like a foul-hooked fish. *Moksha* is capsized. This is it. This is what the dark voice means, and my nightmares. This is the end.

My elbow nudges something hard. I instinctively grab for it. It is a familiar shape – *Moksha*'s gunwale. Is she capsized? The foaming world clears. I see *Moksha*'s white deck and some blue sky. No, we have righted, thank heavens! My ankle is no longer caught; I am free. I cling to the gunwale almost at the stern and wrap my foot around the rudder. I am rigid with fear, knowing full well how close I am to a slow, anguished death. That is death, there, in the churning water right behind us, because the boat is being swept along far more quickly than I could ever swim to catch up and Jason has no hope of pedalling backwards to rescue me. I must hang on here or be swept behind and lost. Where is Jason? And the water-maker?

Jason's face appears through the hatchway.

'Steve, where the hell are you?'

'Jason, the water-maker!'

'I've got it,' he replies, fishing the device from the ocean and holding it aloft. He lets out a great roar of laughter. 'Ha-ha! Wotcha doin' back there?'

'Are you OK?' I ask. I'm amazed that we're still afloat. The hatch was wide open when we capsized. The central cabin must be half-filled with seawater.

'Fine,' he replies casually. I begin to laugh uncontrollably, though I might as easily sob.

I grapple my way back on deck and crawl inside the central cabin. Inside is a semi-submerged disaster area in which the corpses of electronic gadgets, books, charts and cooking implements freely collide. I am in shock and, determined not to contemplate how close to death I came, begin cranking the bilge pump handle to the same rhythm as my thumping heart.

Jason checks the water-maker for any damage and fishes items individually from our new indoor swimming pool.

'Well, finally something exciting happened,' I quip nervously.

'Yeah, we need things like this once in a while just to remind ourselves we're really alive.' I nod mechanically but without knowing why.

'Christ!' He continues. 'One moment you were there, standing in the boat; the next moment I got a wall of water in my face and when she flipped back over again – a flooded cabin and no Steve! I jumped up to the hatchway and saw the water-maker bobbing around in the ocean.'

'You mean it wasn't attached to anything?'

'Nope. You hadn't lashed it to the emergency oar when the wave came. I could easily have lost you and the water-maker in one go – probably would have died of thirst myself before I reached land.'

I begin to shiver with cold and delayed shock and try to warm myself by working harder at the bilge pump. I can still feel the texture and grip of whatever it was that wrapped around my ankle as we capsized and held my body weight alongside the boat just for those crucial seconds, as we hurtled down the face of the wave – *Moksha* upside down, me dragging along in the water beside her. I am shocked to still be here rather than floundering far off behind somewhere, waiting to drown. The voice was wrong. I didn't die. I survived. That terrible presence has gone now, lifted, but why was it in my head in the first place?

It must have been the sea anchor line that saved me. We stow it in long coils that loop around the hatchway and cabin roof, making it easy to deploy in a storm.

I gradually warm up and recover. The full horror of what could and should have been but for the miraculous intervention of the sea anchor line, makes itself known in the grim cinema of my imagination. I would have been swept behind. I would have surfaced, gasping for air, and suffered the helpless torment of treading water while watching *Moksha* disappear forever. I probably would have swum desperately after her; seen and heard Jason – intermittently though, as we rode and fell on different, increasingly distant peaks – screaming encouragement from the open hatch. That would only have lasted a few minutes. Then I would have been completely alone in the middle of the Atlantic Ocean.

I pedal through the difficult pre-dawn hours with the sound of the pedal system reverberating through the cabin. It is so loud that I can barely hear the crash of a breaking wave behind me. The wave is felt instead, as several gallons of ocean find their way through the overhead hatch, soaking me through. I barely remember what it feels like to be completely dry.

Yesterday's capsize destroyed the Walkman. We have no music to mask the heavy grinding noise of *Moksha*'s disintegrating gearbox. I pray for the gearbox to survive just a few more weeks. The storm is thankfully abating, though the heavy swell continues to demand the utmost concentration.

My days of complacency at sea are over. I will now wear a lifejacket attached to a survival line whenever I have to go on deck in bad weather, day or night, and will close the hatch behind me. Jason continues to clamber outside un-harnessed, tipping *Moksha* alarmingly while squatting on the gunwale to have a shit, and leaving the hatch wide open. He vehemently opposes changes to his normal routine, arguing that it is a matter of 'personal risk and personal choice'.

'When a man's weight is resting on one gunwale with the hatch open in bad weather,' I argued, 'it's not just about you anymore. You risk *Moksha* and you risk my life too.'

'Point taken,' he said after a long and thoughtful pause, before shuffling his way into the rat-hole for a sleep.

I look forward to calmer weather and an end to these heart-stopping surges. And I eagerly await the Caicos Passage and the Bahamas, now only three hundred miles to the west. We could also do with a night of sleep tomorrow night, after which I will forward the ship's time, for the last time, to Time Zone+5, and sunrise will not be so horribly long in coming.

Day 89: we are forced to stream the sea anchor, having gained less than twenty miles in as many hours of pedalling against the wind. Exhausted, we wait and watch our slow backward

drift. I think this wind will keep veering round the compass and die out by tomorrow.

Day 90: I was wrong. The westerly blows even stronger. The GPS reveals that we have drifted eighteen miles backwards since this time yesterday. Jason's voice echoes out of the storage compartment to announce that only sixteen days of food remain. He clambers back into the central cabin holding a small plastic bag.

'Take a whiff of what I found,' he says. I smell it. It is, unmistakably, the pungent aroma of cannabis leaf. If smells could only be described by colour, that smell would surely be dark green. Lagos seems a lifetime ago. I had almost forgotten about our Portuguese friend whom we jokingly called 'our major sponsor' for donating a bottle of Jagermeister and a half-ounce of quality weed in those final, surreal hours before departure. The bottle of booze was already half-empty when it slipped through Jason's arms and smashed on the quay. But the cannabis remains intact and untouched.

Using a page from my diary and some heavy-duty glue I manage to roll an enormous reefer. A thick haze quickly obscures Jason's smiling face. Whether the desired effect is a result of the weed, the paper or the glue is uncertain but whatever it is it works. We have our best conversation in a very long time. The subject? Not a clue, I've forgotten it already, but it feels like the best kind of happy nonsense.

Day 91: the westerly wind continues to push us backwards. I can't bear the inactivity a moment longer. I pull in the sea anchor and swap the cog on the gearbox for a larger, fourteen-toothed one to reduce the load ratio. I start pedalling into the wind. *Moksha*'s bow slices cleanly through each approaching wave and we belly flop with a satisfying 'thud' after it.

Day 92: we crawl through our fourth day of adverse westerlies. Our position is the same as it was three days ago. My knees and shoulders are beginning to suffer from the

137

strain. With the Bahamas so tantalisingly close this is a cruel wind that plays upon our hopes. Two weeks of food remain. We discuss the options for fishing and for eating half-rations for the final weeks to Florida, but unless the wind changes we'll need every bit of it just to reach the Bahamas.

Jason has christened the largest of the dorados encircling our boat '107', because we packed only 106 days of food on board. Not that we feel inclined to fish much nowadays. The process of catching, gutting, filleting and cooking is too laborious and unnecessary while instant army-rations remain. The sudden change of diet also gives me diarrhoea – a very unpleasant pedalling experience!

Day 94: it is 2.30 a.m. I stand alone during a break in my graveyard pedal shift, watching the calm black ocean. Sharp bursts of lightning attempt to ignite the south, signifying another storm over the Caribbean. Other lights are from two ships, both steaming into the Caicos Passage from different directions.

The first vessel, a tanker, passes close by. I turn on our navigation lights to give visible form to the puzzling blip on its radar screen. A powerful searchlight swoops down from the ship's bridge. It catches me completely naked in the open hatchway. It flashes three times. I do not respond for fear of provoking another Philippine rescue party. I stand dumb and motionless under the blinding spotlight like an actor who forgot his lines, not to mention his costume.

Day 95: we had a scare last night when the gearbox became very noisy and difficult to turn. The steel bearings inside it are disintegrating after months of metal-on-metal abrasion. I'm amazed they have lasted this long. The gearbox is completely sealed (apart, I suppose, from wherever all the lubricating oil has seeped out) in a mild steel casing. We have no way to fix it and no spare. All we could do was slather every movable part with grease in the hope that some would travel along the shafts and lubricate the internal bearings.

It seems to have helped. Today's pedalling noise is reduced to a menacing growl rather than the 'rabid-dogs-in-fight-to-death' sound of last night.

Day 96: if the easterly wind holds we ought to be passing south of Mayaguana Island in two days. My mariner's guidebook lists a VHF radio channel for the island police, to whom we could inquire for news of Kenny.

A complete breakdown of the pedal system seems imminent, though this alone wouldn't merit an emergency rescue as we still have the oars. I sense Jason almost willing the breakdown purely for the novelty value and the heroic effect of limping to victory. Personally, I'm praying hard for the pedals to keep turning because the idea of sawing oar-holes through the cabin walls and rowing from the cramped passenger seat has never been thought through. I know enough about rowing, having briefly rowed for my university on the River Thames, to know that this set-up would be a thoroughly miserable experience.

The gearbox is having another grinding fit – this time it sounds horribly like its final, agonising death throes. The connecting shafts are wobbling and haemorrhaging brown lubricant.

Jason experiences the same intermittent seizures on his pedal shift. *Moksha* is left to drift as Jason examines the whole mechanism for possible remedies in his own meticulous, ursine way. Fully expecting to begin rowing the last six hundred miles to Florida by morning, I try to grab some sleep.

Day 97: the gearbox has adopted a new, higher pitch of grinding but is still alive and turning. We continue to massage the ailing box with grease and press on as a cold blustery wind descends from the north.

We are beginning to talk to each other again! To call it conversation would be a gross overstatement, but there is a noticeable re-birth of speech. I suppose the gearbox trouble and the fact that there remain many more days of ocean than food supplies are forcing some dialogue. But there is also the exciting prospect of land and all that goes with it. What will America be like? We will be arriving with no money and nowhere to stay. How will we survive there? Jason has made at least one firm decision about America. He doesn't want to cycle. He wants to skate across the continent. Has he any previous experience of in-line skating? Of course not! Don't be ridiculous!

Just after 4.00 p.m. a strengthening north wind whips up white caps, causing us to roll violently on our westward heading. I hear a dull 'hum' over the noise of the gearbox. Strange, is it the radio? The humming gets louder. Vvvvvrrmmm.

'Oh shit!' I whip my neck around in search of a fast moving vessel. It must be upon us.

'Where the hell... ?'

'Up there!' Jason stands and points skywards at a small seaplane. It makes a second flypast.

'It's Kenny!' Jason cries. 'I'll be damned, it's the bloody Scotsman!'

I turn on the VHF. It is Kenny.

'*Moksha*, this is Kenny. I'm amazed we found you. How bad is the injury, over?'

'Kenny!' Jason screams down the mouthpiece. 'I never thought I'd be so pleased to hear a Scotsman's voice. What injury, over?'

'Your previous Argos transmission was a Code Five. The pilot is a doctor but we can't land in this weather and our fuel situation is critical, over.'

Our Argos tracking device transmits a number from zero-to-fifteen every three days. Number five is the code for 'sick/injured person, continuing, no rescue needed'. Several days ago we sent a number three, which means, 'bad weather, cannot pedal, all OK', but one of us must have turned the dial to number five by mistake. Oops! Our families must be frantic.

'OK, I'll relay the good news and apologies,' Kenny replies when we explain. He adds that he only has enough fuel to stay for a few minutes, and urges us to make a quick decision: either we continue pedalling directly to the mainland, in which case we can agree on a position for Kenny to make an airdrop of supplies and a new video camera tomorrow; or we can make landfall on the island Kenny flew from – Providenciales, in the Turks and Caicos Islands.

I quickly take a GPS reading and plot our new position on the chart. It reveals that the north wind has blown us twenty miles closer to Providenciales than expected. The new position puts us only thirty-three nautical miles north-east of it.

'What do you think, Jas?' Jason looks sideways into the sea. It seems there are no easy answers. 'Either we hope the pedal system holds and continue on to Florida, or take a chance with a coral reef and make landfall now to get it fixed.'

'Oh yeah. Not that this'll make any difference,' Kenny adds, crackling through the VHF speaker, 'but Provo's got some really nice people, great food, cold beer...'

We smile inanely at each other. The decision is quickly made. 'We'll be there by morning, Ken. Put the beers on ice.'

The following dawn approaches. I find it increasingly more difficult to contain my excitement. Kenny's unexpected appearance and our sudden change of plan have turned our ocean mode upside down. Land today! The happy prospect is difficult to grasp. It intuitively feels like a good decision. Even the wind and swell are willing us into Providenciales, leaving me with the previously unthinkable need to slow down to avoid reaching the coral reef around Turtle Cove before daybreak. I pedal through the glorious, rolling blackness with ease and enjoy munching my way through the sacred emergency stash of Mars bars in the knowledge that supermarkets are close at hand.

By 7.00 a.m. we are six miles west of 'Provo'. The sight of land is mesmerising – a thin, ragged silhouette of trees and beachfront hotels. It vanishes as the next lumbering swell passes between us. I am struggling not to explode with anticipation.

Our VHF call to Kenny wakes him up. He complains of a cracking hangover, but eventually arrives at speed in a requisitioned speedboat, a chunky white workboat with a large black outboard engine, driven by a young man called Darren.

We pedal behind the escort boat for several miles while Kenny films and shoots roll after roll of photographs. The deep cobalt blue ocean abruptly changes to lighter shades of muddy green and turquoise as we approach the reef. The swell builds into huge waves that collapse into surf nearer shore.

'Darren reckons the Club Med Cut is the safer passage through the reef,' Kenny yells from the escort boat, which pitches and rolls dangerously near our starboard bow. Darren – a sleepy-eyed teenager with long blond hair in surfing shorts – smiles and waves from the helm. 'Just head straight for the blue hotel, OK,' Kenny adds to his instructions. 'We'll go first.' They speed ahead and quickly disappear behind a high rolling wave of water.

I stand in the hatchway with a pair of binoculars and watch for the escort boat to reappear. When eventually it does, Kenny looks frantic. He throws his cameras into a large bag and clings to a handrail. The surf is exploding all around them and the speedboat is completely swamped with water.

'Looks like Kenny's in trouble,' I report back to Jason.

'Bugger all we can do,' Jason replies from the pedal seat. 'And get ready, we're next.'

An enormous cresting wave builds behind us. Realising there is no way out Jason starts pedalling forward for all he is worth to pick up speed. The wave passes underneath us and collapses ahead with a thunderous roar. Jason pedals on, gripping hard on the steering lines to keep *Moksha* on a straight course. The next swell rises up into a massive green wall fifteen feet high; I slam the hatch shut and brace myself as the wave lifts *Moksha* and sends us hurtling down its face. *Moksha* shudders with the colossal weight of water slamming down upon us. The sea, land and sky all vanish behind the dreadful roaring surf. The noise is tremendous. Every muscle and sinew is taught ready for the tumbling, wrecking disaster that we both fully expect.

'CRUNCH!' *Moksha* stops dead.

'We hit the reef!' I yell at Jason who grabs the radio mike and screams for help.

'This is *Moksha*, *Moksha*. We're in big trouble, big trouble!'

The collision with the coral head has hammered *Moksha*'s centreboard through its casing. Water immediately begins spurting through the splintered gap.

Moksha remains stuck fast to the reef and taking on water as the next monstrous wave curls skyward and rumbles toward us. I stare at it, wild-eyed in terror. There must be something I can do. I jump up off the passenger seat, swipe away the seat cushion and pull with all my might at the centreboard, desperately hoping to free us from the coral. The seat cushion lands on the pedals just as Jason prepares to pedal fast ahead to ride the next surge.

'What the fuck are you doing! Get that thing away from me!' he screams and hurls the cushion back. It strikes me squarely in the face as I strain to lift the centreboard free. It won't budge an inch, jammed fast into the back of its casing.

The wave lifts us free of the coral and sweeps us forward again at high speed. I brace myself for the next agonising crunch of splitting wood.

We wait and wait, every muscle tense in expectation of a terrible collision. The crunch doesn't come. Instead we glide shoreward on a crackling, foaming cushion of surf. *Moksha* shudders violently as we fly through the water. We must be clearing the coral by inches. The coral heads appear as colourful blurs of brain-shaped rock beneath. I look over at Jason's red, sweating face. His eyes are totally focused ahead. His neck muscles bulge and his upper body sways from side to side with the effort of his furious pedalling as he tries to keep from being sucked back into the breakers.

We edge forward, eventually pulling clear of the surf zone, and enter the relative calm of a long, snaking lagoon. The colour of the water here is an extraordinary, electrifying turquoise. I have to stop and gasp at its beauty before I can lower my head again to check the damage to the hull. The seawater seeping in through the split centreboard casing has slowed to a manageable trickle. I spot Kenny and Darren bailing water from the escort boat with a big bucket. We follow them along a winding channel between beach and surf to the entrance to Turtle Cove Marina. I feel dazed and numb after our terrifying ordeal and sit on the foredeck to recover and to marvel at the amazing new colours and smells. *Moksha* makes a sharp turn and slips into the marina basin.

It is a quaint little harbour enclosed by a thin bank of white sand and packed with jostling pleasure boats – from old, flaking wooden dinghies to gleaming cabin cruisers and sport-fishing boats with tall, tapering fly-bridges ready for charter. At the far end of the marina, partly obscured from view, a large group of children are crowded together on a rickety wooden jetty. Some of the children are singing a slow and touching hymn in delicate harmonies. They sway their arms and rock their heads like clockwork toys. Others are red-faced and almost bent-double in their strenuous efforts to make conch shells resonate in a low horn sound. A long, deep bassoon of conch horns ripples the air like a silk flag in the wind and makes my skin tingle. We must have arrived in the middle of a special occasion, perhaps a religious event. I feel a bit embarrassed for intruding on an important local festivity, though not nearly enough to make me want to turn around and come back later. Jason steers towards a narrow wooden finger of the pontoon and I get ready to sling a line around a large metal cleat at the edge of it.

The children stop singing, put down their shells and begin waving and cheering. They are cheering at us.

'My God!' I cry. 'They're doing it for us. We are the special occasion.'

What Dat Is? Don' Axe Me!
Turtle Cove, Providenciales: 30 January.

We spent the first two days doing little else but gasp with delight at all the fabulous luxuries that normally are taken for granted: running water, people, conversation, colours, fresh food, cold drinks, hot showers, soft mattresses, trees, flowers, rocks, sand – anything, in fact, that can be relied upon to stay still; and making friends with the islanders. Jason continues to wander about feeling rather numb and lost, finding it hard re-engage himself to the tasks of emptying the storage compartment of garbage and arranging a visit to the local school. I carry out boat repairs and make endless telephone calls to organise our big arrival into Miami. It is vital that we get as much publicity as possible to help attract a financial sponsor. My father Stuart, together with Martin and another of Kenny's friends, Katriona, will fly to Florida from London in time to assist in pre-arrival promotions.

145

The islanders have given us an incredible welcome, a place to stay and some provisions for the remaining weeks of the voyage. They have even organised a fund-raising dinner for us to help pay for *Moksha*'s repairs. Touchingly, we are referred to as the third most famous people to set foot on these shores, after Christopher Columbus – who is claimed to have landed nearby in 1492, and the astronaut John Glenn – who dropped in after becoming the first American in space, in 1963.

Our arrival by no means excites everyone. Two local men returning from a fishing trip have just walked past on the rickety wooden pontoon, close to where I am sitting on *Moksha*'s roof. One wore a ragged T-shirt and chewed on a stem of sugar cane.

'What dat is?' he asked his friend, waving the chewed cane stump at *Moksha*.

'Don' axe me!' replied the other, who balanced a fishing rod on his shoulder. And that was the end of it.

The indigenous people of the region, the Lukka Caya, were all dead – all eight million of them – within forty-three years of Columbus' arrival. Abducted Africans were shipped in to replace them to work at the gold mines, pearl beds and sugar plantations. Today these Africans coexist, uneasily it has to be said, alongside a minority of white business owners and tax-exiles, a proportion of whom, by all accounts, are money-laundering crooks.

Among the rich white minority is the owner of an American fast-food chain called Arby's, who has been generous enough to divert $2,000 destined for the U.S treasury into our hands. All we have to do in return is display a small sticker on *Moksha*'s hull until we get to Miami then send him a picture (to prove it was a legitimate promotional expense). I had the cash in my hands for two seconds before Kenny claimed it for his promotional expenses in Miami, which I readily agreed to. This is our best opportunity to find serious sponsorship. I had momentary ethical reservations about accepting fast food money, considering the damage it does but... well, I suppose my ethical stance wasn't worth two thousand desperately needed bucks.

Principles and practice are proving to be a difficult marriage in more ways than one. Take *Moksha*'s rubbish, for example: we have held on to every fragment of waste we produced – from wrappers to batteries to gas canisters – for the entire voyage. We sometimes even slept among the stinking sacks. What do you suppose happened to all those plastic bags we carefully brought ashore? They headed straight back out to sea on a municipal refuse dumper.

Preparing To Leave
2 February

A friend has invited us to watch the American Weather Channel before we make any decision to depart. I struggle to digest the staggering amount of information they manage to squeeze into a thirty-second bulletin. Back home we get a pasty-faced geek wearing thick bifocals who slaps fog and rain stickers onto a plyboard map. Here you get a glamour-puss presenting satellite movies of storm systems followed by animated charts for Influenza, Pain Index (?), Respiratory Distress and Air Stagnation (??). I think I understood from it that the weather would be fine tomorrow with easterly winds.

The Final Stretch
3 February

We pedal reluctantly away from friends waving at the dock and push hard against a north-west breeze to clear the point.

Then, in open ocean, we head due west, aiming to complete the remaining five hundred miles to Miami in time for the annual boat show that starts on 16 February.

The weather soon turns against us. By the following day the wind veers round to the north-west. We throw out the sea anchor overnight and drift slowly backwards.

The next morning, the hundredth day of the voyage, the wind eases slightly and we resume the usual pedalling routine – two hours on, two hours off, four hourly changes at night.

Each morning for the next four days I find myself waking with a prayer for the wind to change. It doesn't oblige. We keep pedalling into the wind, going virtually nowhere, but forced to try and at least hold on to our position by the Cuban coast, which at one point is only twenty miles to the south.

I tune in to Bahamas Radio to learn that our contrary winds are the result of a vicious gale centred on North Providence Island, where sixty-nine feet waves are reported in open-ocean. Sixty-nine feet!

My knees have become very swollen and stiff, especially in the mornings. I have felt very close to collapsing with exhaustion over the past few days. Sometimes, when gusts of wind blow us backwards, I cannot physically turn the pedals at all. Watching Jason on his shift inspires me to a higher level of grit. His legs of steel just keep turning.

The wind finally turns in our favour on Day 105. I plot a course to take us off the Old Bahama Channel and away from Cuba, onto the shallows of the Great Bahama Bank north of Muracas Reef, which we should reach sometime tomorrow. The big question is whether we are safer or more at risk from another storm in thirty feet of water. And will the sudden, dramatic change in depth cause this deep ocean swell to rise into great cresting waves and break, as it did at Turtle Cove reef?

The following day I change my mind and decide not to risk the bank with this swell. We alter course, looping hard south, and continue along the Old Bahama Channel.

Later in the day, we have several encounters with Cuban fishing boats. The first is a fat trawler with a high white cabin and a sinister-looking crew of about six, who leer and leap about under instruction and seem intent on boarding us. We have no money but we have some expensive equipment aboard. *Moksha* is a slow, defenceless target. All I can think of to do is load a flare pistol, hide it behind my back and stand defiantly in the open hatchway with the evilest 'make-my-day' face I can muster, though inwardly terrified and trembling. They seem rather nervous as well, or perhaps just confused. What is this peculiar boat – a submarine, research vessel, US military? We delay them long enough for Jason to steer through a gap between lines of floating nets where our pursuers cannot follow.

We spot similar vessels positioned every ten miles or so along the coast – all fishing boats without fishing equipment and cruising aimlessly about. It seems very odd and unlikely that they have all deployed their nets at the same time and have nothing better to do than waste precious diesel. The only explanation I can think of is that, rather than being pirates, these crews are fishing for people for the Americans, who pay them to stay out there and net escapees. It must be much cheaper for the US authorities to pay Cubans to apprehend and repatriate their own refugees before they reach US soil than for the Americans to do it themselves.

Later in the day, the sight of an ageing cabin cruiser heading north at top speed and overflowing with people, some literally hanging on for dear life, reinforces my suspicions.

We finally abandon the deep channel for the transparent shallows of the bank at Cay Lobos lighthouse as the pink evening draws in.

Day 107: total calm on the Great Bahama Bank. *Moksha* is alone on a flat ocean that stretches like an endless, perfectly polished slab to the horizon in every direction. I lie on my stomach on the bow deck and gaze down through transparent water at the passing underneath of solitary starfish, clumps of sea grasses and the exquisitely ragged cross-hatching of rippled sands on the seabed. *Moksha*'s bow slices cleanly through the water, creating the faintest ripples that fan out in silent lines behind her and soon vanish. The only sound, apart from a faint whirring of the pedal chain, is the enchanting celestial chorus of a Christian choir on Bahamas radio that echoes dreamily through the cabin.

The cabin temperature is crushingly hot. Months of sweat that have dripped from our bodies into the pedal seat, combined with heat, create the perfect breeding ground for life. Jason is horrified to discover a thriving colony of maggots covering the seat under where the cushion goes. There are dozens of them: identical, cream and yellow coloured, vaguely ribbed bodies about the size of a grain of rice, who wriggle, roll and curl one end up as though begging to be fed. We crouch and stare at them in fascinated horror, before Jason starts rummaging around in our supplies for something to kill them with. Eventually he pulls out a small plastic bottle labelled Biocide containing a chemical we use to clean the filter of our water-maker.

'Here, this ought to do the trick,' he says, sprinkling the foul-smelling liquid over the seat. 'This stuff would take the skin off a rhinoceros's arse.'

The maggots continue to wriggle. The chemical has no effect whatsoever.

'Jeez! I don't believe it.' He laughs raucously in surprise. '"Yum yum," they say, "can I have some more please?"' He empties the entire bottle over them. This seems to do the trick. One by one, they all stop wriggling.

Tomorrow night we leave the shallow bank and join the Santarém Channel that leads to the Straits of Florida. The beginning and the end of any voyage are the most dangerous periods, when good luck with the weather is most essential. Storms that are minor inconveniences mid-ocean become lethal dangers near shore. Over a four thousand-mile distance what did it matter to be blown fifty miles off-course? We merely continued pedalling west when the weather improved. But a storm now would be disastrous because we are almost surrounded by land. Strong winds from the north would run up against the north-going Gulf Stream and create mountainous seas in one of the busiest shipping lanes in the world. Strong winds from the east or west would wreck us on the coral reefs of the Florida Keys or the Bahamas. Our fate really is in the lap of the gods now. The weather must hold.

Day 110: the midday sun bears oppressively down upon us, sapping the strength. There isn't a breath of cooling wind as we slip through the glassy sea, pedalling away inside the humid, stinking cabin. The day is broken up with regular plunges into the ocean but within ten minutes of clambering back onboard we are as hot as before and dripping with sweat.

Steering a course in these conditions ought to be straightforward but the wildly unpredictable currents of the Santarém Channel make a mockery of our efforts. There is a tremendous feeling of latent power ahead, at the confluence of two slow but mighty oceanic currents – the North Equatorial Current from the Atlantic Ocean, and the Gulf Stream flowing out of the Gulf Of Mexico.

We are at the critical edge where these two great currents meet, just a mile from the treacherous Dog Rocks. Our gearbox, which was recently repaired at a marine engineering business in Provo, has broken again. A short time ago the rubber seal split and lubricant started leaking over the cabin floor. Jason carried on pedalling with the bearings grinding noisily against each other, but friction caused the bearings to expand and now the entire mechanism has seized.

Jason remains very calm. He removes the broken seal, cools the unit with seawater and packs new lubricant in through the cracks. I, on the other hand, see the Dog Rocks getting closer and start to panic. I hastily grab a manual drill from our toolbox to bore a hole through the plywood cabin walls on both sides. Next, I thread a wire-saw through the hole in the starboard side and begin working it back and forth, aiming to cut an oblong gap wide enough for our emergency oars to be deployed.

The rocks are now plainly in view, just a few hundred metres away. I am only halfway through cutting the first hole with the wire-saw. My fingers are lacerated and dripping with blood.

Jason manages to get the pedals turning again. He expresses his relief with a flurry of hissing expletives: 'Argh, for fuck's sake! Why can't people fucking fix things properly! If you want something done right, you've always got to do it your fucking self!' And so on.

The following afternoon, both sea and sky are buzzing with traffic as we cross the Straits of Florida heading towards Biscayne Bay. We take turns to race full-speed at the pedals in order to cross the Gulf Stream gunning north at three knots.

Otherwise we are pretending to be terribly busy about the boat, possibly to avoid contemplating an extended period of civilisation after spending nearly one-third of a year at sea in a wooden capsule. The easiest task is to gather our personal things into a bag, because we have so little. A storm carried off most of our clothing from *Moksha*'s washing line, barely leaving us enough to avoid instant arrest. I have a grease-stained T-shirt, a pair of ripped shorts, a foul-smelling pair of cycling shoes, a cap, a toothbrush, some family photos and a hundred dollar bill from the crew of the 'Charlie Brown'.

And how do we feel to be the first people in history to travel from continental Europe to America using our own power? It will take some time to comprehend the achievement. Until today, it was always too vast and overwhelming to contemplate the whole thing at once. But now it is safe to add up all the memories, the millions of pedal revolutions, the long and exhausting nights, the peaceful sunrises and the terrifying avalanches of water and I'm beginning to feel absolutely, incredibly pleased with myself. With a great deal of help from others we have done this amazing thing. We pedalled across the Atlantic Ocean. Whatever happens next, this confidence can never be taken away or forgotten. I know something, something that is priceless, something we should all know: I can do anything I truly want to do.

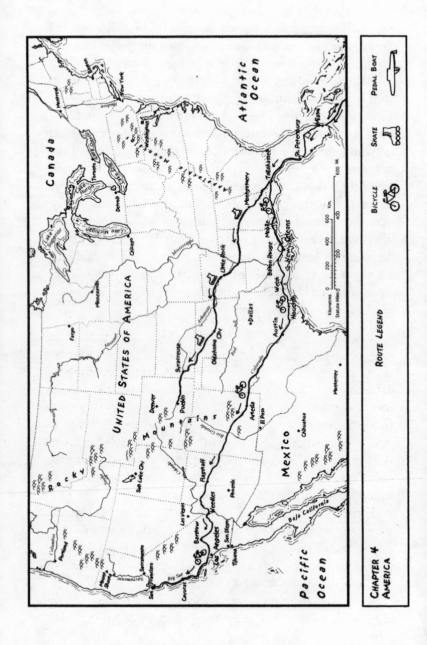

ROUTE LEGEND   BICYCLE   SKATE   PEDAL BOAT

CHAPTER 4
AMERICA

4. America
(February – November 1995)

Out of the Frying Pan...
Miami, Florida

It is our first day on dry land. Jason sits beside me in grim silence in the back seat of Stuart's hire car. I sense my fingers clawing into the upholstery and glance at the speedometer – sixty miles per hour, twenty times faster than we have travelled in a very long time. My father's driving ability doesn't help.

We leave the four-lane freeway and rise above the city on an off-ramp. The landscape is an endless cuboid matrix of lights, metal, concrete and glass: a brightly-lit shop frontage with flamboyantly-posed mannequins, a parking lot, privet hedge, two dogs urinating on a fire hydrant, Italian restaurant, cars waiting at a stop light, pink shopping mall, signs to the freeway, billboard advertising Lacto-Aid – everything disappears from sight before it can be taken in. We swoop between blocks of high-rise apartments; a car overtakes; the traffic lights ahead turn red and the column of cars in our lane slow to a halt. Stuart brakes sharply, forcing us to brace ourselves against the back of front seat head rests, and swerves into the inside lane, which has less traffic.

'We've got free rooms at the Ramada. Look for signs to the airport,' Stuart bellows, addressing us through his rear-view mirror. There are directions and instructions all around me, but none saying 'Airport'. There are several saying 'Stop'; others say 'Look'; and yet more tell us to 'Go'; 'Buy'; 'Loan'; 'Lease'; 'Try Now'; 'Free Trial'; 'Toll-Free'; 'Call'; 'Call Now!'

My stomach is in knots, just as it was on our final day in Europe. But that feeling of pedalling out into the ocean, as I recall, arose from an entirely different class of fear. It was a wonderfully light and tantalising fear. This is a heavy, churning dread. It's the fear of what it takes to survive in a grey metropolis, how it changes you.

My expectations of America were great – I think to myself, as we loop around onto a different freeway and tuck ourselves in behind a boxy suburban with tinted windows. The key reasons for deciding to go west around the world were to pedal the Atlantic first, to make a big splash in America, so to speak, and to prove our sponsorship worth. We are the first people to travel from mainland Europe to mainland USA by human power. I expected that our years of financial struggle, and the worry of how to repay twenty-five thousand pounds of debt, would be over. I thought the corporate world would be so impressed by all the media attention, and so amazed to discover we had come so far without a sponsor, that they would go goggle-eyed and squabble to be the first.

The publicity has been good. A television crew from the British ITN News chartered a boat to document our arrival into Biscayne Bay this morning. Another crew from an American network station trailed us for about an hour from a helicopter. Jason hoisted a flag for them, made from an old white canvas sail bag, bearing a message that had taken ten days to create from cut-out blue canvas lettering and hand-stitched into place. It came out clearly on the morning news. On one side it read 'We Need A Sponsor' and on the other side 'No Sleep Till Florda!' Jason is refusing to explain the mysteriously omitted 'i' in 'Florida'. I think it was mistaken for an exclamation mark and sewn in upside down at the end. Kenny sent a worldwide video link through Reuter's that apparently received lots of airtime on CNN, elbowing aside no less a figure than the Pope on his visit to Poland. We are also rumoured to have made the front pages of several national newspapers, including *The Times* in London. And we were one of Jay Leno's (rather lame) opening gags on last night's show – something about 'Haven't those guys heard of the airplane?'

I ought to feel more appreciative. Stuart, Kenny, Martin and Katriona flew all the way from England and have hardly slept in the past few days trying to promote our arrival. But I wonder whether it was worth all the expense – thousands of dollars in flights, hire cars, telephone calls and room service. All for what, to be today's amusing anecdote? To be the trivial sweet pill (a.k.a. fluff-piece) they tack on to the end of the news to make it more digestible? The publicity is worth nothing to me by itself. It was supposed to be useful, our big chance of attracting a sponsor to repay our debts. But no sponsorship inquiries have come from it.

The Atlantic voyage ended at a remote pontoon below the Miami Yacht Club at 12.30 p.m. Our promotional team had faxed a press release to every newsroom in the country, specifying the venue, the date and the exact time of arrival. Not a single journalist or photographer was there to witness it. I was amazed. Stuart was waiting with the obligatory bottle of champagne next to a pedal-powered vehicle enthusiast called Nancy Sanford, who has been following our progress for some months. A few people drifted down from a barbecue on the yacht club lawn to see what the fuss by the funny little boat was about. A few handshakes and it was all over.

Stepping ashore didn't feel like an ending, more like a fresh twist in the ongoing struggle. Why? The Miami Boat Show began today; only six days remain; despite the kind donation of exhibition space for *Moksha* we arrived with no vehicle or trailer to take her there. Moments after stepping ashore we began begging for help. Stuart has found a printing company to produce five hundred expedition T-shirts and a local businessman to loan us two thousand dollars to pay for them. If we can sell them at the show for fifteen dollars with our signatures on them, then we can pay our bills and have something left over to work with.

My mind wanders as we exit the freeway once more and proceed along a straight boulevard lined with dismal two-storey housing, shops with hand-drawn notices and empty sidewalks. I am overwhelmed by the size of the task. There are so many things to be done before the show reopens in the morning. What about when it ends? We need to find somewhere to live, somewhere for *Moksha* to live. I need an office and telephone to organise fund-raising talks with a slide show, for which I need slides and a speech. I need some clothes to wear, a haircut. I especially need to lose this enormous red beard; I can't eat without chewing bits of it. I stepped ashore with a hundred dollar bill donated by the crew of the 'Charlie Brown' and immediately bought a hamburger and fries, which means I have ninety-four dollars left to begin paying for the above.

I look across at Jason. He looks miserable. I know he wants to pedal straight back out to sea. Stuart takes a left turn and proceeds along a curved road lined with neatly cropped box hedging. There is a large neon sign halfway up a concrete monolith to our right that reads 'Ramada Hotel'.

'OK you guys,' says my father in his chirpy fake-American accent. 'I bet you're looking forward to a shower and clean sheets, eh?' We mumble our assent.

'I didn't expect it to be like a Hollywood premiere or anything,' I say to Jason as we walk from the hotel parking lot and into a large, marble and glass foyer, 'but you know, considering what we did, I thought someone from the press would have turned up to interview us at the Miami Yacht Club.'

'The thing is,' he answers reluctantly, staring straight ahead, 'it wasn't the Miami Yacht Club. It was one of the Miami Yacht Clubs. Apparently there are about six of them. It was a huge fuck-up, basically. The press release our lot sent out included a time and a place, but no address and no bloody phone number.'

Losing The Plot
Ramada Hotel, Miami

I am drowning, drowning in the details, constantly tired and withdrawn. I crawl across my unfurnished room in the hotel basement (literally four bare walls, mattress and carpet) looking for my speech. Layers of papers, lists, maps, bills, dirty clothes and bicycle parts litter the floor. My sixteenth slide show talk begins in two hours. It's a Rotary Club luncheon. My mind jumps from one priority to the next. I try to resolve them all at once in a frenzied tangle of thoughts, achieving nothing. Sometimes I sit in this room for hours without realising that I have achieved nothing but chew my nails until every finger is raw and bleeding.

The misery of debt! The Miami Boat Show raised six thousand dollars. My slide shows and Jason and Stuart's efforts have contributed another four thousand dollars but after expenses we have saved only a thousand. Kenny, Martin and Katriona have returned to England – thank heavens – leaving only Jason, Stuart and myself for the expedition to support. We each live on twenty dollars a day, which means that almost two thousand dollars must be found each month before we can start repaying debts.

Jason and my father found accommodation with different families in Fort Lauderdale. Jason keeps a safe distance from me. I'm the odious, obsessive manic-depressive. He focuses mostly on visiting schools and doesn't seem very concerned about money or debts. My father, who is a children's entertainer by nature, helps him. I think they are happy. I see my father more often than Jason. He does his best to lift my spirits.

Even if I increased my speaking engagements to twenty-five or thirty a month it would still take many years to repay my mother, Maria and Jason's parents. But I don't think I can work any harder than I am. Continual fund-raising is destroying me. I am beginning to despise myself. Every day I see dozens of people. We shake hands and smile and discuss the expedition and they think I'm just being myself. They think I'm interested in them and their questions, always the same questions. Meanwhile, I'm counting down the seconds I have left to get twenty dollars out of their wallets. Will he take an XL T-shirt or a name on the boat? I hate myself because they are such wonderful, warm, positive, generous people.

But how long should our creditors back home be expected to wait? They have their own dreams to pursue. If we can't find the money in the richest, most generous country in the world, where will it be found?

My greatest source of comfort and companionship in this difficult, lonely period is the letters I've received from friends and family back home. I always find it odd that I should exhibit greater concern for their well-being – and they for mine – the farther we are apart. Even distant aunts, from whom I might expect only five words in a birthday card from one year to the next, have taken to posting bulging envelopes filled with lively descriptions of their daily lives, all of which I find delightful. And I respond with funny anecdotes of American life, all the weird and wonderful people I've met – from the hitch-hiking evangelist to the alligator- burger street vendor to the extraordinarily fat people who told me more about Jesus over breakfast at Denny's.

The letters I most cherish come from Ireland, usually in colourful envelopes with funny pictures and postscripts scrawled on them – now at a frequency of two or three a week. These are from a girl I met while cycling down through France last year, a very attractive and bubbly Irish brunette called Eilbhe (pronounced Elva) Donovan. She was working as a horse-riding instructor at a children's summer camp in the Dordogne, but has since returned home to attend art college.

We were together in France for only a few days but it was an intensely magical time. We took horses along the labyrinths of farm trails and woodland tracks and enjoyed a long, giggling afternoon over a picnic in some abandoned field. Then she stunned me by hitch-hiking all the way down to Portugal to see me once more before she had to fly back to Ireland. Her long, endearing, funny letters, all of which I read at least three times, give me no end of pleasure.

Broken Down In The Beast
Palm Bay

I called Melbourne Beach Rotary Club last week to explain that I couldn't make the after-dinner speech because my borrowed car had broken down on Interstate 95. In fact I was just exhausted. Now I'll have to call the Indian River Yacht Club with the same apology, except this time it's true and it's the Florida Turnpike.

The car, a colossal Lincoln we call The Beast and whose chrome plated front bumper alone weighs as much as an English car, is on loan from Howard the cable TV talk-show host. In return one of us had to appear on the show and talk about the expedition. Kenny volunteered. The show's other

161

guests were titled 'The One Legged Lesbians From Hell'. Afterwards Kenny was forced to sit through a screening of Howard's latest video production – a low-budget porn movie featuring Howard. Kenny flew back to England soon after that.

I pull into the parking lot of a shopping complex to let The Beast's engine cool. I might as well sleep here overnight on the back seat and wait for tomorrow's luncheon gig at the Malabar Country Club. In the meantime I have one dollar and a cigarette.

Air-Conditioned Nightmare
Palm Bay

7.00 a.m.: I stumble from the Lincoln with leg cramps and wander across the parking lot to a breakfast diner called Dottie's Kitchen.

Inside, I surrender my crumpled dollar bill for 'all the coffee you can drink'. Accessories to breakfasts I can't afford are placed in neat colonies along a long white Formica bar: dripping jugs of maple syrup, red plastic squeezable bottles of ketchup in the shape of big tomatoes, sachets of salt and pepper in a white china tray, more sachets of jellies and sugar substitutes, a specials menu held vertical in a metal frame, individual tubs of butter substitute in a dainty wicker basket. I settle for a discarded newspaper and an ashtray and listen to a jukebox playing 'Lay Down Sally'. The surrounding tables are filled with burly men wearing baseball caps and short-sleeved collared shirts, most with a single pocket at the front in which pens or lottery tickets are kept. They lay their massive forearms across the table and correct one another on some exotic facts of sporting history and remark how bored they have become of the O.J. Simpson trial on television. Everyone talks about the O.J. Simpson trial, even if it is only to point out how much they hate people talking about it.

I sit at the breakfast bar with my black coffee and cigarette, feeling rather sorry for myself. I notice how cynical I've become since arriving in Florida, which annoys me because I've always been very fond of America. I need to relax and enjoy myself more, have some fun, instead of working to repay debts the whole time. I gave up my career and normality to spend my time doing this! I look around the café once more, and at the glowing ash of my drooping cigarette. The adventure was supposed to be a liberating thing: *Moksha* – Sanskrit for freedom, right? Now I am more a captive of the system than before, and living in Henry Miller's Air-Conditioned Nightmare for my trouble.

Maybe it's just my state of mind, or my long-standing fear that one day I'll wake to find myself a fully paid-up suburbanite without realising how I got there. But there's something horrifying and Orwellian about the Florida good-life – the vast blocks of shopping malls and the spotless Chevrolets parked in driveways between luxuriant, springy lawns, the immaculate golf courses, the dreamy soft-focus television, the novelty mailboxes, the cavernous refrigerators with ice-making facility, the obsession with mail-order gadgetry; there's something about the food – the cheese, milk and bread. It's all a sinister victory of appearance over flavour and yet so seductive and inviting, so easy to slip into and go to sleep.

A New Chapter
Cooper City: 30 May

My belongings are again packed onto two wheels in readiness for the 3,500-mile ride to California. Jason is still adamant about skating across America but has yet to find himself a pair of skates or, for that matter, learn how to balance on them. My father says he's happy to remain in Florida for a while. He shares an apartment close to the beach with a friend and lives on a small pension. We hope to see him on the Pacific coast before too long.

Stuart is a survivor, a larger-than-life character, a showman who loves to make people laugh and – considering that he never knew family life as a child – a pretty good father. His mother abandoned him when he was five and his father worked long hours as a train driver at the ICI chemical works in Middlesbrough, leaving Stuart's guidance in the hands of his miscreant brother George – whenever George was not in front of a magistrate. In 1948, just after his ninth birthday, he was sent to George Muller's Orphanage Home in Bristol for daily doses of the cane and the New Testament until he was fifteen, when he joined the Royal Navy. Stuart was bright and enthusiastic, achieving the rank of petty officer in record time, but also troublesome, constantly in and out of military prison for insubordination, absence-without-leave and drunken brawling.

Eventually he met my mother Sylvia, who was a Wren, and who succeeded in channelling Stuart's energy to better ends. They married, started a family, left the Navy, and my father worked hard to become one of the most successful life insurance salesmen in the country. He gave motivational speeches at business conferences around the world. He also devoted considerable energy, after the death of my brother, to children's charities and became a regional chairman of the Variety Club of Great Britain. He failed to spend enough time with his own children, but was always very generous, supportive and fun to be around. I loved him, but we were never friends, not until I left university, by which time my father had made a series of staggeringly foolish decisions – both personal and financial – that left him jobless, homeless, divorced and practically penniless, all within the space of two years. I was also feeling pretty sorry for myself at the time, having split disastrously with my college sweetheart, and we moved in together to a flat in Ealing, West London. We continue to marvel that, had it not been for my father's misfortunes, we might never have been close. The expedition has also given him a renewed sense of purpose and belonging. The key to understanding my father is this powerful need to belong and be loved.

Jason and I have agreed to travel together across Florida to St Petersburg then split up for the remainder of the journey across the country. We were once the very best of friends but that seems a very long time ago. It was an intimacy born in the wild and carefree years at university and which continued to thrive in the early, bright years of full independence in London. We still have occasional good times, but these are generally propped up by the presence of third parties and quantities of alcohol, where we resurrect the ghost of friendship past and retell old jokes. Mostly we tolerate each other. Perhaps this long separation will help us both to heal wounds and reconnect in California, refreshed and ready for the greater challenges ahead. Or perhaps it will be the end of us.

On the practical side, Jason once asked me whether I fancied skating across the country too, although he didn't suggest I do it with him. 'Bugger that for a game of soldiers!' was my immediate reply, which did nothing at all to communicate the real depths to which I had gone in considering it, or the admiration and respect I have for his courage in doing it. I struggle to admit an element in me that rejects the idea of skating across America just because he thought of it first, which is ironic because this is precisely the sort of petty rebellion I most like to accuse Jason of. The main reason I'd like to carry on cycling is that I love travelling in that way, especially on the quiet, gravelly back roads and interesting trails where skating would be impossible. Jason's route will be largely confined to busier, well-managed highways. I fail to see the attraction in that. Nor am I particularly smitten with the novelty value of being the first person to skate unsupported across the continent. I choose to stick with the mode of human-powered transport that suits me best.

Our timing is typically atrocious. This summer is widely predicted to be one of the hottest since records began and we will be travelling through the Deep South at the height of it, in June and July, in temperatures over 100°F and humidity approaching one hundred per cent. The alternative would be to wait until September but we have done all we can here and are anxious to move on. As we learned from the ocean, anything can become normal over time and what scares me is how used to suburban living I have become after three months in Florida. I am truly grateful to the various individuals who have given me shelter but, as my favourite American hobo would have put it, my shit ain't hard no more and it's time to move on.

Moksha will remain in dry storage at a marina in Fort Lauderdale until we decide how and where to ship her next. Several thousand dollars have been thrown at the debt mountain, at least showing good faith, and thousands of children in dozens of schools throughout southern Florida have been introduced to the expedition. Sometimes we bring *Moksha* along to these school visits but otherwise we arrive with just a slide show. The aim is to inspire and to expand their understanding of what is possible. Given how exposed children are these days to all that is fast, aggressive and money-oriented, I particularly enjoy balancing that with something that is slow, simple and non-competitive. We remain unsure of how to develop the schools network as we progress, but the idea of an interactive web-site looks to be the most promising.

San Francisco appeals to me purely by gut instinct as a destination. I don't know a soul there but I've been given the name of Marcus Cook and an address in the Mission District for somewhere to initially stay.

Winners
Okeechobee

Our journey across America began four days ago, on 18 June. A small crowd of friends and reporters gathered outside the Elbow Room bar on Fort Lauderdale 'Strip' to see us off. Jason took his first nosedive into a gravel driveway half a mile to the north. Forty miles and countless spectacular falls later we reached Lake Worth. It was Jason's sixth attempt on skates, the previous five having been supervised circuits encompassing a few blocks of downtown Fort Lauderdale.

It is interesting to note how differently people react to the idea of a complete novice skating, entirely unsupported, 3,500 miles across America. Their responses – disbelief, delight, encouragement, criticism, advice and even downright anger – reveal a great deal about them.

'Why are you putting yourself through all this?' asked a kind-eyed matronly woman at a café where we had stopped briefly for shade.

'It's just a personal thing,' Jason replied for the umpteenth time, leaving the concerned woman none the wiser. He tried again with greater thought. 'What I mean is,' he continued, while strapping on his elbow and kneepads again, ready for the road, 'it's not like I need to get to San Francisco. If I needed to go anywhere then I'd drive or fly or take the train or whatever like everyone else. Do you see?' She shook her head. He persevered.

'Look, I'm a beginner at this, as you can tell.' He stood shakily on his skates and steadied himself with a hand on her shoulder. She flinched a little, perhaps feeling momentarily alarmed at the unsolicited use of her body by this unfathomable longhaired boy with his dark eyes and neatly sculpted goatee. But then she smiled, took his elbow in her hand and hardened her stance helpfully. He continued.

'Thanks. But there's a trick to it. There's a skill, a flowing movement that uses the whole body. I'm interested in that. I'll figure it out soon enough.'

'But it's such a long way!'

'Yeah. But I'm in no hurry.' He let himself roll down the pavement and waved goodbye to the woman, and again to a boy with a dog who shouted good luck. 'If you keep going you've got to get there eventually, right?'

Jason seems to have no doubt he will skate to San Francisco. It is not a matter for debate, only a matter of time. Thus far it has also been a matter of considerable pain. By the morning of our third day, heading north-west from Indiantown, Jason's shins were a mass of oozing, bloody holes and bruises from the constant rubbing of his boots. The conditions are unpleasant enough on a bicycle – murderous heat and humidity and mosquitoes everywhere. We can't even lie down to rest without being attacked by hordes of biting red ants. But skating demands double the effort of cycling. It exhausts me just to watch him wobble along these badly maintained farm roads, mile after sweltering mile. The salt in his sweat burns like acid into his bloody shins and still he struggles on, trying to master the swaying rhythm of skating.

Because of this swaying motion a skater uses more of the road than a cyclist does and is thereby more vulnerable to passing cars. After several near misses I now ride behind Jason and take up a fraction more of the road than I need. This is by no means guaranteed to make cars overtake safely. Many

Floridian males seem unwilling to respect anything smaller than what they are driving (usually a pick-up truck). After countless whirlwinds of abuse, honking horns and flying beer bottles, I can only guess that veering a few feet to the left for the sake of a cyclist is considered the ultimate humiliation.

Legally it is as much our road as theirs. They don't see it that way. The way they see it, anyone over the age of fifteen who cycles must either be too poor or too stupid to drive, in which case they might as well get flattened along with the other road-kill vermin – the possums, the snakes and the armadillos – that litter the road. I have yet to come across another cyclist on the road, either living or flattened.

I suppose it is normal to be intolerant of the abnormal. Only a lifetime ago the motorcar was an infernal machine that frightened horses. A lifetime from now it will be the pick-up truck's turn for abuse from passing gyro-hover jets, or something similar.

There is nothing normal about my present situation at the public launderette in Okeechobee. Dressed only in my last clean pair of underpants, I am loading a machine with the foulest-smelling garments in creation. The remainder of my belongings cover the floor: a hammock (for sleeping out of ants' reach), a mosquito suit, a cooking pot and utensils, food, a medical kit, bike spares, soap, a toothbrush, mosquito repellent, a flashlight, batteries, a map, a journal, a waterproof jacket and a wallet containing a hundred and thirty bucks. By some miracle Jason stuffs all his gear into a small backpack, although he doesn't carry food.

The noise is unbearable: washing machines tumble and spin; the air-conditioning drones; mosquitoes buzz in my ear; a 'Final Fight' video game machine delivers its martial arts 'Hee-aarrs!' and 'Whacks!' at full volume, followed by the victory jingle. I stare at the video game screen, horrified at the numerous ways in which I could mutilate my enemies – from ninjas to gangsters – before taking my winner's wave holding aloft a spinal column dripping with blood. The video game preview resets itself to an opening statement. In view of the bloodthirsty game itself, the irony tickles me:

From William S. Sessions (Director FBI)
Winners Don't Use Drugs

Armed with fresh-smelling socks we pack and rejoin State Road 98, a quiet single-laner that meanders through grazing land to Fort Basinger.

I am delighted to be reunited with my bicycle, which was kindly couriered over from Europe by DHL. It is a gloriously smooth, practically silent machine, a Cadillac among cycles. Again I become the silent drifter, observing the passage of rain clouds and the scurrying of startled rodents.

Dusk: pinks and oranges bleed from the dying sun. The air is saturated and dense, making my sinuses throb. It begins to rain in heavy bulbous blobs that drown the chirruping din of cicadas. Out in the pasture a white egret stands motionless on a cow's back.

The Cracker Trail
Wimauma: 25 June

Yesterday we covered fifty miles along the old Cracker Trail from Basinger to Zolfo Springs and the same again today to Wimauma. Both days were scorchers, about 110°F with the humidity factor. A century ago this route across Florida was renowned for the sound of cracking whips as ranchers drove herds of cattle to coastal markets. I can understand the animals' reluctance. No living thing travels of its own accord in this climate.

Zolfo Springs was reached within minutes of its only store closing for the night. The kindly storekeeper was so impressed by us that he wouldn't allow payment for our food. He then directed us to the nearby Camp of a Thousand Adventures, where enormous recreational vehicles with names like 'Amazon Explorer' and 'Himalayan Trekker' were parked in military rows. Here we found cooking water, a patch of ant-less ground and some dead branches for a fire.

We shared a stew of tuna and rice, then lay on a groundmat and tried to sleep through rain showers covered only in our mosquito suits. Our neighbours, the jungle explorers, watched television from a sofa and retired to air-conditioned bedrooms and cotton sheets.

Twenty miles into today's ride Jason collapsed onto the verge with heat exhaustion and nausea. We found shade under a picnic table at Duette Elementary School, where Jason took sachets of electrolyte powder with water. Half an hour later we set off again at a slower pace.

Tonight's deluxe accommodation is a garden shed next to an alligator-infested swamp. Since my cooking fire was extinguished in a torrential downpour we have been crunching our way through a semi-cooked mixture of rice and sardines in the tiny shelter. Our dismal situation is illuminated with a torch that Jason made from a broom-handle wrapped in strips of cloth and soaked in vegetable oil.

Only ten miles now separate us from the eastern shore of Tampa Bay. Nancy Sanford, whom we met on arrival in Miami, will be waiting for us there with three of her commercially made 'Escapade' pedal boats for a crossing to her home town of St Petersburg.

I first made contact with Nancy, who is very active in a worldwide organisation called the International Human Powered Vehicle Association (IHPVA), while we were still in London. We had just decided to pedal west across the Atlantic instead of going east around the world, and had no useful contacts in the USA. I feel incredibly fortunate to have picked Nancy. She is a super-efficient and well-connected, energetic single woman in her late forties, who formerly worked for a US senator and now manages a small hotel in St Petersburg. As a hobby, she also promotes a range of recreational pedal boats.

Nancy's plan for an enjoyable day's pedal across Tampa Bay has also been organised for press coverage, thereby promoting both Nancy's boats and the expedition. We desperately need funds, having only forty dollars left between us. Jason also needs medical attention and a dry, clean environment for his infected feet and legs.

The following morning, we vacated the garden shed early and covered the final ten miles to a small marina near Apollo Beach, at the shore of Tampa Bay. Nancy was waiting there for us. The pedal boats we had been given to use were very handsome white plastic capsules about the size of a compact car with two seats, a windscreen and a green awning for shade. We pedalled through a blisteringly hot day, stopping only for a brief packed lunch, and by sunset we made it across to St Petersburg.

Nancy kindly gave us a large room at the hotel and helped to organise everything from school visits to fund-raising talks to equipment repairs. We discussed how Jason and I would maintain contact as we progressed across country and Nancy agreed to be the base coordinator to whom we could both report.

A week passed quickly in busy preparations. Jason and I shared a room but spent little time together during the day. I sensed him becoming very focused upon his own mission and mentally preparing for the harsh and solitary life ahead.

The day before I was due to cycle on alone, north towards Tallahassee, I received another letter from Eilbhe Donovan, the Irish girl with whom I have developed a strong connection through letters over the past few months. She had completed her college course and was looking for something to do for the summer. It was Jason who urged me to give her a call and ask whether she fancied the idea of cycling across America. Jason had left his bike with a friend in Fort Lauderdale, but it was there to be used if Eilbhe wanted to ride with me.

I was incredibly nervous as I picked up the phone. Eilbhe answered. The sound of her soft Irish accent made my heart melt. I came straight to the point.

'Eilbhe, what do you think about cycling to San Francisco with me?'

'Wow! Um, sure, that would be fantastic!' she replied instantly. 'When were you thinking?' She sounded more hesitant. I knew she would be shocked by my reply.

'Next week.'

'Next week!'

'Yes. It'll take me a few days to cycle to Tallahassee. Then I could hire a car and drive back to Miami, pick you up from the airport, grab Jason's bike and we can drive back to Tallahassee together and head west on the bikes.'

'Err, OK. What should I bring?'

'Cycling shorts, T-shirts, you know, summer stuff. We'll worry about warmer clothes when we get to the Rockies.'

'Great. Anything else I should know?'

'Yeah. You can't take the piss out of folk over here. They don't appreciate the humour.' I had to stress this point. Eilbhe means 'Little Fairy' in Irish, though 'Mischievous Pixie', however translated, would have been more fitting. She has a relentless impudence, developed to an art form: when travelling she makes money drawing scathing caricatures of tourists, who mostly pay for the pleasure of being laughed at in the most enchanting way. 'Oh, I nearly forgot. It's really hot here.'

'Yeah, it's hot here as well. Dublin was seventy-eight degrees yesterday!'

'You don't understand, honey. It's really hot here. Never mind, you'll see.'

It was fantastic to see Eilbhe's smiling, freckled face as she walked out of the arrivals gate at Miami Airport. Her cascading brown hair was longer than before. She wore a pink cotton vest, green combats, an orange and gold flat cap and two pendants on leather necklaces that swung together as she walked and which dug into me as we threw ourselves into each other's arms. Her breath reeked of booze – 'Malibu,' she explained, giggling, from a bottle belonging to 'A fella from Limerick, Jaysus, wuddja believe it! In the very next seat!'

'Whew, it's so hot in here I can't breathe,' she remarked as we headed back to the car park. 'I can't wait to get outside.'

'Look up, darling,' I said. 'This is outside.' Sure enough, there was the open sky.

Eilbhe was silent for a while as we drove from the airport. She had never been beyond northern Europe, had never subjected herself to fitness training for any sport and had never ridden a bicycle more than a few miles in her life.

We set out from Tallahassee late one afternoon, managed fifteen miles and made camp behind a disused gas station. The following day we cycled another fifty miles west. Eilbhe is adjusting incredibly well not only to the heat, the insects and the physical effort, but also to being Irish and vegetarian in western Florida. A typical conversation might begin:

'Aah lurve yer accent. Where ya frum?'

'Ireland.'

'What island?'

'Ireland.'

'There's an island called Island?'

Eventually she learned to say 'Eye-err-laand' and most people had heard of it.

Another begins:

'You're a what, sweetie?'

'I'm vegetarian. I don't eat meat.'

'Wayll, never mind darlin'. How 'bout Aah fix ya'a turkey sandwich instead?'

We are finding it extremely hard to find proper food. West Floridians stock up on groceries during weekly trips to the nearest city hypermarket, but here in the country there are only the appalling convenience foods offered at gas stations and roadside cafés.

Ebro City
Florida Panhandle: 16 July

We rode starving into Ebro yesterday evening and found 'The Ebro Café – Home of Country Cooking'. A second display board promised, much to Eilbhe's amusement, 'Hand-Grated Cheese'. It turned out to be the home of pre-cooked microwaved pies and canned okra. Eilbhe settled for the last muesli bar in her pack and bought a cup of black coffee. She added 'cream' and 'sugar' or, more accurately, she added 'corn syrup solids, partially hydrogenated soybean and/or canola oils, sodium caseinate, dipotassium phosphate, sodium silicoaluminate, artificial colors, mono-and-diglycerides, lecithin and artificial flavours' and mixed it with 'dextrose with maltodextrin, aspartame (contains phenylanine), calcium saccharine, cream of tartar and calcium silicate'.

We left Ebro half an hour later and began cycling eagerly towards a camping spot on the Gulf of Mexico, which we hoped would offer a cool breeze and few insects. Broken glass on the road wrecked our plans only minutes later. I tried

repairing the puncture with patches but the gash was too big.
It was my last inner tube. We spent the night on waste ground
behind the Ebro Café.

It is now steaming hot at noon. Our things are laid out on the
dirt, covered in ants, in an attempt to dry them after a night
of solid rain.

We start chatting to the café owners, Edward and Janice.
Edward's brother Roger, who is mayor of Ebro, generously
offers me a lift into Panama City to buy new inner tubes.
Eilbhe stays behind to give Janice a hand in the kitchen. 'Maybe
I could grate some cheese for you,' I hear her say as she
disappears inside.

I lift my bicycle into Roger's pick-up truck, slide into the
passenger seat and slam the door behind me. Roger's opening
topic of conversation stuns me.

'Listen here boy,' Roger growls, thumping one great fist on
the steering wheel. 'There's only two things wrong in this
world, an' that's AIDS an' niggers.'

We are already heading south on the highway – no escape.
Besides, I must have the inner tubes. There is little choice
but to sit and listen to the mayor's politics. Thankfully he can
identify only two wrongs in this world. We should turn the
schools into military academies, Roger insists, weed out the
queers and the lazy niggers – who could then be neutered or
killed, and the survivors could then create a healthier, stronger
country. I stare out the passenger window and bite my lip.

I am relieved to find that the hypermarket has a sporting
goods section that stocks bicycle inner tubes. I return to Ebro
on my bike. We pack up our bags. It starts raining heavily
again.

'You leavin'?' Edward yells from the back door. 'Heck! I
figured you'd be white enough to stay out of this rain.'

Florida Avenue
New Orleans, Louisiana: 25 July

How lucky am I! I watch Eilbhe cycling ahead, the movement of her deliciously firm, long limbs and flowing brown hair. She loves the simple life of the open road; she thrills in the finding of a fresh campsite each night and the grubbing around for firewood; she'll just as readily sit on the concrete kerb at a filthy truck stop to sip her coffee as a comfortable dining chair; she can drink beer and belch with the best of them and can slurp soup from the pot. She abhors pretension, all make-up, frills and glamour, yet she is a divinely feminine, natural beauty.

In the twelve days since leaving Tallahassee we have cycled almost five hundred miles, west through the Deep South, through extreme heat, thunderstorms, insects and hostile traffic. Eilbhe arrived unfit, porcelain-white and un-acclimatized, and almost immediately began pushing her wispy, eight-stone (one-hundred-and-ten-pound) body to the limit on a bicycle that (with panniers) weighs about the same as she does. Today's ride will be eighty miles long.

We reached the Gulf coast at Grayton Beach soon after escaping Ebro. On the following afternoon we took shelter from a severe storm in the porch of an abandoned summerhouse at Destin Beach. An entire day and night passed blissfully by as we lay naked, watching a great lightning display, playing cards and eating fruit.

On the evening of Wednesday, 19 July we stumbled upon an enormous beach party at Navarre Beach on Santa Rosa Island. There we danced all night and made sweet love on the beach until, exhausted and entwined, we fell asleep.

The Alabama state-line was crossed on Sunday, 23 July, but by nightfall we were already through to Pascagoula, Mississippi. A casino waitress in Biloxi kept supplying us with free cocktails throughout the afternoon of the twenty-fourth, until our luck with the fruit machines finally dried up. Not surprisingly, Eilbhe's intake of White Russians dried her up during the onward journey. She collapsed with heat stroke and slept for fourteen hours under the pier at West Biloxi.

8.45 p.m.: the Louisiana swamplands have gradually given way to the squalid outskirts of New Orleans. Now deep inside the dark city, my mood has also transformed to a state of intense, nervous vigilance.

I am always wary upon entering a strange city by bicycle, but I don't remember feeling this tense. My primary concern is for Eilbhe's safety. We obviously have no money, but a beautiful young girl on a bicycle dangles like a jewel waiting to be snatched.

The streets become dirtier and more threatening the farther we cycle. Two carloads of rough-looking men follow close behind. We stop at a gas station, hoping to find a public phone to call our contact in New Orleans for help. The cars pull in behind.

An enormously-built black man approaches from the shadows. He wears a white string-vest and has a huge python dangling from his shoulders. He greets us gently and begins a conversation with Eilbhe. Instantly I feel a great sense of relief. He seems, somehow, to understand the situation and his presence is instantly effective. The sinister characters slink back into the night, presumably in search of easier prey lacking big friends with snakes. Hurriedly, I dial our contact's number.

'Hi Michael? It's Steve and Eilbhe. We're in east New Orleans, still about fifteen miles away.' I explain the neighbourhood. He knows it and is shocked – good sign, maybe he'll come and pick us up.

He isn't coming. His fiancée is annoyed that we'll miss dinner. To my dismay he starts giving me directions to his home on the other side of the city... left into Florida Avenue... junction... turn right... left... through the park... I take down the instructions, thank him and hang up.

The man with the snake has disappeared. We quickly cycle on.

The atmosphere becomes even more menacing. We pass an abandoned burnt-out car; a lonely drunk haunts the sidewalk, scattering litter as he goes. There are no street signs or directions to Florida Avenue.

Eilbhe spots a police patrol car on the opposite side of the road. We cross and wait for him to finish talking on the radio.

'Excuse me.' Eilbhe taps him on the shoulder

The officer turns, startled.

'I think we've missed the turning for Florida Avenue. Could you help us?'

His facial expression could either be anger or disbelief. He looks at me, then at Eilbhe, then at our bikes and back to me again.

'You gotta be kiddin' me! Yo' outa yo fuckin' minds, right?'

'Well, err, we didn't see the sign. Was it that obvious?' The officer shakes his head and groans loudly

'Ya don' unnerstan'. Listen t'me. Ya see this vee-hicle?' he asks, slamming one hand on the roof – we nod our heads – 'This vee-hicle's got ree-inforce' steel on'a sides. An' ya see this-here windshiel'?' He continues, stepping backwards and pointing – we nod again – 'Iz made o' bullet-proof glay-uss. An' ya see this?' He rests his right hand on the handle of a handgun holstered to his hip. We nod. 'Well, I still ain't goin' down Florida Avenue! Y' unnerstan' now son?' Eilbhe and I glance at each other in open-mouthed terror, look back at the irate policeman, and slowly nod.

The officer gives directions for an alternative route through the city and recommends that we 'Go like the god-dayumm wind till we get there. Go through red lights. Do whatever ya gotta do, aright. Just don' stop.'

179

The French Market
New Orleans: 28 July

Curtains of rain pelt the sidewalk beyond the perimeter columns of the French Market, muffling the sound of live jazz at a nearby café. Eilbhe drifts lazily by each stall, intoxicated by the warm humid air laced with the smells of jambalaya and gumbo mixes, chilli peppers, incense and dried flowers. Past the sellers of red beans and dirty rice the market becomes more haphazard and eclectic. Cute plastic dolls from China with fat bowed legs, synthetic blond hair and long eyelashes are propped up alongside stuffed alligator heads with red plastic eyes, lacquered hides and gaping jaws; huge glass jars stuffed with pickled pigs knuckles take centre stage at a stall selling sweets, tobacco and steaming trays of spicy peanuts.

New Orleans is a heady mix of peoples – African, Indian, French, Caribbean and Irish – all stirred and steamed up into the most powerful urban brew you're ever likely to experience. I feel more alive than ever before. Maybe you have to be. Rather like being in the jungle, the intensity of New Orleans demands one's full attention.

We frequently stop to check our street map as we cycle around the city. A navigational error of just a few blocks can make the difference between a quaint leafy avenue and a dangerous ghetto. New Orleans has more than twice as many murders as the whole of Canada. We found a magazine article on the subject on Mike's kitchen table. The locations of all four hundred and seventy six murders committed in New Orleans in 1994 were pinpointed on a map of the city. The length of Florida Avenue was an almost unbroken string of red dots. We can only assume that Michael and his fiancée never got around to reading it.

How To Cross America With No Money
Beaumont, Texas: 8 August

The experiences of New Orleans and Baton Rouge have clarified in my mind how to cycle across America with no money. We spend twenty dollars a day, mostly on food. Every few weeks, when funds drop below the two hundred dollar safety net, we must visit a large town to raise more.

We roll into town poor, smelly and anonymous and if we're lucky there is a pre-arranged place to stay with the friend of a friend. The first thing I do is check the local telephone directory for any newspapers and television stations, schools, sporting goods stores, Rotary clubs and cycling clubs. The sequence of phone calls is important – schools first, then media, then fund-raisers. I have to call the schools first in order to attract the media, because local reporters understand that people aren't interested in foreigners crossing the country on bikes or pedalling the Atlantic Ocean. It has nothing to do with them. But if foreigners are going to cycle into school to tell our kids all about it! Well, that's worth a story and pictures too.

With our names in print, and especially with our faces on television, clubs and stores become more willing to host a slide show. Sometimes they will agree to it before the media exposure, thereby enabling us to include the venue details in the article. I never ask for an entrance fee to these events. After a good show people are either willing to donate twenty dollars for their name to be inscribed on *Moksha*'s hull or they aren't.

This sequence works because everyone benefits: the schoolchildren get an exciting adventure, a break from routine and hopefully a seed is planted in their heads – the seed of limitless possibility – teachers also get a break and some fresh ideas for free; the local news media get a good story; slide-show audiences are entertained and inspired; we have a wonderful time with everyone and cycle away with an extra five or six hundred bucks.

On Saturday, 5 August, we cycled through the drizzling remnants of Hurricane Erin as far as Welsh and were invited to stay at the home of the delightful Daggett family. For one unforgettable Sunday we became 'Miss Elvie and Mister Steve', part of a real southern family. All the Daggett children, their cousins and neighbours' children, took us around their world on a magical tour of places of interest and family legend. One story led to another – The Day The Giant Gator Came, The Secret Wood, The Rattlesnake's Tail – each one told by a different child, wide-eyed with the certainty of its great importance and of our duty to retell it to the world.

The family raft was loaded up with children and food and we disappeared deep into the bayou. Birds darted and lizards twitched in a jungle dripping with colour as we glided through the swampy maze of creeks and coves. An uncle sang songs in Creole and finally we arrived at a large lagoon. The children dived headlong into the murky water without a care and began screaming for Miss Elvie to dive in after them. Eilbhe watched nervously as they swam to a big tree, climbed it, then took turns swinging from a suspended rope and letting go for the biggest splash. For much of the previous hour we had been playing 'Spot The Alligator' and with some success. This new game therefore came as quite a shock. The adults were already busy playing cards and making sandwiches. Trusting in their love of their own children, we jumped in.

We cycled from Welsh on a wet Monday morning and the rain poured all the way to Texas. A garden bench at Deweyville church became a bed beyond the reach of ants for three hours, then we made coffee at sunrise and cycled through to Beaumont.

We are currently nested in our hammock at the park eating lunch. Eilbhe refuses to let me sleep until I've done my *obair bhaile* (Irish for homework). She is determined that I learn to speak her language. I don't mind. I'm in love – hopelessly and completely so, and I'm enjoying every minute of the journey with this funny, bright, tender, beaming woman.

Land Of Extremes
Marble Falls: 1 September

I managed to reach Jason by telephone while we were in Houston. He was sheltering at a skating centre in Little Rock, Arkansas. He seems to be taking a parallel route to ours across the continent, but five hundred miles to the north. Staggeringly, he will probably be in San Francisco before us, as he regularly skates from sixty to eighty miles a day and is on the road for longer periods than we are. His experiences are similar to ours: the constant battle with heat, insects and traffic; and the alternate extremes of kindness and hostility, tolerance and prejudice.

It was great to talk to him again. We laughed and exchanged our observations of the Deep South – such as the astonishing fact that in Louisiana you have to be eighteen to buy a beer but only seventeen to buy a gun. I cried with laughter when he explained how, on reaching Mississippi, his last pair of shorts fell apart. Two women in a convertible tossed him a pair of tartan pantaloons, which he put on. 'They were perfect,' he explained. 'Loose and so much cooler to skate in.' I tried to picture this longhaired, semi-naked hippy wearing an earring and what would have appeared to be a tartan skirt skating along the roads of Mississippi, and marvelled at his nerve.

Apparently – and I had to remind myself at this point that Jason loves to embellish his own stories – he suffered two days of non-stop wolf whistles, flying beer cans and abuse before a police patrol finally pulled him over. The officer, predictably, was the clichéd big-bellied, tobacco-chewing cowboy type who 'don't take kindly to no freak shows on my highway'. Jason, now in the squad car on his way to the police station, had a brainwave. 'Och! For the love of Robbie Burns!' he cried. 'It's the Scottish national holiday today. My da would kill me if a' wasn'a wearin' ma kilt!'

The redneck cop stopped the car, turned around and said, 'Well, god-dayumm son! Why didn' ya say so before? My great-great-great grandaddy was from Scotland.' He then drove on to the Dairy Queen, treated Jason to lunch and waved goodbye as he cycled on toward Columbus.

Jason admitted to feeling lonely skating day after day with little humour or cultural variety to spark his interest. Fortunately Eilbhe and I have each other. We have also enjoyed interesting breaks from cycling in New Orleans (one week), Baton Rouge (two days), Welsh (two days), Houston (one week) and Austin (twelve days).

Houston was an infinitely more rewarding place than we had been led to believe, thanks largely to our host Jeff Debevec. Jeff guided us on architectural tours of the city, took us to a performance of Pericles at the open-air theatre and treated us to sumptuous dinners at Tim Son's Vietnamese restaurant. He also engineered a donation of four hundred and fifty dollars from Wholefoods supermarket in exchange for recognition in an article in the *Houston Chronicle* – one of the finest newspapers in America.

Austin was even better. Austin seems to have it all: a fabulous climate; beautiful buildings, monuments and parks with pure, natural springs; all kinds of arts and cultural facilities; a first-class university and a thriving intellectual community. The area has always been a powerful centre of alternative thinking, which is perhaps why it is known as 'the last refuge of the

Texas hippy' – an island of progressive liberal thought in the heart of Republican Texas.

We stayed at the home of an eminent academic and liberal activist called Sherwood Bishop, through whom I was invited to speak to the American Institute for Learning, The Natale Institute, Hostelling International, Greenpeace and other environmental groups as well as a number of summer schools, clubs and retail outlets. We left Austin yesterday well-provisioned with food, a camping stove and thermal clothing in readiness for the Rocky Mountains, as well as twelve hundred dollars in cash. It could be enough to see us through to California.

We creep so gradually west that the subtle changes in climate and vegetation escape notice. This morning I was delighted to see dew clinging to our tent for the first time. Previously the air was never cool enough for it. These rolling, forested hills between Austin and San Angelo appear to be the natural border between the steamy, sub-tropical lowlands of the Deep South and the drier, scrub plains of the Midwest.

We reach Kingsland at sunset and stop for coffee and donuts at a roadside gas station. It is an unremarkable, dull white-brick building with a tin roof and oil-stained double forecourt, but with the addition of hundredweight brown sacks marked 'Deer Corn' stacked to head height along the front wall. A wizened old-timer in filthy brown dungarees limps slowly towards us. I sense a life story about to be told.

Americans have a peculiar willingness to open up to people they've never met. I suppose one must accept the good with the bad. The openness with which complete strangers unravel their life stories at gas stations, when all we asked for was directions to the park, must be the same openness that offers a welcome bed for the night. I find Europeans – who would sooner drive tent pegs through their own kneecaps than reveal anything of themselves – far less welcoming.

'You two's bikin' cross-country, huh?' We nod in unison, sipping our coffee.

'Yes sir.' I answer. I've become used to addressing people in this way – sir and ma'am. People of the south expect it. 'We've been on the road for...'

'Guess how old I am?' Here it comes.

'Eighty-six. Yesirree! Been here fer fifty-two years. But ah wasn't born in Texas. Ah was born in Missouri. Y'know – '

'Excuse me but – ' Eilbhe tries to interrupt, pointing to the sacks of corn.

'Back then we'd take a horse 'n' wagon to town,' the old man continues. 'Git evithin' we needed fer a month. We'd ride all day to git there, an' all day to git back agin. Up at first light, take the dirt road in – '

'Excuse me,' Eilbhe interrupts again. She has a question on her mind. When Eilbhe has a question on her mind there is no recalcitrant toddler in the world who can match her for dogged persistence. 'Sorry to interrupt, but what is deer corn?'

The old man slaps himself on the knee and begins to shake violently in a fit of chuckles.

'Y'aint never come across deer corn missy?' He gasps. 'He-he! You know the difference 'tween deer corn and regular corn?' He almost whispers the question, as though it were some great secret. We shake our heads and wait for the answer.

'Absolutely nothin'! Hee-heee! But folks round here ask fer deer corn an' won't take nothin' else. I started selling deer corn back in 1963 when Margie... th-that's my second wife...'

A rambling personal history involving four wives, six horses and twenty-two children finally reveals why men in pick-up trucks are queuing up for deer corn at this old man's garage and paying twice the price of regular corn for their trouble. The hunting season begins on 1 October. For several months leading up to this date, deer corn is spread daily on a patch of ground at a 'sporting' distance from a covered shooting gallery. The local population of white-tailed deer become used to congregating at one place for an easy meal.

This simple innovation renders obsolete the traditional process of tracking and wilderness survival that used to make hunting such a laborious and inconvenient affair. Today's hunter need only furnish his hideout with comfortable chairs and wait for friends to arrive with snacks and coolers of weak beer.

The Edge Of The Rockies
Artesia, New Mexico: 9 September

We rose early enough to vacate an anonymous park before anyone could complain. For the past week we have ridden hard and fast, tending to sleep at the nearest patch of open ground we come across after the decision to stop for the night. At Big Springs, for instance, we found a roadside recreation area; at Lamesa we tucked ourselves under a beech tree on a fairway of the golf club.

I agree with the vagrancy laws because people generally can't be trusted to be invisible and leave without trace. We regularly break these laws knowing that we can and we do. There is also a certain romance, as in old western movies, in 'making camp at sundown' wherever one happens to be. You can't legally do that anymore. Every square inch of ground is owned, fenced and fumigated with rules. We could plan our route to stay at designated campsites, but when all we require is a patch of earth I object to being placed, suburban-style, in a numbered row with facilities and be expected to pay for it. Besides, there are vast acreages of lost America – beside roads and rivers, under bridges, behind buildings, on wasteland.

The experienced nomad can so easy disappear in a patch of nowhere without causing offence.

By late morning it occurred to me why our progress feels so sluggish. We have been cycling up the same imperceptibly gentle gradient for the last four hundred miles, ever since we crossed the Colorado River.

The morning mist has lifted to expose a corrugated horizon. This immense and gentle incline will soon head skyward at the Sacramento Mountains, part of the great backbone of America – the Rockies!

We say farewell to the Texas prairie, to the evening silhouette of cacti and scrub, and to the glorious carpets of purple and yellow wildflowers. It is strange to no longer hear the rhythmic clanks and screeching of the 'nodding donkeys' that substitute for trees on the oilfields of west Texas. And we'll never forget the great migration of tarantula spiders scurrying across the hot asphalt. At night they would instinctively leap at the sound of approaching wheels and bounce off our legs. We won't miss them! But I sincerely hope we haven't seen the last of 'all you can eat' buffet lunches for five dollars.

11.30 p.m.: it has been a long, hard climb. We finally stopped half an hour ago, just four miles shy of Mayhill, when Eilbhe spotted a dilapidated hay barn in the valley.

We rearrange hay bales into a double bed and stare out into dark forest and pouring rain. We are both too exhausted to care whether the rustling in the rafters is from bats, rats or birds.

My Birthday
Cloudcroft: 10 September

My birthday began with a panorama of the Sacramento Mountains from our hay-bale nest.

We climbed four miles to breakfast at the Fire House Café at Mayhill, then another twelve to a large ranch with a rodeo stadium. Swapping cycles for horses, we trekked through the forest trails, breathed the dizzying, pine-fresh air and listened to our guide's local folklore of Billy the Kid.

I loved watching Eilbhe cycle up and around the final bend into Cloudcroft at the summit. She was on fire, burning with pride in her achievement. And she was doubly pleased then to find fresh fruit and vegetables, quality bread and cheese at the mountain store. 'Why should we have to go up almost nine thousand feet to find decent food?' Eilbhe wondered. 'But it's worth it.' She took great delight in dumping our old stocks of Wonder Bread and rubbery Kraft cheese – still alarmingly fresh after five days in a hot pannier, and we shared a sumptuous picnic at the park.

Jason's Birthday
Pueblo, Colorado: 13 September

Disastrous news!

On the evening of 10 September, Jason suffered terrible injuries after being hit by a car and left for dead on a road outside Pueblo, Colorado. I only found out last night when I called Nancy to let her know that Eilbhe and I were about to leave Cloudcroft. She didn't have many details, only that he is still alive. My father Stuart flew immediately from Florida to be with him at the hospital.

We arrive at Parkview Hospital as the sun is setting on Jason's twenty-eighth birthday. Stuart greets us with the news we most hoped for: Jason is going to live. But despite eight hours of surgery, doctors fear he may never walk again. The car hit him from behind at over forty miles per hour, smashing his legs to pieces.

We walk into Jason's room. His face is scarcely recognisable with all the bandages, tubes and bruising. He is heavily drugged but conscious.

'It was a miserable day,' he explains in a slow, croaking voice. His hands are shaking. 'I reached the Colorado border. I remember thinking the roads were crap; took a bad fall trying to avoid a truck... took some skin off my legs and arms. Then it started raining.' He pauses for a while.

'The sun went down. I reached a gas station. I kept telling myself to stop there and spend the night. I was exhausted. But there was the offer of a soft bed in Pueblo. I'd skated eighty-five miles... only two more to go. I decided to turn on the strobe lights I carry on my pack and keep skating along the hard shoulder. Then wham!

'The car bumper hit the back of my legs. I felt the snap and the bones tearing through the flesh on my shins. My pack smashed the car windscreen and probably saved my life. I rolled off the roof and fell into the ditch. The pain was unbelievable. I sat staring at the bones sticking out of my legs and started to wave my flag for help. The road was full of cars but no one would stop.'

'Oh Jesus!' Eilbhe cries out. She sits at the far end of Jason's bed with her hands covering her mouth. 'How long did you have to lie there on your own?'

'I don't know.' Jason shakes his head. 'It seemed like ages. At least fifteen minutes. And then I had to wait in the ambulance for even longer. They said they were looking for part of my ear.'

It turns out that the driver of the car, an eighty-one-year-old man, didn't even stop. Another driver who witnessed the accident had to chase him down and force him go back.

'What a bastard!' I cry.

'Actually he's a very sweet old guy,' Jason croaks. 'He's been to visit twice. He seems genuinely very sorry.' Jason's eyes start to roll. He must be tired. The strong drugs make him drift in and out of consciousness. We must leave him to sleep.

My father fills us in on the rest of the story. He looks very tired after a long flight from Miami and has had little sleep since arriving, having had to deal with lots of hospital forms, legal proceedings and police statements. He is also very angry that the police didn't arrest the driver for hit-and-run or even test his breath for alcohol, especially since he was using the hard shoulder as a lane when he hit Jason and admitted to being on his way home from a party. The driver claims he thought he had hit a deer, which is why he didn't stop. My father refuses to believe that.

After more surgery and the insertion of metal rods in both lower legs, it is hoped that Jason will be out of hospital in six weeks and able to get about on crutches by Christmas. Stuart, who says he was bored with Florida anyway, has offered to nurse Jason through his recovery and oversee his appeal for medical expenses and damages from the driver's insurance company. Jason's surgeon, Dr Ken Danylchuck, has most kindly offered them both a place to spend the winter at his buffalo ranch in the mountains south-west of Pueblo.

It is difficult to speculate on what may happen after that. If the splintered bones knit back together he may take his first steps next spring.

Later that evening, Jason wakes again as Eilbhe and I prepare to leave. I know my friend well enough to understand that nothing is going to stop him making a full recovery and rejoining the expedition. I lean across the bed and take his hand in mine.

'I don't want you to worry, Jas. I want you to know that when we get to San Francisco, I'm not going any further on this trip until you get there on your own two feet. Agreed?'

'OK then.' He smiles and closes his moistening eyes.

Pedalling to Hawaii

Inspired By Jason
Magdalena: 20 September

Jason's accident inspired us to change our route. Before hearing the terrible news, Eilbhe and I were about to take the fastest, most direct route to the Pacific Ocean – through the deserts of southern New Mexico, Arizona and California to San Diego. It was the easy option that would avoid the most hills and satisfy our yearning to dive headlong into the Pacific surf.

Yet Jason, up until his accident, was about to tackle the widest stretch of the Rocky Mountains on skates. He wasn't looking for the easy route. Why should we sacrifice the magnificent beauty of these mountains? Why hurry along a boring, dusty freeway and a thousand miles of scrub?

After our hurried detour to Jason's hospital bed, we returned to Cloudcroft. But instead of flying down the Sacramento Mountains to Alamogordo we headed north-west, along the tough, mountain trail to Ruidoso, past the splendid forests and glistening pastures that border the Mescalero Apache Reservation.

At first, Eilbhe was not entirely happy with the change of plan. Twice she broke down in tears and refused to go on. She cursed me between gasping breaths and felt that the mountain passes were too much for her.

'I just collapse sometimes,' she sobbed, 'when I look up and see a huge mountain and a steep, winding road that never seems to end.'

'But isn't this the part we've been talking about and looking forward to for so long, darling? Indian country, forests, cool mountain air!'

'Oh I love mountains! I'm just not so into cycling up them. It's just a lot harder than I thought, that's all.'

It is hard, even in twenty-fourth gear. Mountain roads are painful, a relentless, burning pain in the legs and arms and back. We struggle to climb at a snail's pace for twenty minutes to reach one crest or bend in the road only to find that on reaching it we are at the bottom of another stretch of road exactly like it, and then another, and another. In order to acquire a level of fitness that allows one to appreciate the experience, the scenery and so on, one must accept a lot of pain. Actually, more than that: a long-distance cyclist should see the necessity of pain as part of the whole, fulfilling package and thereby create a reason to enjoy pain.

For me, it all comes down to desire and commitment. I am absolutely committed to cycling to San Francisco. I don't question whether I can do it. My mind simply doesn't conceive of any other way. In that sense it is much easier for me than for Eilbhe, because my mind is relieved of tempting alternatives. Courage doesn't come into it, because courage is the emotional struggle to deny easier options. Instead, my head is free to concentrate on how to optimize the experience – including thinking up ways to accept and even enjoy unavoidable pain. Eilbhe, on the other hand, decided to do this on a whim and for reasons that have little to do with cycling up mountains. She's here to see the country; to be with me; to experience cycling and living outside. But I suspect she would just as soon skip the steep bits and cycle the flat bits. Eilbhe loves good food, fun people and interesting places – probably in that order of preference. But she has never been interested in physical fitness. The fact that she keeps battling on, despite the tears and the tantrums, demonstrates her extraordinary courage.

We flew down the western slopes of the Sacramento Mountains to the Tularosa Valley and arrived at a desolate campsite west of Carrizozo in darkness. The morning light revealed a black volcanic wasteland called the Valley of Fires. Eilbhe spent hours climbing over the swirling patterns of solidified lava taking photographs.

Yesterday's ride took us over the San Andres Mountains and down the eastern slopes of the Rio Grande, which we crossed that evening. Today we climbed slowly up its western flank and onto the high plains of San Agustin.

Yesterday Saloon
Springerville, Arizona: 22 September

Frances Morse, a reporter with the Apache County Observer, intercepts us at Springerville. We find a roadside café where we can sit outside.

'Oh, by the way, there's another group of cyclists in town,' she says upon finishing her interview. 'You'll find them at the inn.'

'What! After two and a half thousand miles on the road, our first contact with another cyclist!' Eilbhe exclaims while brushing her matted hair.

We ride directly to the place, excited by the prospect of some fresh company, some stories of the road, a few laughs and maybe a few beers. We have been riding solidly for four days. It's time for some fun.

The parking lot at the inn is packed with support trucks, their sides emblazoned with the 'Ride Across America' logo. Dozens of riders in garishly coloured skin-tight suits mill about while support engineers in blue overalls tweak spokes and tighten chain links. Eilbhe pushes her bike over to a tall lady with pink glasses wearing a pink and green suit and white bicycle helmet. She looks about forty. She looks at Eilbhe, who is dressed in a loose sleeveless green army vest, brown shorts and sandals, with a mixture of mild bemusement and disdain.

'So what's this all about?' Eilbhe asks her, putting her hands on her hips and giving the woman a big smile. I can already guess that she isn't going to like the answer.

'It's the Ride Across America Challenge,' the woman replies impatiently. 'Cycling coast-to-coast, happens every year, you probably won't have heard of it unless you cycle competitively. You're not from around here, are you? Where you headed?'

'San Francisco.'

'Oh OK. You're going the wrong way, you know.'

'Err, no. Last time I looked San Fran was on the west coast.'

'No, I mean you're going against the wind. You should have gone west to east.'

Further details are extracted from other passers-by as Eilbhe becomes determined to have the full story. We learn that the convoy of support vehicles and crews drive ahead, prepare regular food and drink stops, organize medical and other special needs and reserve hotel rooms. Every detail is pre-planned, right down to the exact mileage to be covered on each day of the twenty-three day race across America.

We get chatting to a couple of men about my age but neither one cares for a beer or even a soft drink at the bar and a good yarn with a couple of dusty hobos. They have some laundry to do before bedtime.

It quickly becomes clear that our mode of transport is the only thing we have in common with these people. 'They're racing across their country!' Eilbhe concludes with dismay. 'Good luck to the lot o' them,' she says as we walk away pushing our heavy loads, 'but they might as well be doing the entire thing on a bicycle machine in their bedrooms for all they learn about their land.'

We hit the first bar on our way out of town, the fabulously named Yesterday Saloon. There are a handful of cowboys inside steadily getting drunk. We join them. One is a barrel of a man with a surprisingly gentle manner called Don, who tells the most gripping true stories about rattlesnakes – how they like to slip into your sleeping bag at night for warmth – and household security. Don (not his real name) is a survivalist and has enough explosives, ammunition and weaponry stashed inside his modest farmhouse to make a Panamanian drugs baron green with envy.

We stumble out of Yesterday's Saloon rather worse for wear and cycle on to St Johns in time to take up Frances the reporter's kind offer of a bed for the night.

'Well, we're happy to have you,' says her husband Jim warmly. 'But you'll have to excuse me. I'm going to bed now. Been through one hell of a day.' Jim is the local Sheriff. He is wearing a T-shirt with 'War on Drugs' on the sleeve next to a cannabis leaf with a thick red line across it.

'Why? What happened?' Eilbhe asks.

'Heck! It must have been another one of those low fly-pasts by the Air Force. Every time that happens we get overwhelmed with calls from every damn redneck in Apache County. You wouldn't believe how many guys around here believe the United Nations is trying to take over the world.' Eilbhe lets out a shrill chuckle.

'Yes, I think we just met some at the bar,' she explains and gives Jim a big smile. 'But even if it was true, why would the United Nations pick on St Johns, Arizona? Wouldn't Washington or New York City be a more sensible target?'

'Yep, there's a whole bunch of paranoid folks round here. These guys just dig themselves in. They got their combat gear; they got their farms all alarmed with trip wires and such. Heck, they got enough weapons and ammunition to take on a small country.'

Frances leads us by candlelight to a small caravan in the garden and leaves us to unpack our sleeping bags and overnight things. Eilbhe and I sit up a while longer, staring up at a sky so full of stars that it's hard to say whether it is black with starry spots or the other way round.

The Wrong Way Across America
Flagstaff: 3 October

O.J. Simpson was today found not guilty of murdering his wife and Ronald Goldman on 13 June 1994, despite being covered in their blood as he tried to outrun police in his Ford Bronco and clutching ten thousand dollars in cash. Callous though it may be, I ceased caring about the verdict a long time ago. I just pray the country starts talking about something else.

We rode into Flagstaff nine days ago after an eighty-mile uphill battle against the wind. Eilbhe found it particularly hard going and at one point broke down in tears and refused to go on. The racers in the Lycra suits are right – we are going the wrong way across America. The wind has been against us for five hundred miles and will continue to be for the remaining thousand miles to San Francisco. We leave again tomorrow having refilled our empty coffers after giving talks at two Rotary clubs, a bike store and a sponsored feature article in a local newspaper.

Cherry Garcia by Moonlight
Williams: 5 October

We had a late start from Flagstaff yesterday, managing only thirty miles west on Interstate 40 to the forest beyond Williams before the day was gone. After stumbling about the roadside forest under a full moon for about twenty minutes we found an ideal campsite with a thick carpet of pine needles for bedding. We placed ourselves on a big log and bathed in the warmth of our campfire while passing a shared dinner – a pint of Ben and Jerry's Cherry Garcia ice cream bought from a nearby gas station – back and forth in blissful silence.

For dessert there was clam chowder and cold beer, the latter earmarked as an ingredient for campfire beer-bread. Eilbhe to her credit saved enough for the baking experiment, though the resulting bread had the consistency of pig iron.

Today we coasted effortlessly down to the desert forty miles beyond Seligman where a road sign reads 'Next Turnoff 75 miles'.

The Mojave Desert
Ludlow, California: 9 October

California! We relive the great feeling of deliverance felt by millions of pioneers and dustbowl refugees before us.

For Eilbhe and me, much of the relief is on account of our escape from the terrible noise and turbulence of freeway traffic. We have had no choice but to brave the shoulder of the freeway across northern Arizona, it being the only east-west road. An incident at a filling station near Kingman compounded our sense of vulnerability and frustration.

At the station store Eilbhe was approached by a truck driver who shoved his hand into her crotch, laughed and walked away. She was shocked and distraught when she came to tell me what happened. We walked around the cafeteria and I asked her to point the man out. He was sitting at a table with some other drivers.

The station manager refused to get involved or call the police. He merely implored me to take any trouble outside. I started walking to the table. The pervert spotted me coming and bolted through a side-door. The others at the table stayed in their seats. Good, I thought with relief; they weren't his friends. I ran out after the man and began hunting through the truck stop.

As I hunted around the trucks for the driver it suddenly occurred to me that we were the only touring cyclists in north-west Arizona on the only road into California. We had no option but to carry on cycling that night to the rest area at Yucca. It was the worst possible time and place to be on a trucker's hit list. Reluctantly, I stopped looking and let it go.

The following day we celebrated reaching California with an afternoon of picnicking and swimming at Lake Havasu, followed by the luxury of a motel room in Needles. It was only the second time we have paid for accommodation.

Today's ride was a monstrous one hundred and five miles across the Mojave Desert. Stupidly, we began late morning, when the sun was already high and the temperature racing towards a hundred degrees. Eilbhe developed heat exhaustion near the top of the second summit west of Needles. We were lucky to find a parked truck for shade and a sympathetic driver offering cold water.

California state law prohibits cycling on the freeway. We managed it for fifty miles, all the way to a rest area beyond Essex, before a highway patrolman spotted us. We were booted unceremoniously onto old Route 66.

The national affection for this historic road does not extend to financing its maintenance, at least not in the long looping section across the Mojave Desert. In places it was easier to push our bikes across dried-up creek beds than negotiate what remains of the original road. The final twenty-five miles to Ludlow has been a tortuous uphill slog against the wind and in pitch-blackness.

2.00 a.m.: at Ludlow. There are no obvious places to camp here. The town of Ludlow consists of a gas station/convenience store, a breakfast café in the shape of a Swiss mountain chalet and not much else. We erect the tent on a disused parking lot, where tall strands of desert weeds pick out the pattern of sun-baked split asphalt, and groan our aching bodies to sleep.

To The City Of Angels
California: 14 October

For the next four days we cycled hard and fast through the desert heat. The first of these days was a blisteringly hot ride as we rattled along the bumps and craters of old Route 66 through the desert scrub to Barstow. The second day delivered a succession of grubby mining towns from Barstow to Hesperia and eventually we came to the mountain pass that would take us off the high desert plateau, through the San Bernadino Mountains, and down to the coast.

Following local advice, we managed to avoid the frenetic arterial route to Los Angeles by locating the dirt track that services the Santa Fe railroad. After snaking our way in glorious solitude through the mountains for half the night we finally camped by a stream near Clayhorn.

The heaven-to-hell transition at the outset of the third day was partially anticipated, but not the grotesque scale of its extremes. Upon waking, at an elevation of three thousand feet, to the gurgling chatter of a mountain stream, we breakfasted before a crisp clear vista of emerald-green valleys and blue skies. But within half an hour of rapid descent we slid beneath a thick yellow blanket of haze that denied all sense of direction of sun, sky or topography. The world recoiled into a single demented street.

The immensity of Los Angeles became gradually understood as the hideous day wore on. When, at Claremont, we realised we had no hope of traversing the metropolis in a single day, I made a desperate call to friends in Austin, Texas, who arranged sanctuary in nearby Pomona at the home of Robbie Lopez.

Robbie's place is like a little square of a Constable painting cut out and pasted onto Picasso's 'Guernica'. It is an atoll of bucolic bliss: a simple house and lovingly tended garden – with its neat rows of eggplant, squash, peppers, corn and herbs, even grapes – thriving in an ocean of loveless concrete, dereliction and street gangs; where children (I imagine) fall asleep by counting distant gunshots.

We heard no shooting that night. For us, death came much closer on the following evening in the plush suburbs of Bel Air and Brentwood Heights. We had entered Hollywood as night fell and, wishing to avoid the seedier neighbourhoods of Venice and Mar Vista, chose Sunset Boulevard as our route to the coast. It was a shock; rather like shambling along the sun-kissed Mediterranean back alleys of Monaco to fetch the morning papers only to find oneself suddenly on the grand prix circuit on race day. Once upon Sunset Boulevard there was no escape, no shoulder and no sidewalk, only the wailing of engines that hurtled round bends and the screech of hot tyres occasionally making contact with cold asphalt.

Here on the wealthiest street in the world, I felt more at risk than in any Atlantic storm or murderous ghetto. We cowered and crawled along occasional slivers of pavement that soon disappeared under the bushes and razor-wire fencing of millionaires' mansions, forcing us into a frantic dash along the race track to the next sliver or a perilous crossing to another on the opposite side. In this fashion, a five-mile journey along Sunset Boulevard lasted several hours. Finally, we fell exhausted onto a patch of grass by a roadside public convenience.

We woke early this morning to the distant pounding of surf. The Pacific Ocean! We stuffed sleeping bags hurriedly into panniers and freewheeled down the final stretch of Sunset Boulevard, crossed the Pacific Coast Highway, and drove our bikes straight onto the beach. The first headlong plunge into the salty glistening surf was worth every mile of dust and sweat and grime. I had imagined little else for days but the shocking ecstasy of the real thing was unimaginably better.

We let the sun dry us now as we sit in the sand below Gladstone's fish restaurant at Malibu, sharing another tub of Ben and Jerry's ice cream, this time the aptly named 'Wavy Gravy'. The waves are watched in silence; there is no need for words. Relief, joy, pride, the simple overwhelming pleasure of this moment, these are enough.

Discovering the Real California
Cayucas Beach: 24 October

What more could life possibly have to offer than this? I wake to find myself in the glory of an autumn sunrise, on a Californian beach, entwined with my naked lover. A gleaming film of dew covers the golden sandy beach. A flock of sandpipers scuttle back and forth at the water's edge, as if playing 'chicken' with the waves. I kiss Eilbhe's head, wriggle out from under the sleeping bags and run down into the crashing surf, scattering birds as I go.

It is our third day of lazing on Cayucas Beach. Before this we spent three days in Morro Bay celebrating Eilbhe's birthday with a wonderful fellow called Ryan – a chunky, bouncing man with a big smile, wild blond hair and a bulbous red nose – whom we met at a gas station in Los Osos. This is what I love most about Americans, their unmatchable openness and generosity. Ryan was walking to his pick-up truck with a six-pack of beer in both hands when we asked him simply if he knew whether the nearby state park was open to campers this time of year. Within five minutes of chatting together he had insisted that we stay at his house, whereupon we bundled our bikes onto the bed of his truck, bought even more beer, and there Eilbhe's birthday celebrations began. Ryan also invited his daughter and his girlfriend and others turned up uninvited. It was more like a mini-festival than a birthday party. We bought three kinds of fish – tuna, swordfish and wild salmon

– from the fish market, baked cranberry nut bread, and sat around eating and drinking on the AstroTurf balcony of Ryan's simple wooden home and accompanying Ryan, who plays piano, with whatever instrument – guitar, bongo, maracas – happened to be closest at hand.

We have covered ten miles in a week, which is exactly as it should be. Learning from Eilbhe's enchanting ease and companionship I have finally managed to relax completely and bury time in the sand.

The news from Colorado is also good. Jason has left hospital and is convalescing well with 'Nurse Stuart' at the surgeon's buffalo ranch. My father describes Jason, all too believably, as a carer's nightmare. Despite being under strict instructions to rest, he wheeled himself outdoors on his first day from hospital and was caught chopping firewood for the winter. There is talk of him being able to walk with a stick by early spring. All I can gather of Jason's therapy program is that it seems to be dominated by daily trips in the wheelchair to Olzan's bar at the base of Rye Mountain, augmented by the occasional outing to Aloha Gloria's strip joint in Pueblo.

The Old Coast Road
Big Sur: 28 October

Eilbhe wants to get off the beaten track for a while. We turn off the highway at the entrance to Pfeiffer-Big Sur State Park and come to a stop outside the visitors' centre, a low brick building with decorative mock-pioneer wooden panelling.

'I don't suppose there's any road towards San Francisco other than the main highway?' Eilbhe asks a woman ranger, who stands next to a large information board, wearing a smart green tunic and brown leather hat. 'We want to get off the beaten track, you see, more into the forest out of the noise of traffic and stuff.' Eilbhe is desperate to see a herd of wild deer.

Even a lone racoon would mollify her, but not the streetwise sort who scavenge among garbage containers and picnic areas. The ranger puts her mind to it.

'Oh yeah!' she remembers, eventually, with great enthusiasm. 'There's the old coast road. You'll find the start of it at the bottom of the hill on the right. No one goes up there any more...'

'Not since the old man died, eh!' I interrupt. 'Sounds like the opening line of a Scooby-Doo cartoon.' I laugh. The ranger responds with a withering look.

'No, I was going to say, not since they built Bixby Bridge.'

'Up, you say?' Eilbhe asks, suspiciously. 'No one goes up there? How far up, exactly?'

'Oh, it's not so bad, ' she insists and paws the air dismissively in front of her. 'It's no biggy. You'll be fine.'

It is already late in the afternoon. We sail down to the coast to meet a chilling sea breeze. Just as the ranger described there is a dirt track on the right-hand side, directly opposite a campground.

We embark on a steep winding climb of about five hundred vertical feet before the dirt road comes to a plateau. A grey pick-up truck is parked at its edge overlooking the ocean.

'Oh shit, this isn't the summit,' I notice, gasping for breath. 'Look Eilbhe, it's just the beginning.'

Four young men sit on the bonnet of the truck quietly enjoying the view. An impressively long, tapering reefer passes between them.

'Hey dude. You goin' up there?'

'That was the idea,' I reply. We stand and visually follow a sinewy brown trail that snakes wildly upward like a prematurely released party balloon to the tree line, where it disappears, only to reappear on a higher, more distant peak.

'Jesus Eilbhe! Whose idea is this? Off the beaten track, eh. Wilderness! Why do wild things always pick such bloody inconvenient places to live?'

'Guess you won't be needing any of this then?' says the stranger, holding out the smoking trumpet. 'Finest KGB dude – Kalifornia Green Bud.'

'That's where you're wrong mate, thanks. The stoned-er the better, I think, is the only way to proceed at this point.'

They all laugh and seem pleasantly shocked. Eilbhe reaches into her pannier and pulls out a can of beer for them in return. 'It isn't very cold but it's yours if you want it.'

'Whooh girl! You guys sure know how to pack!'

It is past midnight. Even with twenty-four gears the steep gradient has still beaten us. We have been walking and pushing our heavy loads up this pot-holed bastard of a trail for four hours.

The night is pitch black and now we are enveloped in fog so thick that the beam of my headlight barely reaches down to the stony, rutted trail. The lack of vision, however, may well be an advantage, since the lethal precipice to our right might otherwise have rendered us immobile with fear. Stoned, scared and stubborn, we see no option but to stumble on through the ghostly white night. Occasionally we stop and stand, electrified by the creeps, crackles and howls of invisible creatures in the trees. Eilbhe stops, listening intensely.

'Would a bear attack, say, if it was really hungry?'

'No way darlin'.' I don't really know.

'What about a mountain lion?'

'Nah, they're scared of people too.' I lie again. I read in a local paper only last week that a jogger had been badly mauled by a lion and his dog was killed.

Eilbhe's strategy for calming any fears of what might be out there is compulsive questioning. As the potential dangers –

real and imaginary – have gradually changed by geographical region as we cycle across this vast and varied land, so Eilbhe's questions have changed. I chuckle to myself over a cherished memory.

'What are you laughing at?' The tone of her voice is high and slightly pleading, as though she wants to be distracted. We push on into the thick, swirling white haze.

'I was just remembering... do you remember what you said you would do if you ever got caught in a tsunami on the Gulf of Mexico?'

'Oh Jes! You're not going to let me forget that one are you!'

'You,' I am laughing so hard I can barely get the words out, 'you said you'd figured out a foolproof escape plan, remember?'

'Yes, yes...'

'And if you lived near the beach you'd always make sure to carry around with you a really long bamboo pole and a spade, so if the giant wave ever came crashing in, you could quickly bury yourself in the sand and stick this pole in the air to breath through.'

'It was just an idea for God's sake!' She is laughing with me now.

'What came next? Oh yeah, Louisiana, and your obsession with alligators.'

'Do you remember,' Eilbhe joins in now, ignoring a loud screeching sound that echoes through the fog 'what yer man at that gas station said you had to carry around and throw into the water behind you if an alligator attacked?'

'Cheese Puffs!' we cry in unison.

'Did we have a plan for tornados in Texas?' I ask.

'Nope. The only thing for that is Dorothy slippers.'

'And how about rattlesnakes getting into your sleeping bag?'

'That was Don in Arizona wasn't it? He said not to worry because they can't strike if they're lying in a straight line. You just have to make sure there's not enough space left in your sleeping bag for them to curl up in.'

The heavy curtain of fog lifts for a moment to reveal a bend to the left before the inclined track disappears once again behind dark columns of pine trees.

'But what about the bears?' I knew she could not be diverted for long. 'Are you sure that brown bears are timid?'

'Quite sure.'

'How timid though,' she continues, 'compared to, say... ducks?'

'Oh Eilbhe please! This night is freakish enough. We're stuck in the freezing fog in the middle of the night, pushing a bike up a track to God only knows where, and you're asking me to decide how timid bears are compared to ducks. Am I dreaming or is this really – '

'Oh fuck off then.'

Two hours later the trail finally levels off. There is an area of grass next to some fencing and a metal gate. Exhausted beyond care we let our bikes drop... crash... and erect the tent with final reserves of will.

Why can't we sleep? Why does every cell tingle? Why does each sound, each movement, each moment, vibrate in its own infinite tension? I stick my head out of the tent flap. In an overgrown hedge on the opposite side of the trail a vague silhouette shifts slightly in the gloom. Perhaps I imagined it. I say nothing.

We wake to a cold, clear morning. Eilbhe instructs me in the baking of campfire flatbread for breakfast. As we have no water left I have to make the dough with our last beer. I tend to the smouldering package in tin foil on the fire while sipping on the remaining few inches of beer in the bottle. Eilbhe is pacing in circles around the tent. The crisp morning air leaves a wispy trail of hot breath behind her. She bends over to inspect a patch of bare earth.

'Jesus! Fuck! These prints are bigger than my fist. Jesus! Look! They're everywhere!' She circles the tent again, following the tracks of a mountain lion.

'Do you remember the size of the paws on that stuffed one in the Morro Bay Museum? Look at the stride! It's definitely a lion. And look at how deep they press into the dirt. My footprint doesn't dig in that deep. Does yours? I'll try it. No! Look, see? And I'm what, hundred and ten pounds? And it's got four legs to spread its weight as well. How heavy does that make him, four hundred... five hundred pounds?' I've never seen Eilbhe so excited.

In Native American tradition a visitation from a mountain lion is considered a great honour and very powerful medicine. I don't know what to think about that, but there's no mistaking the incredible euphoria and well-being that we woke with.

A crumpled tangle of ridges and valleys meander down to a distant blue band of ocean. Having repacked the tent and provisions we begin freewheeling down the dusty trail. Our high spirits fly ahead of us. The morning sun pushes long kaleidoscopic sunbeams through a towering forest of giant redwood trees. We surprise the birds and deer at each bend in our effortless, magical descent.

The old coast road finally flushes us back onto the highway north of Bixby Bridge and the fairy tale abruptly ends. We return to the rushing and raging of motorised humanity. I have ridden the entire descent with a flat front tyre, which in fairyland didn't seem to matter. My air pump is broken. I wait in hope of a passing cyclist while Eilbhe cycles dreamily on and out of sight.

I flag down two racing cyclists heading south. They kindly stop.

'Hey man, you're going the wrong way.'

'Against the wind yeah, so I've been told. Look, I've got a flat tyre and my air pump is broken. Do you have a pump I could use please?'

'Oh, OK. Here you go. You from Australia?' asks the one in the red suit.

'England, but my American is improving, don't you think?'

'How far have you come?' asks the other in the green and purple stripes.

'Florida. How about yourselves?'

'San Francisco; we've got to be in Los Angeles by tomorrow night.'

'Wow! I'll be as quick as I can then.' I struggle to tip my loaded bicycle upside down for a speedier change of inner tube. Two empty beer bottles slide out of the rear pannier bag and begin rolling away... clink, clink, clink... down the hill. I chase after them.

'Sorry about that. Right, now, this'll only take a jiffy.'

Several strained attempts are made at conversation while I hurry to swap inner tubes and re-inflate the new tyre. But we are too stunned by each other's appearance to speak and men can only do one thing at a time. They can only gawp open-mouthed in disbelief at the dishevelled wreck in five-dollar shorts and beach sandals. They are wondering how he could ever have pedalled all the way from Florida on that filthy old jalopy. And I, in turn, can only stare back wondering how it is possible for anyone and his equipment, outside of an operating theatre, to be quite so surgically clean. I fail to spot a speck of dust or dirt or bead of sweat; not a single whisker of hair sprouts from the smooth skins of The Immaculate Riders.

209

Journey's End
San Francisco: 2 November

The change from country to city never fails to astound me – how people can utterly transform everything, including themselves. We both sensed, with growing agitation, the quickening pace of life between Pacifica and Daly City. Now, as we enter the Mission District, the noise and smell of city traffic is overwhelming. We pass Mexican women selling cheap shirts on the sidewalk. Drunks lurch around in the gutter and spit onto the road. Long rows of grubby stores offer colourful plastic goods and the exhaust of the subway steams up through street-level vents.

We stop by a public phone booth. I try calling the number for Marcus Cook, the only contact we have in the city.

A girl called Abigail answers the phone. Marcus, she tells me, no longer lives there, but she has heard of us. We are welcome to come and stay provided it's only for a few days.

Eilbhe leans her bike up against a shopfront window and goes inside to buy milk. I wait outside and experience a growing sense of trepidation.

We have been avoiding any discussion of what it means to end the journey – how it will feel to live indoors, to be in the city, to find work. We have only a hundred and fifty dollars left to survive on. Throughout the morning we have been weaving our way through the stale suburbs with a vast continental openness still in our hearts and with the salt ocean clinging to our skins. We are woefully unprepared for this change.

I scan the display ads in the window looking for offers of employment. The first one reads, 'Applications invited for the Gay and Lesbian Downhill Ski Team.'

This could only be one place, I think to myself: San Francisco. And the thought suddenly hits me: we made it, it's over.

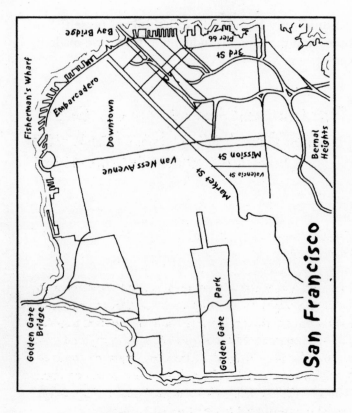

San Francisco

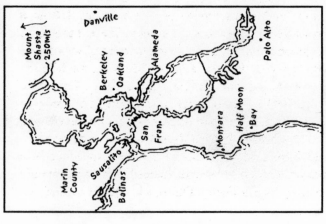

Chapter 5: The Longest Winter I Ever Spent...

5. The Longest Winter I Ever Spent Was The Year In San Francisco
(November 1995 – October 1996)

1419 Valencia Street
San Francisco: 5 November

Abigail's rented apartment reminds me of my student days: the threadbare carpet, the peeling walls and that sort of damp, echoing emptiness that transient people and their things can never quite eliminate. The walls of our room are lined with posters of old music festivals. There is a bare mattress on wooden floorboards and a cheap lamp on a cardboard box. The hallway is littered with colourful junk mail and unopened telephone bills addressed to one Emelia Earhart.

'Return to Sender' is scrawled on one envelope, followed by the irresistible 'Whereabouts unknown. She just took off'.

The neighbourhood is also changing identity. Once an Irish migrant stronghold, then Italian, then Mexican, the Mission District is now being gentrified by white-collar professionals. Stylish cafés, with espresso machines that gurgle excitedly in the business of mass caffeination, sprout up on street corners where haberdashers and nicotine-soaked bars once stood.

The old ethnic identities have blended together in a phenomenon known as 'world fusion'. The apartment's longest serving tenant Danny Dunn, a.k.a. JimBo Trout, is a prime example: JimBo, twenty-three, is the American son of Polish Jews, whose favourite food is sushi, who drinks Guinness and earns a living busking bluegrass music on a street full of Mexicans. Abigail, thirty-two, is a beautiful and emotionally-complex blonde with talents for singing, fine art and picking the wrong guy, who works in a bar on Haight Street. A frequent visitor is her estranged husband Billy, who is busy suing her for 'loss of spousal services'. He blames the demise of their sex life on Abigail's cycling accident. She in turn is suing the driver of the car involved. In the unlikely event that the case ever comes to court, the sloppiest of insurance investigators need only spend two minutes in the Mad Dog In The Fog to discover that Billy's spousal services are being denied, not by Abigail's back condition, but by the affections of a handsome young plasterer from County Cork. It is an altogether bizarre household in a crazy district of the weirdest city in the world that we have come to rest.

But we are here to stay, at least until Jason is fit enough to resume the expedition and *Moksha* can be delivered and made ready for the next phase – the Pacific Ocean. Being stationary is no less a challenge as we are down to our last fifty dollars and need to find work and a place to live.

Eilbhe and I arrived destitute and apprehensively at the door of 1419 Valencia Street. The idea of living within walls was daunting. Equally, I feared a return to the months of obsessive fund-raising that had plagued my life in Miami. The simple joys of the open road in Eilbhe's company helped me to understand what a twisted character I had been there. San Francisco would be different.

We could not have been more fortunate than to arrive at Valencia Street, where, as the days and weeks unfolded, we quickly blended in with the most sincere, funny and colourful community of friends one could wish for. The only drawback was that most of them were struggling to survive in the big city just as we were, and none were in any position to spare a room or offer cash-in-hand work.

We lived on couches in five different apartments through November. I took whatever work I could find, from office work to nude modelling for a life-drawing class.

Marcus Cook, our initial contact in the city, and his girlfriend Carla, helped to organise a few expedition slide shows for San Francisco's bicycle messenger community. These venues were a blur of drug-crazed bikers flinging projectiles across one hellhole of a bar after another. Marcus' band, my warm-up act, was hard-core thrash. He would agitate the mob with gut-wrenching guitar solos and scream out the lyrics:

'I'm so glad I gotta new trance mission / the key broke off o' the new ignition / but that's OK / cause I gotta new / I gotta new trance mission and / I gotta get outta town / I'm in a d-d-d-d-dizzy condition / but that's OK.'

And he delivered them to an increasingly violent, sweat-drenched crowd. I was then expected to step up onstage with a slide show, talk about life on the ocean and try to adapt anecdotes designed for portly middle-aged Rotarians to work on rabid lunatic bike messengers. Zeitgeist, the Covered Wagon and Mission Rock were a succession of utter-disaster venues. With the greatest delicacy, I implored Carla not to organise any more.

Some good came of them. Therese Ortolani – a gorgeous, sultry, brown-eyed Portuguese-American diva – witnessed me dodging missiles on stage at the Covered Wagon and introduced herself. She invited me to advertise a more effective fund-raiser at her home and photographic studio – a cavernous, corrugated iron hangar at the corner of Twentieth and Shotwell. The event was successful, especially because of the interesting group who came – artists, local councillors and business people – to offer their support.

For her part, Eilbhe made a difficult living situation look easy. She transformed scraps of food into exquisite dinners wherever we stayed; she bought fabrics and made them into clothes, both for us to wear and to sell. Where I might have thrown money and stress at a situation, Eilbhe simply devoted time and patience and created something wonderful with it. I have never been so poor or felt so well-blessed.

After a month in the Mission, though, we were tired of couch-surfing and of the relentless noise and pollution. We were also becoming more aware of, and drawn into, a very complex social network with deep grievances and personal problems. Abigail and Billy's doomed marriage was just the tip of the iceberg. The complete picture was much more complicated. Marcus, for example, once the heart and soul of this circle of friends, had become a serious heroin addict. And he would repeatedly, with a calm conviction, confess his determination to kill himself. One by one, all his friends who tried to help had failed and eventually gave up on him – one too many lies; one too many valuables gone missing. Only Carla and Marcus' sister Kim remained, and they were running out of ideas.

On 1 December we moved to a house in Montara twenty-five miles south of the city. It was a very strange-looking, though not unattractive, pueblo-style cottage nestled in the coastal hills above a beach community. The rent was unusually low. Every room in the place had at least one doorway to the outside, making eight exits in all. There were secret panels and compartments in every wall. Behind one shelving unit in the utility room we discovered a hidden doorway that led down a long flight of wooden stairs to a damp cellar. The roof of this crypt was the base of a 1920s Ford truck. All of this seemed to confirm what our housemate John Gray – a heavily-built, reclusive, middle-aged man with shifting eyes and a bushy grey-tipped moustache – claimed to know of its original purpose: a stash-house for illegal whisky during the prohibition era.

Within days of moving in it became clear that a truck was not the only thing that moonshine gangsters had buried in the foundations. The house was prone to sudden temperature fluctuations; locked doors would burst open at all hours; John's cats would hiss venomously at thin air. There were other, invisible tenants. John had been well aware of this for some time. He also failed to point out, until later, that the previous occupants were two (alleged) lesbian sadomasochists, whose house parties we dared not imagine, who used to keep goats in our bedroom. This accounted for the dried-up droppings stuck fast to the carpet.

We cleaned and redecorated as best we could but it was clear that something had to be done to improve our situation. I scoured the Bay Area phone directories for clubs and organisations likely to need a guest speaker. A week later I gave my first slide show to the Bay Area Sea Kayakers, which was a great success, and by Christmas my engagements calendar was booked solid through to March.

For Christmas itself we commandeered John Gray and his ancient minibus to take us north towards Mount Shasta, near the Oregon border. We bundled Abigail, JimBo, Therese and two of Therese's friends in with us and drove for nine hours to Big Bend, in the mountains east of Redding. It was an extraordinary week.

Our campsite was a clearing at the bottom of a treacherous dirt road that doubled as a flood ravine. We arrived on the night of the solstice and unpacked mountains of food, tents, sleeping bags, cooking pots, tools, musical instruments, axes and lanterns. We looked around. It was a magical spot between a river and an old Indian burial ground. To the north a frozen meadow followed the bank of the river and to the south, a short dash from the fireplace and our circle of tents, was a series of five hot springs.

Earlier visitors had contained the springs with baths built of the river stones that lay all around. We spent our days scampering naked from one bath to another, and occasionally jumping into the icy river for an almighty shock. Long conversations flowed as we simmered and stared at the river, into the forest and up to the snow-capped Cascade Mountains. All-day bathing was blissful. The difficult part was the temperature outside, which never rose to zero degrees for the entire week.

A feeble winter sun barely tiptoed over the treetops at noon, never managing to melt the ice in our cooking pots. Even the olive oil had to be thawed before use. Daylight, for what it was worth, lasted seven hours. Otherwise we were in freezing darkness.

Yet the most elaborate, exquisite meals were made on an open fire. Not a word of command was needed for the fire to be kept lively, for fresh wood to be at hand and for warming teas of ginger and spices to be constantly passed around. At night JimBo and Abigail sang and played guitar, while the rest of us provided a migraine-inducing percussion with spoons and empty bottles. As the nights went on a few more locals from Big Bend, solid unassuming country folk with names like Tammy and Gaylord, would come down to hear the music and share our fire, bringing with them heavy logs, lanterns and local stories.

The magic flowed. You could see it rising like a phoenix from the crackling flames; it was silhouetted in the dancing shadows that projected onto the pine forest; and it rang in the shrill echoes of laughter and in the gurgling of the stream. It was in each long, tapering, misty breath. The magic was its own inspiration and catalyst. It fed on its own power, because each person's gift of service – every time a carrot or onion was carefully chopped with frozen hands, every trip to the river's edge to scour a pot of burnt porridge – inspired us to do more, to create something even more special. We lived like kings in the freezing forest.

It was only for a week, true enough, and we were more than ready for an un-sulphurous hot shower and a soft bed when the time came. But the experience was real. We turned competition and selfishness – what some people call human nature – on its head without having to think about it. It was as though we were competing for the joy of contribution. And it reinforced my faith in an ideal, a happy community that lives and thrives on generosity.

The homeward journey south got no further than Abigail's couch in Valencia Street, Eilbhe having flatly refused to set foot again in the haunted house at Montara. Luckily there was a message on the answering machine inviting us to take care of a beach house in Balinas, twenty miles north of Golden Gate Bridge.

On the morning of 3 January, Marcus's body was found slumped and semi-naked on a bench on Sixteenth Street. He had given himself a massive and fatal injection of heroin. The needle was still sticking in his arm. Other addicts had scavenged everything of value from the corpse – his jacket, boots, watch and his beloved bicycle.

'I just want to die, Steve. Why live?' It was the last thing he said to me. I didn't know what to say and so I said nothing. This was a highly-intelligent young man, musician, social activist, a founder of the (now worldwide) Critical Mass cycling protest movement and of the World Bike Messenger Championships. He had a family and a girlfriend who loved him. If these weren't enough to save him, what good were a near stranger's words? Why live – what can one say?

I felt anger towards Marcus at first, and sorrow for those he left to grieve. But as I was a latecomer to his life I was both least affected by his death and least qualified to judge his decision, if anyone had that right. The living carried on as best they could.

In the month of January I earned over two thousand dollars at speaking venues. By early February I felt confident enough about our immediate security to hire a car and drive out to Flagstaff, Arizona to see Jason and Kenny – who was visiting and filming Jason's recovery. They drove from Pueblo, Colorado; thus we met halfway.

The meeting place was El Rancho Grande, a Mexican bar in a rundown part of town. I was nervous as I swung the saloon door open and scanned the faces for my friends. For some reason I was convinced that Jason was going to announce he was leaving the expedition. They too looked nervous, but I could not have guessed why.

Jason looked well. With the aid of a tall wooden staff he limped towards me, smiling under the rim of a leather hat. He wore ripped jeans, a white shirt and a long ponytail. Kenny also looked well and happy. I hadn't seen him for a year. We found ourselves a table. The place was as squalid as we'd hoped for, with toothless bartenders, tipless pool sticks and beer like fizzy drain water. By the second pitcher of beer it was clear we had all relaxed well enough into each other's confidence to spill the beans. It was all about Kenny's big idea.

'Why confine the expedition to the northern hemisphere?' Kenny began. 'Why don't we cycle down through Central and South America to Peru? We could have *Moksha* transported there on a container ship. You and Jason could then pedal through the South Pacific with the south-east trade winds to Australia.' Jason looked at me, expectantly. I could see he already loved the idea. They were anxious that I wouldn't go along with it.

We were all mistaken. Jason wasn't leaving the expedition. Nor was I about to resist such a bold and agreeable plan. The South Pacific! How could anyone object to that? I agreed immediately and we sealed the treaty by getting horribly drunk.

I drove back to San Francisco the following day, eager to give Eilbhe the news. I missed her terribly after three days – the longest we'd been apart in eight months. She had spent her time making clothes to sell at the market and walking the house owner's dogs on the beach at Balinas. Surrounded by beauty and solitude at the beach house, I found her lovelier than ever, happy, peaceful and radiant. She was delighted at the news, especially as it meant an end to the idea I had been mulling over to cross the frozen wastes of Alaska and Siberia by bicycle and kayak. She was terrified of me doing that. The new route opened marvellous new opportunities for her to join us at intervals on the way. She also loved the idea of crossing the South Pacific – as crew on a sailboat.

Unfortunately the house owner returned from Europe a week early. We headed reluctantly back to the Mission and gratefully accepted a few nights at Therese's hangar on Shotwell Street.

The following week I spoke to the Berkeley chapter of the Sierra Club. This was an obdurate bunch of octogenarian Republicans, Old Money, the kind of people who hand over entire inheritances to stop homeless dogs becoming dinner in Manila, but who stare blankly at the suggestion of helping homeless people in Berkeley. The expedition's aim of visiting schools to encourage children to think for themselves made even less of an impact. I fell back on my 'beauty and beast' show instead, focusing on easy-to-please slides of sunsets and grossly exaggerated stories of wild animal encounters. They expressed their appreciation with a polite patter of hands.

Eilbhe and I autographed and sold a few expedition T-shirts. Dejected, we made our way to the door.

Waiting there for us was a most engaging, delightful woman who introduced herself as Deanna Ferrera. Deanna more than made up for the others' lack of enthusiasm. Her's was wholehearted and sincere. She wanted to know everything about the expedition, where the idea came from, why the educational focus, what the Atlantic Ocean was really like, and could I come and talk to schools in the East Bay.

'What kind of training do you do to prepare?'

'Oh there's a lot of wait-training,' I replied.

'Oh really, weight-training?'

'Yeah, I always wait until the day we leave to start training.' It was a well-worn gag and entirely true. Deanna laughed out loud.

We talked and laughed for another hour or more, by which time Deanna was adamant that we should come and live with her family for a while – husband Norman and daughter Laura – in Danville.

And so, it is here in Danville, at the beginning of March, that we welcome the arrival of spring. The Pacific is pacified. Eucalyptus trees no longer shed their slick purple bark or drop fat splattering globules of rainwater from the canopy. It has been a long wet winter – wetter than England, in fact. But we are assured that, unlike home, the weather is guaranteed to improve.

It is wonderful to feel at home with the Ferrera family, with all of the chaos, the love, the laughter, the banter, the bickering, the dogs, the cats and the scattered heaps of laundry that go with it.

In stark contrast to the Mission District of San Francisco, Danville in the East Bay is a very white and wealthy neighbourhood, with immaculate lawns and gated estates. An article in the winter issue of *Danville Today* illustrates how determined some people are to keep it just so. Entitled 'Neighbourhood Watch Works', it reads:

'A resident of Clydesdale Drive recently observed an older model van slowly driving through her neighbourhood. She jotted down the licence plate and called the Danville Police Department. Patrol officers reacted quickly and detained the subject, and in all probability a burglary was prevented.'

In With The Cream
Danville: 13 March

Another of my standard slide show gags, one about a regular intake of Ben and Jerry's ice cream being the secret of eternal happiness, produced more laughs than it should at a breakfast meeting of Fisherman's Wharf Rotary Club. After the meeting, Roger Kaufman introduced himself as the owner of the Ben and Jerry's franchise in San Francisco and offered whatever assistance he could give.

One good fortune led to another. Roger offered office facilities to produce the latest expedition newsletter and he will cover the postage for our eleven hundred American subscribers. He also invited me to a Rotary Club dinner and auction in support of schools in Chinatown, at which the guest of honour was San Francisco's Chief of Police. I donated a 'Pedal Around San Francisco Bay' in *Moksha*, which went for five hundred dollars, the buyer being the gentleman seated to my right. I almost choked when told I should stand to acknowledge an ovation from the assembled elite, and even more so when I sat down again and the gentleman introduced himself:

'William Simon; please call me Bill.' He handed me his business card. It read, 'President, The North Face.' I arranged to visit their head office in San Leandro to discuss the expedition with his sponsorship manager – world-famous mountain climber, Conrad Anker.

There is renewed hope that sponsorship might finally deliver us from years of desperate struggle and debt. At this point I'm ready to endorse practically anyone. Well, not really, but nothing works like poverty to soften one's cynicism. I suppose I've also become more realistic about the relationship between an event, its sponsors, the media and the public. Everyone uses everyone else to get what they want: expeditions get funded; sponsors get the right image and brand recognition; the news media get a quirky 'filler' between crime and murder stories; and the public get momentarily amused. And a few, one hopes, get inspired enough to pursue their boldest dream.

At the beginning of April Eilbhe and I moved onto a rented sailboat, *Aqui No Mas*, on Pier 39 at Fisherman's Wharf, and spent a week making her habitable. The following week Jason arrived in a donated car (a Ford Galaxy – another monstrous relic of the 1970s, which he nicknamed The Behemoth) towing *Moksha* and accompanied by her builder, Chris Tipper, visiting from England. By some miracle The Behemoth had managed to drag *Moksha* across the continent, surviving snowstorms, mountain passes and a dozen breakdowns, before growling and spluttering her dying breaths along the length of Jefferson Street and finally depositing *Moksha* at the Maritime Museum on Hyde Street Pier.

Reconnecting With The Wild
Yosemite Valley: 28 April

Eilbhe and I gratefully accepted the opportunity to test North Face products for Conrad Anker and quickly organised a hiking trip in Yosemite National Park with Therese and her partner Todd.

It is the afternoon of our third day of hiking and we are well beyond the limits of day-trippers, marked trails, scavenging squirrels and blue jays and those ridiculous signs that say 'Viewpoint Here'. We have entered the raw, splendid wilderness.

The following morning I wake at the river's edge in a frosted sleeping bag. I lean across to Eilbhe. She is cocooned snugly in her bag and only the tip of her multicoloured woollen hat is visible. She hears the rustling of my bag, pokes her head through and tries to mouth the words 'good morning' through a long yawn. Therese and Todd are also stirring on the other side of Eilbhe.

Having made the decision to unzip and let in the cold, we each hurry into our outer garments, stuff sleeping bags vigorously into backpacks and begin preparations for breakfast. Todd resurrects last night's fire from the glowing embers deep inside its ashes; Therese collects an armful of twigs; I stir a pot of drinking chocolate and Eilbhe melts butter in the flat pan for pancakes.

On the first day Therese and Todd had argued bitterly and Therese was afraid that she wouldn't cope with the weight of her backpack. Now the dynamics of our group are much different, relaxed, settled down like the fragrant bed of pine needles that carpet the forest around us.

Any remnants of knots and tensions are flushed away under a waterfall shower – a powerful, ice-cold mountain stream that drops about twelve feet off the craggy, moss-covered slopes into a plunge pool big enough for a person to bathe in. Todd is first to strip and take the plunge, then Therese, then Eilbhe and finally me. I watch each of them disappear into the falls and then emerge, laughing with intense joy, bursting from the numbing cold, reborn as hyperventilating, glistening creatures with pink, goose-pimpled skins and dripping hair, stretched sinews and heaving ribs, nipples hard and erect; clenched fists and jaws; 'Whoooah!' Each makes his or her yelp of ecstasy, which tumbles on down the valley and floods the forest with its echo.

By late afternoon we have walked all the way back to Therese's jeep. We drive back to San Francisco through the dusty pesticide-laden winds of the San Joaquin Valley. The atmosphere inside the car is happy but subdued.

Five hours later, Therese and Todd drop us off on Jefferson Street in front of Pier 39. We wave goodbye and slowly make our way to D Dock, through the steel mesh security gate, down the ramp and along the long lurching wooden pontoon to our rented sailboat. We lift our backpacks high over her wire railings and dump them down into the aft seating area. I clamber over after them, unlock the main cabin hatch and climb down the wooden stairwell. Eilbhe climbs down behind me and switches on the cabin lights.

'Oh damn, what am I going to wear for San Luis Obispo tomorrow?' I have rummaged through several drawers where clean clothes are usually kept, and in the thin locker by the forward sleeping cabin where smarter stuff can be hung. 'None of this stuff will do for a formal dinner gig.'

'Well de tings won't clean demselves now, will dey?' Eilbhe puts on a broad Limerick lilt to make me laugh. She proceeds to elbow and bustle her way through the cramped cabin, emptying drawers, holding garments up to the light, giving them a good sniff without the slightest qualm. 'Now!' – she always announces that word sharply whenever she feels decisively on top of things – 'I'll sort through everything and find your decent shirt and trousers. We can do a wash at the harbour office launderette. What does the machine take, quarters? OK then, I'll get the laundry sorted out; you see if you can get me five dollars worth of quarters.'

I jump off the boat, walk briskly up the ramp and onto the mainland, extract a twenty-dollar bill from the cash machine in the arcade and begin my hunt for quarters along Jefferson Street. It is a warm airless night in the city, much warmer than our previous nights in the mountains. Looking down I notice how filthy my legs remain from the day's hike. I am wearing sandals, boxer shorts almost hidden by a long T-shirt, and a red North Face raincoat. Never mind, the street is deserted. I'll be back for a hot shower in five minutes.

The stores are all closing for the night. None have quarters to spare. I buy a frozen yogurt at the first place I try, a 1950s theme parlour called Johnny Rockets, and carry on walking west towards The Cannery.

A small nervous-looking Korean man at a leather-goods stall takes my note and hands me some change. He can only manage three dollars in quarters. I go into an adjacent shop where the assistant exchanges another two dollars worth.

I walk slowly back on the seaward side of Jefferson Street. I finish my pot of frozen yogurt listening to the clatter of sail rigging and the barking of resident seals.

Back now at Pier 39, I yell down from behind the security gate at D Dock. 'Eilbhe. Shall I meet you at the launderette?' Her head bobs up through the cabin hatch.

'No,' she replies. 'Come down here. I need a hand with the bags.'

'Righto.' I reach inside my pocket for the gate key.

'Hey! You!' I turn my head to the right. Four men in dark clothes are running along the quay, pointing guns. Instinctively I look the other way, fearfully imagining what kind of gangster's retribution I might have walked right into the middle of. There is no one there. I look back at the men. They keep running towards me. I see now that one is in police uniform.

'Hands on your head! Get on your knees. Now!' They mean me. I am terrified. The gun barrels look as big as cannons, all pointed at my head. I do as they say.

'On the floor; face down; arms behind your back.' I am pressed to the ground with my cheek on the concrete floor. One of the men stands on my back, crushing the air out of me. I feel the soles of his boot dig in. Handcuffs click tightly around my wrists. Someone drags me to my feet. I am pushed backwards until the backs of my calves meet a bench. I am told to sit. A gun remains levelled at my head.

'What the fuck you doing?'

'Shut up! You want to get tough?'

'I want to know what the fuck you're doing?' My fear has turned to rage. Eilbhe opens the security gate and tries to walk to me. She is pushed back and ordered not to approach. The security gate slams shut with a heavy clang. She stands this side of it, visibly shocked and close to tears.

'What have I done?' I ask.

'Grand larceny, now shut yer mouth,' the officer replies. His badge identifies him only as 'Welsh'.

'What the hell's grand larceny?' They ignore me. All eyes turn to a blue and white squad car that has just pulled up to the dock. A man opens the rear passenger door, looks at me and mutters something to another officer.

'That's it. We have positive ID. Let's go.'

I am bundled into the back of a different squad car. Eilbhe is crying and screaming and flapping her arms as she tries to reason with the nearest man.

'Where are you taking him? Can't he give me our keys? This is where we live. I can't get back inside now.' The policeman refuses.

We drive away leaving Eilbhe alone in tears on the pier and without keys to get back to the boat. I stare helplessly back and watch her shaking figure as we speed away.

I arrive at a police station within minutes. Officer Welsh pushes me down onto an empty bench, un-cuffs one hand, feeds the chain around a rail behind my back and re-cuffs me. I am utterly shocked and confused. I feel like screaming my head off.

I remain handcuffed to the bench for several hours. A colourful, scantily-clad line of prostitutes marches through from a holding room on their way back to the streets. Some other prisoners have been brought in and sit alongside me, though untied: two enormous black men loudly exclaim their innocence; a drunken ex-fireman hurls constant abuse. He spits and snarls and finally vomits over himself.

I am alone again on the bench. Ahead of me to my right is a sad lunatic who languishes alone in a cell. He wails and groans and fiddles with his penis under a pair of putrid underpants. Another large black man is bundled through the door and deposited next to me on the bench by a plain-clothes Asian detective, whose face I recognise from the pier. His name is Liu. He is very angry, continually pacing back and forth in front of us and rubbing his face. When he has calmed down sufficiently to speak, he addresses the new arrival with a spine-chilling aggression.

'You don't see it, Theo? Well I see this, man! I see you running, Theo. I see the dope – remember throwing the dope into the garbage can, Theo?'

Theo shakes his head. His massive frame jerks and wobbles continually as he blubbers through his denials.

'Why run then, Theo? Why run?' Liu's is close to exploding. 'Eight years, man. Look, it's fucking simple. Count it, Theo. Eight years. This man here,' Liu points at me, 'he's grand theft. He's going down for two. But you, Theo…'

'But my name's Michael, who's Theo?'

'Wait a minute,' I interrupt. 'You say I'm going to prison for two years for theft? What did I steal?'

Surrounded by dope dealers with amnesia, prostitutes, vomiting drunks, repulsive lunatics, and now a thief playing the innocent, Detective Liu has clearly lost all patience.

'Six hundred bucks from a store at the corner of Jefferson and Taylor,' he spits. He emits a long painful sigh and throws me a look of pure contempt.

'What! You searched me! I've only got change for the laundry. I'm no thief. Look, you can check with my bank. I took out twenty bucks with my cash card to get quarters. Why would a robber do that?' But Detective Liu is too experienced, too long in the front line of a losing battle, too sick of dumb excuses and most of all too tired to listen to this crap. He turns on his heels and disappears into a back room office.

A lieutenant removes my red jacket to be used as evidence – Exhibit A; not the sort of publicity North Face was counting on, I'm sure! He empties one pocket of its bundle of quarters, the marina keys and my cash-point card. I am transferred to a solitary cell directly opposite the deranged man, who is now rubbing faeces over his stomach.

This is a dramatic fall from grace. Last month I dined with the city's finest, was even applauded by the Chief of Police. Now I find myself beginning two years behind bars, in a cell opposite a man who likes the feel of his own shit. And if that wasn't bad enough all I have on is a dirty T-shirt and a pair of *Batman Forever* boxer shorts.

In the early hours of the morning I am taken by squad car to the San Francisco Hall of Justice for 'processing'. Photographs and fingerprints are taken. I am searched and thrown into a bare concrete cell measuring thirty feet long by eight feet wide. I share this space with about forty other men. Many of them are sprawled across the floor asleep. I crouch in one corner and wait.

The next day around midday – it is hard to tell in this strip-lighted dungeon – I remain huddled in my corner of the stinking room of bodies. My name is called. I walk through to the processing area.

I sit and wait for another hour. Finally, more photographs are taken. More fingerprints are taken. There is a medical interview and another interview with an Official Recognition Officer. He allows me a phone call. I try Therese's number. I get an answering machine. I leave a message. I ask for another call, which is granted. I call Kim Cook, Marcus' sister, who is a lawyer. I get an answering machine. Bollocks! I leave another message.

I am returned to the main cell. Many of the other inmates are now shaking violently and grimacing with the pains of withdrawal, from either crack or heroin. One addict, a sickly, skeleton of a boy in his late teens, tries to stand and shuffle around, but forgets that the police confiscated his belt. His fashionably baggy jeans fall to his ankles. He drags them pathetically back up to his waist and sits down again. He fidgets and stands up shakily. The trousers fall to his ankles again. After the fourth and fifth times, this really begins to annoy me. I want to cry out, 'Stop dropping your fucking pants, man!' But looking down at my bare muddy legs and boxer shorts I see the weakness of my position. I focus instead on the guy shouting instructions down the public telephone line in the far corner.

'No Sugar, listen careful. First thing is, ya go ta Mama's wardrobe, arright. Ya put the bags in there. Now, ya gotta take the TV to Barney's, arright Sugar. Now you listenin'? Cuz there's more I wancha ta do fer me.'

How come other people were allowed to keep the change from their pockets? Or did they come prepared with a block of quarters stuffed up their backsides?

A respectable-looking prisoner (someone wearing trousers) hammers on the iron door with his fist. He complains loudly about the foul smell, the heat and the lack of space. The door opens in response. A hand grabs the man's throat.

'You want some space, huh?' A voice bellows. The man is lifted off his feet and thrown against the far wall of the corridor outside. He doesn't return. There are no other complaints.

The hours drag on. Eventually I am instructed to walk down a long corridor to a dormitory cell. Along the way I am told to pick up a mattress and bed sheet, a toothbrush, toothpaste and a razor. I pass men who press their faces against the bars of a long line of other cells. 'Matches?' they whisper. I shrug my reply and walk on.

The dormitory cell holds six iron beds, a toilet and a table around which a group of men are playing cards. They seem entirely at home, laughing and joking. One looks up and nods briefly before continuing with his hand. There is a bible on a bedside stool. I place my mattress down and open it at Psalm 110 – glad to least for somewhere to bury my eyes and remain unworthy of attention.

I have reached Psalm 134 when I am instructed to move again, this time to an interview room. Inside, to my huge relief, I find Kim Cook sitting on the far side of a small square table.

'Oh, Jesus! Thank God you got the message.'

'No I didn't. Eilbhe called me. She said they arrested you for grand larceny. What's the story, Steve?'

'I wish I knew Kim. They tell me I'm going to jail for two years.'

'Not here you won't. You'll be deported back to England first. They tell me you're an immigration case. You been here longer than you should?'

'Um, yes. I meant to talk to you about that, Kim. My tourist visa expired about eight months ago. I meant to leave the country and come back in again but, I don't know, I guess I was afraid they'd refuse me entry since I couldn't show funds to support myself for another six months.'

'Then we'd better get you bailed out of here – fast, before the immigration people do their sweep. They're going tough on you Steve. Your bail has been set at five thousand dollars.'

'Five grand! How am I gonna find five grand? Look, can you give me some quarters? When the gangsters get off the phone I can start calling round for help.'

'Sorry, I'm not allowed to hand you anything. They're watching us. I'll ask Eilbhe to phone people for you. But we don't have long, Steve. We need you out of here now. Immigration could come for you anytime. I'm surprised they haven't already.'

There is a knock on the door. The interview is over. I am escorted back to my cell. The situation appears quite hopeless. I'm to be deported as a criminal unless Eilbhe can find five thousand dollars in the next few hours.

A short time later someone shouts over to me. 'You're out, man. Good luck.' One of my cellmates has spotted a guard heading our way. Somehow he knows he is coming for me. He returns to his game of cards with the others. They all appear comfortable with their predicaments and resigned to whatever happens next. 'You don't belong here,' he adds as I turn to leave, with a curious mix of cold indifference and touching sympathy.

'Follow me,' says the guard. 'Take your mattress. Put it in the box.'

We take the elevator down to the first floor. The elevator doors part. Eilbhe, Therese, Todd and Kim are standing, grinning, in front of me. We hug each other. I feel rather embarrassed by my smell.

'I don't believe this. Eilbhe, where the hell did you find five thousand dollars?'

'It was Therese. She put up your bail.'

'Well we couldn't have you sent back to Old Blighty now could we,' Therese adds with a big smile.

'Oh, Therese, I... I don't know how to... thanks.' I am tongue-tied with gratitude and relieved to be out of that dreadful place. I haven't slept in thirty-six hours and have had no food or water in the last twenty-four, though they were offered this morning.

'Don't worry about the money now. I've put it on my credit card. We'll sort it all out tomorrow. What do you want first – shower, eat, sleep?'

'No, I have to sort this out now. Can you drive me back to Fisherman's Wharf?'

Therese drops me at the corner of Jefferson and Taylor. A thin, pale, casually dressed man in his mid-forties stands at the leather-goods stall.

'Hey there.' I call out as I walk towards him, still dressed only in my T-shirt, boxers, muddy knees and sandals. 'Did an Asian employee of yours have someone arrested last night?'

'Err, yeah. Jay Park, the Korean guy. But he doesn't work here anymore.'

'Oh really. Why not?'

'What's it to you?'

'Quite a bit. I'm the guy he had arrested. When did you get rid of him?'

'This morning, about nine o'clock. The boss was here. He found six hundred bucks under the tray in the cash machine. He fired Park on the spot.'

'Your boss found the money at nine in the morning! Why hasn't he told the police? I spent the past twenty-four hours in jail for a crime that never even happened. I'd still be there now if it weren't for a friend who stuck five thousand dollars for my bail. Doesn't that bother you?'

'Err, well. We were told you'd been released,' the man stammers, obviously lying.

'Oh really! And who told you that?'

'Jay Park.'

'Oh, I see! How could he have known I'd been released? And why would you believe him anyway? You only just fired the man!' I struggle to control my temper. I must get a signed statement out of this guy first.

I am so angry. I'm angry that a shop assistant could, in theory, rob his own till, point a finger at the first down-and-out who walked by, and the police would require no further evidence to subject that person to the terrible fear and humiliation of arrest at gunpoint. I'm angry that the recovery of the missing dollars was the shop owner's only concern. So what if some deadbeat was left wallowing in jail. It wasn't even worth a phone call to him.

And I'm angry that if immigration officers had found me and deported me back to England, I might never have known what really happened. I would have been branded a criminal and barred from re-entering the United States. The expedition and all these years of effort would have been over for me.

The following afternoon I stand outside the impound yard of the Atlas Towing Company, at the corner of Eighteenth and Harrison Street. Gripping the perimeter fence, I shake it in violent anger and frustration. I want to cry. Instead I scream out loud. *Moksha*, our pride and joy, sits on her trailer between two rusting hulks destined for the scrapheap. She is not, as far as her captors are concerned, the world's only ocean-going pedal powered boat, Queen of the Atlantic Ocean. She is merely a two hundred and fifty dollar ticket that increases by twenty five dollars a day.

Pedalling to Hawaii

It was a hectic morning on the telephone at the Ben and Jerry's office. My first calls were to the police department. The detective in charge of my case wasn't yet aware I had been released on bail, or that I was innocent. An hour later, Assistant District Attorney Candy Hysler called to offer her sincerest apologies. She told me I was a wonderful person, so very brave, and that the bail money would be reimbursed to Therese immediately. I made the mistake of immediately reassuring her that I wasn't going to sue the city for damages, before asking for help in arranging expedition slide shows for Kids At Risk groups in the city. The moment she realised there was no danger of a financial backlash or scandal for her department, her tone completely changed; the shallow toadying dried up and she stopped listening.

I then had to call and make my own apologies for the missed engagements in San Luis Obispo. Next I checked for messages on the expedition's freephone number: there was one from Jason, which was three days old, telling me that, due to an argument between Chris Tipper and Bill Doll – the manager of the Maritime Museum at Hyde Street Pier, I had until today to find another home for *Moksha* or Mr Doll would call a towing company to have it removed.

I called up a friend of mine who owns a tow vehicle and we raced over to the museum. But we were too late. *Moksha* was already gone.

I don't have $250. I was relying heavily on the San Luis Obispo gig to replenish my funds. I gave Chris and Jason $400 of my savings and our bicycles to enable them to cycle back to Colorado – to test Jason's recovering legs and to give Chris a pedalling adventure. This is the thanks I get. They skip town and leave me to sort out their mess.

Now I have to figure out the bus route back to Fisherman's Wharf. I check to make sure I have enough change for the bus fare. The police still have my cash card and the banks are closed until Monday. This moment scores high among the all-time expedition low points.

I decide to walk as far as Van Ness Avenue and wait for the number forty-nine bus.

A very untidy-looking black man wearing an old pinstripe suit and sandals bounces toward me, grinning madly. In one hand he holds a dustpan, in the other a crumpled piece of paper.

'Hi there! My name is Theodore Harrison Junior,' he volunteers with great formality. 'But most people call me Smooth.'

I sense this is going to be one of those conversations that require absolutely no indication of interest on my part.

'I have a dream,' Theodore continues, 'to establish a wholly scientific, not-for-profit organisation in order to build cities on the Moon.' His words, although nonsense, are delivered with such poetic grace and charming enthusiasm that he makes me smile.

'I'm pleased to meet you, Smooth,' I say truthfully.

'You know, I always knew I was somebody special. You know how?'

'No. How?'

'Coz I was the first black man born in Los Angeles on New Year's Day.'

'Is that so?'

'Yessiree. But also because, you know how most babies is born with they eyes all squished up?

'Um, yeah.'

'Well mine was wiiiyde open!'

'That is unusual. And what's the crumpled-up piece of paper for?'

'That's a sign, which I felt obliged to tear out of the Not-for-Profit Corporation Handbook, a sign of my destiny that instructs me how to establish such an organisation.'

'And the dustpan?'

'That signifies how I was too efficient an' too intelligent to stay in Africa, so I was born here in America, where I can be self-employed. The dopers an' the boozers I hang out with say I ain't goin' nowhere, but I know I'm intelligent.'

He is intelligent. Confused, but intelligent. And smooth.

'Well, I'm sayin' like the farmer said to the p'tater – watch me now... I'll dig ya later.' And with that poetic farewell, Theodore Harrison Junior skips away, leaving me in a thoroughly good mood. Even though I am stony broke – again, even though the pedal boat is impounded, and even though these four years of the expedition have been one relentless struggle. Life is rich with surprises.

An Unexpected Visit
San Francisco: 6 June

About a month after rescuing *Moksha* from her prison (with a loan from Eilbhe's father), I am barbecuing sea bass on the pontoon next to our boat, *Aqui No Mas*. Eilbhe is in the galley steaming vegetables. Our guests, Matt and Tracy, sit cross-legged on a bench at the stern.

'Yeah, The Pier 39 Corporation grosses one-point-four billion a month,' Matt explains (they both work in the marketing department of Pier 39, which is the hideous complex of tourist shops and amusement arcades immediately ashore from us). 'And until Underwater World is finished the only thing to see here are the seals!' Eilbhe pokes her head through the companionway and nods politely in recognition of the vast sum. I smile, thinking how novel it is for us to have friends with real jobs. They are a delightful couple: sincere, interesting, kind-hearted and beautifully clean. Normal people, perhaps!

Just as I am clearing up the empty plates, Jason appears, quite unexpectedly, at the entrance to D Dock. I run up the jetty to let him in. He explains that he has driven all the way from Colorado to tell me something important. He brings along a friend, Leslie. She is very drunk.

The two groups of guests mix like oil and water on the stern deck of *Aqui No Mas*. Leslie is incoherent in her tale of the road journey. Jason tries to fill in the gaps during her bouts of laughter. I gather something about being hounded by F-16 fighter jets across a nuclear test site in Nevada. Matt and Tracy offer their thanks for dinner and make a speedy exit.

Sensing Jason's urgency to unload the burden that thickens the air around him, I suggest a pint of Guinness at the nearby Irish pub, Fiddler's Green. We get up to leave. Eilbhe is left to tend to the increasingly unstable Leslie. She understands the situation and gives me a meaningful kiss goodbye.

Jason and I walk slowly along Bay Street, allowing for his still pronounced limp.

'I'm going to be a father, you know.'

'Oh, Jeez! Congratulations mate. That's great... isn't it?' I stumble, unsure.

'Um, yeah.' We carry on slowly, and in thoughtful silence.

'I'm married too,' he announces a minute later.

'Hurhumm!' I clear my throat in shock.

'Well, except for – slight technicality – she's already married to someone else. So I guess it doesn't legally count. Great service though, at one of those little chapels in Vegas; reception was at Taco Bell.'

'Ah! Yes. Wow! You have been busy.' I shake my head, wondering what on earth will come next. 'So, is the baby the reason for the marriage, or did the marriage come first?'

'No, they're actually not connected. In fact, they're different women.'

'Different women? You mean the woman you married, who is already married to someone else, isn't the woman having your child?'

'That's it.'

'And are they aware of each other?'

'Oh sure. It's all very cool. Julie, the one having my child, is happily married anyway to my friend Tom. He knows everything, it's cool.'

Jason continues to unravel the soap-operatic web of intrigues he has managed to weave during his nine-month recovery in Colorado. But he wouldn't drive all the way from Colorado just to tell me this.

'How are you and Eilbhe getting on?'

'Oh brilliantly mate. Gets better all the time. We've had two, maybe three arguments since she arrived in Florida. Cycling across the country and living from hand-to-mouth was a big test, and then we had the stress of creating a very different life here in the city. But none of it pulled us apart; in fact quite the opposite.'

'Well I envy you then. I can't seem to be comfortable with anyone for very long. Familiarity breeds contempt. The longer I stay with one person, the less fulfilled I feel.'

So why would you marry someone, legally or not?'

'Oh, it's hard to explain. It was pretty impulsive. We're not committed for life or anything.'

'No, only for about three years if they catch you.'

There is another long silence. We arrive at Fiddler's Green, a lively traditional Irish bar on the street corner opposite a grassy square. The place is busy and smoke-filled. Everyone is absorbed in shouting conversations. I stand at the bar and wait for two pints of Guinness to be poured. All the seats inside are taken. We go outside and sit at a picnic bench. Jason sips the white head off his Guinness, shifts uneasily, and comes back to our previous conversation.

'What we were talking about, you know, familiarity, I guess that's what I came to tell you.' Jason fixes his gaze on the glass in his hand. His cheeks are flushed. He looks very serious and determined. 'It's been a year and a half now since we arrived in Miami. We've been apart for most of that time and let's face it we've changed.' He looks up at me for agreement. I nod my head slightly. He lowers his eyes again, shuffles in his seat, and continues. 'Well, I know I have. I suppose it was deliberate on my part, in that I chose to separate myself – mentally as much as geographically. And it's given me the space to reassess things.'

'Reassess things?' I repeat after him, raising my brow.

'Yes. I've been thinking a lot about my own growth and happiness and I think, for me, that growth requires constant changes of associations and partnerships.' He starts to frown, perhaps struggling to voice the theory as elegantly as it was rehearsed, over and over again, in his mind on the long drive from Colorado.

'As you know,' he continues, 'I've been developing my own ideas and, um, my own way of doing things and... I think it's time for me to carry on alone.' That is it. He has said it. The thing is done. He relaxes his shoulders and looks at me.

'I see.' I look up and around me, at a curling, old-fashioned streetlamp and at the glowing rows of lit office windows across the street. I don't think anything. I am numb. It feels as though the atmosphere around me is electrified. Jason waits for some added response, and receiving none, continues to unload himself.

'Believe me, Steve, this is just my way of finding my own path. It's not anything personal against you. I do respect you as a friend. I'll always appreciate the brilliance of your idea and for getting me involved in the expedition.'

'And how do you propose to continue alone?' I ask, genuinely puzzled.

'Well,' he takes a deep breath. 'Obviously I can't expect to take *Moksha*. She's more your boat than anyone's. So, time is short, but I'm planning to cycle north pretty soon and follow that overland route to Asia you came up with a while back – Alaska to Siberia by bicycle and kayak. Maybe we could join up again somewhere in China or even Europe. I would love to cross the finishing line with you.'

'Europe! The finishing line!' Jason's words leave me utterly bewildered. 'If you and I somehow manage, separately, to cross the Pacific and travel all the way through Asia by human power, I hardly see the point of us crossing the English Channel together.'

We finish our beers and walk slowly back to the boat, deep in thought. I have to find a way of talking Jason out of this. It won't be easy. He must have thought very carefully about it already. He was totally sincere – except about going north. There was something fake about that part. Jason hates cold climates.

We walk down the jetty to *Aqui No Mas*. I stop Jason before we go aboard.

'If you had the choice, Jason, wouldn't you be happier to pedal *Moksha* across the South Pacific?' His whole face lights up at the suggestion.

'Yes,' he replies. 'Desperately.'

Jason steps aboard and retires to his bunk opposite Leslie's in the saloon cabin. I sit out on deck a while longer and watch the twinkling dance of city lights on the water.

It has been a sad day. The morning paper brought news that our English friend, Peter Bird, had drowned in his attempt to row across the Pacific Ocean. He leaves behind a partner and an adorable little son called Louis. And now Jason's decision to go it alone: it changes so much for me; practically, personally; in terms of the expedition's heart, what it represents.

I agree with him – every man has to follow his own path, with integrity and courage. It's just that, as far as this journey is concerned, Jason has always been part of it. Our partnership, despite the disagreements, was a fundamental part. His decision isn't a complete surprise. I have often wondered where our long separation was leading. But there was a commitment there. I would have liked to see it through.

I have to laugh at myself. I am a romantic idealist, always hoping for that perfect love, that unshakeable bond, in lovers and in friends – musketeers, all for one and one for all. And I feel rather foolish now, having waited so long for his recovery. Maybe the commitment, the ideal, never existed. Maybe it was only in my head. I feel a great loss, something irretrievable.

The following morning, I awake tense and early in a fragile light. I leave Eilbhe sound asleep in the forward cabin of *Aqui No Mas* and creep silently through the saloon cabin where Jason and Leslie lie in their separate bunks. I climb the polished wooden steps, yawn and stretch my arms on the stern deck and breathe in the damp salt air. Jason appears minutes later. I tell him I'm going to spend the day working on *Moksha*'s repairs. He offers to come with me.

Jason follows me up the ramp at D Dock. We mount our bicycles and I lead him along my daily route to *Moksha*'s new home.

We cruise easily along the wide flat pavement of the Embarcadero, heading south. We pass under the Bay Bridge, cut through South Beach Marina and stop at the Java House Café for scrambled eggs and coffee.

Continuing on, we cycle across Lefty O'Doul Bridge and past the inline hockey stadium on Third Street. We take a left at Sixteenth Street by the cement works, past the Bay View Boat Club and a line of colourful house-buses parked along China Basin Road.

Sandwiched between a commercial boatyard and a fish wholesaler is a tiny boatyard called Pier 66. Inside the wire fence stands a dilapidated wooden shack ringed by rusting oil drums and discarded blocks of wood. A handwritten wooden sign above the door reads 'Office'. Another sign reads, 'No Tools Loaned: Min. Rental Charge Six Pack Miller Light.' The manager, Rudi, a tall shaggy caustic German whose smell is a blend of sawdust, acetone and marijuana, can occasionally be roused from his armchair in the workshop to haggle over a price for plywood. The exchange rate currently stands at a bottle of tequila per sheet. If it's marine-grade you're after, better make it Cuervo Gold.

Out in the sloping yard lies a scattered colony of a dozen decrepit boats, each propped up with planks and crates and bits of rope. Half of them are destined for bonfires and scrap. The others will be painstakingly resurrected for another life at sea, but even the owners are unsure which way theirs will go. *Moksha*, sadly, does not look out of place here.

We circle *Moksha* a few times as I explain my plan for repairs and preparations for the South Pacific Ocean.

'There's a lot to do. The hull looks pretty sound. Here, she needs repairs on the foredeck, and some more aft. There's some fibreglass reinforcing to do here. The centreboard and its casing are still damaged from the coral reef at the Turks and Caicos. Nearly all the stainless steel and brass fittings need replacing. All the wiring will need to be stripped out and replaced. None of the electronics are worth a damn. And I'll have to check all the safety gear and see what we can salvage.

Obviously the whole boat needs to be stripped down, sanded and repainted.

Once the boat is done, I'll need to find six months' worth of dehydrated food from somewhere. That's just to get me, and maybe a new pedal partner, across from Peru to the islands of the South Pacific. I could rely on fresh and tinned stuff and island hopping from then on. Then I need to find a shipping company to deliver *Moksha* and the supplies down to Peru... somewhere.

I haven't even begun planning the cycle ride from here to Peru. But I do know that you can only cycle as far as Panama. Then you have to walk through a hundred miles of swampy jungle called the Darian Gap to get to Colombia, and apparently it's full of mule trains of armed drug smugglers.'

'And what about all the educational stuff, the schools program?' asks Jason.

'Exactly. That's becoming a full-time job by itself, isn't it? You've been working with all those kids in Colorado, visiting schools and so on. And there's the whole business of setting up a website.'

The size of the task ahead is overwhelming. We take our thoughts with us and walk back to the road and down to the garden at the Bay View Boat Club. We find a bench to sit on overlooking China Basin. Jason finally breaks the silence.

'Let me ask you this. Did you ever feel that the expedition required me? Am I an essential part of what it means for you?'

'Yes, definitely. I know we've had our ups and downs but I couldn't imagine doing the trip with anyone else. How about you?'

'No, I feel very differently. For me, the expedition has always been very much a personal thing. I don't feel necessarily connected to both you and it in that sense.'

'I think I see that now. Mind you, I still think that travelling separately at this point would be a big mistake. It's always been a struggle with two, even with Stuart's help and Kenny and all the other people who made it possible, I mean, I...' I am choking with emotion.

'I can't do this on my own!' I blurt out. 'It's too much. I could try, but it wouldn't be a life. I'm already working at my limit now. It's always been that way, for me anyway – in London, in Portugal, in Miami. It's all so bloody huge! And look where we are now – at the edge of the Pacific. It's like starting all over again, except it's even harder. The cycle ride from here to Peru is ten times farther than London to Portugal and through poor, possibly dangerous countries. The ocean pedal to Australia is two or three times as far as the Atlantic. The educational part of it is potentially huge by itself. Isn't that hard enough, without making it twice as hard by splitting into two expeditions?

'Besides Jason, you hate the cold! If anyone can slog through thousands of miles of tundra and kayak across the Bering Straights, I'm sure it would be you. But I've got a very bad feeling about that whole northern route into Asia. I mean we're pretty good at muddling along; knowing bugger all about what we're doing, learning as we go along. We make fun of it, don't we, all our stupid mistakes, the way we never manage to leave or arrive on time, but...'

'Yeah, I know what you're going to say,' Jason interrupts. 'The cold is different.'

'Yes absolutely. I think our approach would be deadly up there. There's no margin for fuck-ups. You hate military precision. You think I'm too militant! You told me last night that you'd much prefer to pedal *Moksha* across the South Pacific?'

'Yes, I would.'

'And yet you'd still go north rather than carry on working with me?'

'It's not you personally; it's being forced to be with one person all the time that I can't handle.'

'Well, maybe we can figure out a way of staying a team but getting more people involved.' I lean against *Moksha* and pick at some flaking paintwork as I consider the idea. 'Maybe we could cycle with other people on the way to Peru. Maybe there are other ways of travelling between the South Pacific Islands by human power, instead of always having to be together on *Moksha*. We could ask different people to pedal parts of it with us.' Jason's face brightens with the fresh possibilities.

'Yeah,' he replies enthusiastically. 'I've been thinking about expanding the trip, getting different crew members like Kenny or Nancy Sanford or Stuart to do parts of it with me. I'm just a bit sick of the Jason and Steve Show.'

'I know Eilbhe would love to do a stretch.' I add. 'Haven't we been saying all long, 'There's no limit to what you can do'? What better way to prove it?'

'Sure, why not anyone – women, kids, older people. Yeah!'

Jason is someone who consistently inspires me to new expanded visions, and I'd like to think I do the same for him. We've always been able to catalyse each other to greater things, a combination that is greater than the sum of our parts.

The Harbour Queen
San Francisco Bay: 29 July

I'm working for six dollars an hour as a snack bar attendant aboard the *Harbour Queen*. For five minutes every half an hour I sell overpriced junk to over-weight tourists before they are herded onto Alcatraz Island. Between stampedes I think and write and read the newspapers.

On days off I cycle to China Basin to work on *Moksha* and write begging letters to marine equipment suppliers. Thanks to Eilbhe's beautifully illustrated expedition brochure the necessary fittings and gadgets are flooding in.

On the other hand, rejection letters are the only response to proposals for corporate sponsorship. I have never understood why, given the amount of publicity we have generated over the years, no company has been willing to sponsor us. Perhaps our journey is too long, too risky, or too slow to match their campaigns.

Instead, *Moksha*'s rebuilding costs are being met with hundreds of small donations from slide-show audiences and with a single monumental effort from students at California High School. For two weeks in July, Bill Pence's eleventh-grade class raised $2,700 for the expedition by selling chocolate bars in the community.

Exactly one month ago today, Jason strapped himself back into his inline skates and continued rolling west towards San Francisco from the place where his legs were shattered nine months before. He is due to cross the California border tomorrow, after skating a thousand miles on legs held together by inserted metal rods. I am so happy and proud for him that my throat goes into spasms and tears fill my eyes every time I announce this to my lecture audiences and I hear a room gasp with admiration. It is the most inspiring part of our story and it is happening now.

Cycling alongside Jason and carrying both of their baggage is April Mann, a primary school teacher from Rye, Colorado. Her challenge is also amazing, as this is her first ever bicycle trip and because she dares to do it in the face of universal disapproval. April has spent her life in happy service to her family, her students and her community. When Jason announced that he needed a cycling partner to join him and carry his gear, since his legs couldn't cope with added weight, it sparked April's imagination – could I do it? Could I cycle over mountains and cross deserts and live on the open road all the way to San Francisco?

All the people who profess to love April most can't see beyond their own needs. To them the idea is 'just lunacy'; it is 'selfish and inconvenient'. Adventure and self-discovery, they believe, are unacceptable urges for mothers in their mid-forties. April, to her eternal credit, thinks differently.

The Frankenstein Syndrome
San Francisco: 29 September

Roger Kaufman paces around the secretary's desk at the Ben and Jerry's office. His head hangs low as he walks with his hands fidgeting inside his trouser pockets and his heavily-lined, troubled face is obscured with a lank curtain of greying fringe. I watch him disappear into his private office and shut the glass-fronted door behind him.

I knock warily on the door and enter. Roger surfaces from a sea of papers that overhang precipitously, like the coin cascade machines in an amusement arcade, from the edges of his enormous desk.

'Hello Roger, I just popped in to finish emptying my desk. I don't think I'll be seeing much of you any more. We'll be spending all our time getting *Moksha* seaworthy before heading south. I don't know how I would have managed without your help though; you've been a godsend. Thank you so much. I'll take care of any outstanding telephone bills today.'

'Oh... fine,' Roger answers inattentively. 'Glad I could be of help. I do admire your cause and your determination.'

'Likewise. I don't think I've ever met anyone who works as hard as you do. You're in here, what, eighty, ninety hours a week?'

'Yeah,' Roger sighs. 'I work all the time.' His hand releases a fat document. It lands on the desk with a heavy slap. He rubs his eyes. 'I guess you think I must be doing all this to end up with a big fat pile of money one day, huh?'

'I... I suppose – '

'Well, that's not the case. I started business as a challenge.' He emits a stunted, bitter laugh, almost a painful hiccup. 'The idea of creating something really excited me. But, you know, somewhere along the line, somewhere...' – he looks at his desk and shakes his head – 'it started to take over. It's hard to notice when, it... it just happens, little by little, over a long time. And now I'm stuck. It rules my life, Steve. I can't stop it. I can't even slow it down.'

Roger's confession frightens me. I feel deeply sorry for him: for the hopelessness in his tone, and for the life he feels imprisoned in.

Maybe Roger's life isn't so unusual, I think to myself, as I walk along the busy streets leading home. After all, how many of us, when we're really honest with ourselves, can admit that we have created our own Frankensteins? It's always a noble purpose isn't it, to begin with? You start off feeling in control, and then it grows, and grows, and takes on a life of its own. Eventually you're doing all you possibly can just to keep up with it. The idea, that noble creature, becomes the monster – the master that controls its own creator.

This expedition was created for a kind of liberation: liberation from the normal, the habitual, the material, the expected. And yet it has developed so much obligation and debt that I feel less free than before. It is still enjoyable and challenging, but I can't pretend to be its master any more. My obligations command, just as they command the vast majority of lives. My biggest motivation now, ironically, is to be free of its control, free of the obligation of debt. That is not to say that I necessarily want to give up the expedition, I just want the freedom to know that I could. To be free means not to be confined – to be free to choose – to do or not to do. I don't want the answer the question 'Why are you doing this?' with 'Because I can't do anything else'.

I'm tired. It is time I took a break from the expedition.

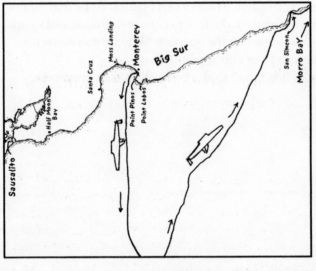

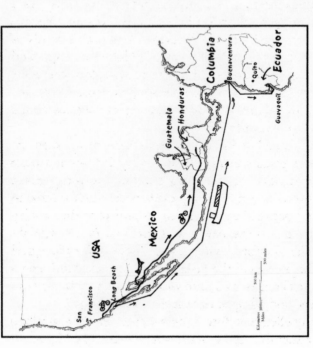

Chapter 6
More Snakes Than ladders

ROUTE LEGEND:

BICYCLE KAYAK PEDAL BOAT CARGO SHIP

6. More Snakes Than Ladders
(October 1996 – September 1998)

A few weeks later, Eilbhe and I decided to spend the winter away from the expedition. I left without knowing whether I would return to it. I just knew I had to get away, away from Jason, away from the whole struggle. We left San Francisco and flew to Ireland, arriving on the morning of Eilbhe's twenty-third birthday – to surprise her parents, who hadn't seen her in over a year. We had intended to rent a cottage somewhere nearby in the Wicklow Mountains south of Dublin, but in the end we accepted Eilbhe's parents' kind invitation to stay with them, which seemed to please everyone. The warm family atmosphere developed further with the arrival of my mother, who took lodgings in the same village in a large house overlooking the sea.

Jason remained in San Francisco to organise the redesign of *Moksha*'s pedal system, which was carried out as a team project by engineering students at Stanford University. Jason had discovered a commercially-made pedal unit for boats in which the pedals, gears, crankshaft and propeller are all connected as a single device and enclosed in a watertight casing. The Stanford students cut a hole in *Moksha*'s keel directly below where the pedals should be and fabricated a stainless steel box or well, into which the new pedal unit can be dropped and clamped tight at the correct height.

The propeller, therefore, is now suspended midway along the hull rather than at the stern, which seems an odd place to have one. But according to Todd Taylor, a hydrologist at MIT's Water Tunnel Lab, it makes no difference to a propeller's efficiency where it goes – bow, middle or stern.

The advantages of this new all-in-one pedal system are considerable. It is more efficient than the system with which we crossed the Atlantic, and therefore *Moksha* can go faster. It replaces our troublesome gearbox and the heavy, vulnerable, three-metre long propeller shaft with a light removable unit that can be serviced on board. It means an end to James Bond-style leaps into the abyss in foul weather, knife gripped between the teeth, to free the sea anchor line from the propeller. Never mind, we'll have to find other ways to amuse ourselves.

Just after Christmas, Jason decided to pedal *Moksha* south, in five one-day voyages, from San Francisco to Monterey. It was a valuable test – both of the new pedal system and of our new concept to make the expedition more inclusive. The inaugural voyage was supposed to have been a two-hour affair, pedalling on the ebb tide from China Basin out to the Presidio Yacht Club, near Golden Gate Bridge. Unfortunately Jason and his crew (Arf Pitney, Commodore of the Bay View Boat Club) had already swallowed a few too many toasts in their honour before they set out, became completely disoriented in heavy fog, did several laps around Alcatraz Island and arrived six hours overdue.

Several other friends – Annette, Sherri and Sonny – then crewed with Jason in relays using an escort boat, down the coast to Half Moon Bay. By all accounts everyone was violently sick and thoroughly enjoyed it.

My father flew across from Colorado – to resume his invaluable support and fund-raising role – in time to accompany Jason on the leg between Santa Cruz and Moss Landing. Therese crewed the final stretch with Jason to

Monterey. It was apparently such a gloriously sunny day that they had to do it naked. He's a jammy bastard!

Soon after that, Jason began cycling south towards Mexico with Therese and three other friends – Olivier and Carole from France and Jenny, an American. Stuart stayed in Monterey raising funds from *Moksha*'s exhibition space outside the Maritime Museum. I would often call him from Ireland to ask how he was getting on there, to which he would reply, 'Oh, like a pig in shit son!' – which translates as a very enjoyable thing.

Jason's team had all dispersed by the time he reached halfway down the Sea of Cortez, where he kayaked across to the eastern shore and cycled on alone as far south as Honduras. Eilbhe and I had recovered our appetite for travel and had returned to California by then, from where we hitched a ride on a cargo ship down to Ecuador (along with our bikes, in order to scout for a suitable departure point for *Moksha*'s voyage across the South Pacific – and hence where the cycling section should end). We were in Quito, the capital of Ecuador, preparing to join Jason in Honduras and cycle on with him when we received some very bad news.

It was 5 September, 1997, a day of bad news. I remember Eilbhe and I sitting having breakfast at a café on the outskirts of Quito. The café – well-known among western travellers for its coffee and selection of desserts – comprised the front room of a guesthouse that overlooked a small, neat garden on a residential street. The place was what I call backpacker-chic – colonial-era, scratched wooden floors and cheap Peruvian art on peach-coloured walls. Reggae music wafting from a single speaker was barely audible over the scraping of cutlery on plates, simultaneous conversations in several European languages and the irregular harrumphs of noisy plumbing emanating from the kitchen. The waitress cleared the table next to us but left behind a newspaper. There was a portrait of Princess Diana on the front page and the word 'Muerto' typed in large black letters underneath. Even though I knew that word and could translate much of the article that followed, I still tried desperately to disbelieve it, hoping that I had misunderstood. And as the grim reality sunk in I felt the distance that separated me from my homeland and that strangely disabled me from sharing its grief. All I had was in print, in foreign words, and the face of a famous woman wearing pearl earrings.

Minutes later, a friend with contacts in the Ecuadorian Interior Ministry came to the table to tell us that all the forecasts were predicting the worst El Niño weather event in history. The government was preparing for massive storm- and flood-damage, evacuations of coastal areas and funds for emergency relief. It might take a year or even two, he said, for the westbound prevailing winds and ocean currents to reassert themselves across the South Pacific.

We were suddenly left with no choice but to abandon the southern hemisphere part of our journey. We would have to cross the North Pacific instead. Jason travelled for three days on a bus to return to Monterey. Eilbhe and I made the journey back from Ecuador on a container ship loaded with bananas, which took nine days.

The weather isn't all that has changed for the worse. My relationship with Eilbhe, while not exactly stormy (Eilbhe hates confrontation), has become distinctly overcast and gloomy. I try to recall when we were last truly happy, and have to admit that it was probably in San Francisco. Ireland was not an unhappy time, but neither was it especially fun. It was just restful and undemanding, which was the whole point. Eilbhe had made hats to sell at Galway market and I had found work as a nude model for a life-drawing class, which was chilly but paid rather well. We saved money and lived quietly, spending the long winter evenings around a peat fire and the short days walking in the hills. For the first time in four years I kept no lists of 'Things To Do' and was required to master nothing more complicated than the baking of soda bread.

Where it really started to go wrong was in Ecuador. For much of our time there we lived at a farm and retreat centre high in the Andes north of Quito, run by an Ecuadorian-American family. In contrast to our time in America, where I had largely supported Eilbhe, she now found herself in the position of having to support me, because what our hosts asked for in return for free lodgings were drawings of their farm and surrounding scenery. Although she agreed to it, Eilbhe did everything but the drawings. The owners, for whatever reason, kept coming to me rather than her to inquire what was wrong, and I in turn vented my embarrassment and frustrations upon Eilbhe, sometimes loudly, which only made her more determined not to draw. She felt that I ought to have trusted her to do things in her own time and way. She withdrew and spent long days by herself or riding her favourite horse. Two months later four exquisite drawings were completed, by which time we had exhausted our savings and I had lost her respect. The voyage back to California on the banana boat was miserable. We spent our days in separate parts of the ship and in bed we merely slept or read books.

Now, back in Monterey, we don't even share a bed. I am devastated and haven't yet given up hope of winning her back but, as the days and weeks pass, that hope looks ever more foolish and forlorn. The main reason she is still here, I suspect, is that she hasn't yet decided where to go next.

Jason has also changed in the year that we've been apart, but in a positive way that mirrors my own thinking. We both admitted to feeling rather bored – or perhaps fulfilled – in our personal ambitions to travel by human power. We agreed to further expand the purpose of the expedition beyond the 'Jason and Steve Show' by giving not just one but both crew places aboard *Moksha* to other people. We would continue to manage and promote the expedition but – at least for the first leg of the Pacific journey from Monterey to Hawaii – two new pedal-powered adventurers would be born. And we knew the ideal candidates, two bright, determined, resourceful masochists desperate for the opportunity, Casey Dunn and John Walker. Casey is a blond, lanky, formidably intelligent Californian, prone to grinning madly and saying 'Hey, it's all good!' no matter how bad it really is. He is one of the Stanford students who helped to build *Moksha*'s new pedal system. John is a more physically powerful, older and more circumspect British Naval Officer who recently attended an Arabic languages course at the military base in Monterey.

We rushed to get *Moksha* ready – installing electronics and other fittings, loading provisions, doing capsize drills and a thousand little details – before the winter weather set in and this morning, 23 November, just one month after our return from Ecuador, Casey and John pedalled out of Monterey Harbour bound for Hawaii. I forgot to ask Jason whether he felt any pangs of regret as we watched them disappear over the horizon. It was, after all, a lot to give up after six years' wanting to be the first human-powered circumnavigators of the world, five years of organisation and three years (on-and-off) and over ten thousand miles of blood, sweat and tears. I fully expected to feel those pangs, but they never came. I saw the same mixture of joy, fear, and determination on John and Casey's faces that I had once felt myself and just knew that it was the right thing to do.

At least I hope we've done the right thing. The two men are now five miles offshore and pedalling hard west between a light sea and an overcast sky.

I step into a small café at the wharf. Casey's mother is there, being comforted by other members of her family. She is inconsolably distraught, having just seen her only son pedal off into the Pacific Ocean in a boat no wider than the table on which she rests her elbows and onto which her tears gather in a little puddle. My reassurances have little impact on her. Unsure of what to say next, I stare at the misted window behind her and at a falling trickle of condensation that gradually coalesces with smaller dots, building in speed.

A Faint Signal from The Void
Monterey: 30 November

The duty officer at Monterey Coastguard Station telephones to say that a faint VHF message from *Moksha* has been picked up. The news is a tremendous relief. This is the first communication in more than three days. I jump into a borrowed car and race round to the coastguard station.

It is the evening of John and Casey's seventh day at sea. Everything had been going smoothly for them for the first few days: the pedal system was running well; the weather was fine; they sent back such positive emails on the Inmarsat transmitter that even Casey's mother was beginning to relax.

On the third day the wind picked up and the clouds rolled in; then a blade fell off the new wind generator, putting it out of action. The generating power of *Moksha*'s solar panels alone was insufficient to recharge the batteries. John and Casey should have minimised their power consumption at this point until the weather improved – when they could then have climbed out and replaced the wind generator blade, but their fear of colliding with a ship compelled them to leave the navigation and cabin lights on all night.

The last transmission three days ago placed them about a hundred miles offshore and described the weather as getting worse. The batteries must then have dipped below the ten amps required for the Inmarsat. They were well beyond range of VHF radio. The three silent days without emails that we have endured since have been agonising. The telephone receiver practically glows red after Casey's mother's increasingly frequent and hysterical calls. Understandably she wants her child home safe, but the downside of having the latest technology on an expedition is the instant they stop working, mothers start fearing the worst.

I park the car in the coastguard station parking lot and run through the drizzling rain around the sides of the low brick building until I find an entrance. The cold, unsentimental interior of the station, with its polished linoleum, strip lighting and cork notice boards, instantly unsettles me. It is the same feeling I get in any building – hospital or police station – that exists for emergencies. Two men in blue coastguard uniforms wave me into a glass-enclosed office. There is a huge map of the coastal area between Santa Cruz and Santa Barbara on the far wall, and a bank of communications equipment on an adjacent side where the two men stand.

'Hello. I'm Steve Smith. You called me... about the pedal boat guys.'

'OK Mister Smith, This is what we have.' The larger, more senior of the two men reads in strict police-statement fashion from a thick logbook on the desk in front of him. 'Paddle Boat *Moksha* transmitted a message at 20:39 hours PST. Position given was fifty miles west and ten miles south of Point Lobos. Not currently under power, using a sea anchor due to bad weather and drifting south at an approximate speed of one knot. Next communication will be attempted at 21:00 hours.'

'Good. That's only a few minutes from now. Can I speak with them?'

'Sure. But you'll have to listen hard. Their signal is weak and intermittent.'

The signal is picked up exactly on time. It is John's voice, though weak and crackling. I hurry across to the radio desk and pick up the microphone.

'*Moksha* this is Monterey CCG, Steve talking. John, what is your situation, over?'

'Steve... headi... ho... we're head... home... Mon... rey... Over.' I look across to the two coastguard officers.

'Sounds like they're trying to get back here.'

'Yes. That was our understanding as well from the earlier message.'

'Standby John.' I leave the radio mike on the desk and walk across to the large map. 'Hang on a minute, they're already south of Point Lobos and getting pushed south by wind and tide, right? And there's no sign at the moment that they can make any headway north. Now to get safely back to Monterey they need to get north of Point Lobos AND north of Point Pinos. What if they come inshore and can't do that? Below the Point there's nothing but sheer cliffs for... a long way.'

'Yes. They need to stay well clear of the coast south of here. The closest safe harbour is Morro Bay and that's a hundred miles away.'

'Then that is where they'll have to go. Thanks guys.' I walk back to the desk and pick up the mike. '*Moksha, Moksha.* This is Monterey, Steve here, over.'

'Ste... this... John... O... r.'

'Head for Morro Bay. Is that clear? Morro Bay. We'll wait for you there. And John, for God's sake stay well clear of the coast until you get there.'

Too Close Too Soon
Morro Bay: 3 December

Casey's grandfather is waiting for us as we walk into the operations room at Morro Bay Coastguard Station. He is a formidable, stout, retired soldier in his late sixties with short grey hair, dressed in a polo neck pullover and corduroy suit. He shakes my hand, then Jason's, and immediately insists that we go and have a private talk. Jason and I glance meaningfully at each other. We all walk outside and find a restaurant open a little way along the harbour front. We go inside, choose a table and order coffees.

'Gentlemen,' begins Casey's grandfather. 'I know we all want the same thing here. Casey's mother is going crazy with worry. We just want him to be safe. Now I think we should authorise the coastguard to go get them right now, just in case.'

'None of us can do that,' Jason replies, 'even if we wanted to. The coastguard can only respond to a request from Casey and John, or they can make their own decision if the guys are in immediate danger.'

'Look,' I add, going further along Jason's tack, 'I appreciate how your family must feel but, please, let's give the boys a chance. They have radio. Let them ask for help. Imagine how disappointed they must feel already. At least allow them the small victory of bringing *Moksha* safely home with some dignity.' Casey's grandfather shakes his head. He is still not convinced.

'I'm not interested in dignity,' he growls. 'I was asked to come down here by the boy's mother to guarantee one outcome – his safe return.'

Jason, sensing the rising emotional level, suggests that we go back to the coastguard and wait for *Moksha*'s next scheduled radio transmission.

Back inside the operations room, the commanding officer reports that events have reached a critical point. Casey and John have now made a request for immediate assistance. They are only five miles away from being smashed against the cliffs while still a good thirty miles north of Morro Bay.

'Damn it!' Jason mutters under his breath. 'They came in way too soon.'

'Are you the registered owner of this pedal boat?' The officer addresses me.

'Yes, I am.'

'The rescue controller is on the phone and needs to speak to you.' He hands me the telephone. The voice identifies itself.

'We're launching the lifeboat now. We've also scrambled a helicopter from San Francisco. If your vessel gets within a mile of the rocks before the lifeboat reaches them, the helicopter will lift the crew clear and the boat will be left. Is that clear?'

'Y-yes.' I hand the telephone back. 'My God! Jas, they're not interested in the boat. If the helicopter pulls the guys out first, that's it! They're talking about letting *Moksha* drift into the cliffs!'

We run out of the coastguard station and sprint to catch the lifeboat crew as they prepare to launch the rescue. 'You've got to get to them first,' we plead. 'Bring back the guys and *Moksha* together!'

We wait and pray for the lifeboat to get there first. It does, but only just. John and Casey look very tired, cold and dispirited as they jump off the lifeboat in the early hours of the following morning and shuffle along the jetty wrapped in blankets.

Moksha has been saved, they tell us over coffees at a nearby 24-hour McDonald's, but because the lifeboat skipper was unwilling to spend the whole night chugging slowly back at towing speed, she was left tied to a coastguard mooring at San Simeon Cove, seventeen miles to the north.

We grab a few hours' sleep and drive north. John and Casey come with us, while Casey's grandfather returns to Oregon with the happy news.

'Actually it was a fishing trawler who got there first,' Casey explains on the drive up to San Simeon. 'It arrived within twenty minutes of our Mayday call and towed us until the lifeboat arrived.'

'And don't forget the helicopter!' John prompts him.

'Oh yeah!' Casey laughs. 'The highway patrol chopper arrived first, that's right. The whole situation was so surreal, my God! The cliffs were only a few miles off; we could see little white explosions of surf at the base of them; and it had been the most beautiful sunrise I've ever seen; just spectacular colours; anyway, we were just deciding whether to call for help and it was like the voice of God coming from above: "Attention little yellow boat, little yellow boat." You couldn't hear its rotors or anything, just this booming voice and I looked up and it was a tiny two-man chopper with a loudspeaker.'

'And then we made the call to the coastguard,' John continues. 'But the fishing boat got there first and the most amazing thing happened – '

'Yeah! Oh my God!' Casey interrupts, animated in his recollection. 'The trawler backed up and threw us a line and I had to crawl up to the bow in this big swell, getting soaked, and I remember struggling to get the line through that eyebolt in the prow and tie a good knot; and just at that moment, the entire ocean came alive with dolphins – '

'I'm not joking,' John picks up the story, 'there were dolphins as far as you could see, back and dorsal fins breaking surface and rolling, some jumping – '

'Yeah, some were jumping over the tow rope I was holding on to!'

'And in a way,' John concludes philosophically, 'it made us both feel really lucky and grateful for the whole experience, even though we didn't make it to Hawaii.'

We arrive at San Simeon. A stone's throw north of the small town of Cambria, San Simeon is a shallow exposed bay with a steep shingle beach. There is also a pier, which the eccentric billionaire William Randolph Hearst had built to receive supplies for nearby Hearst Castle. We walk through pouring rain to the end of the pier. We can clearly see *Moksha* tied to a mooring buoy only few hundred metres away. She is pitching and rolling in heavy waves but seems to be riding them well. There is nothing we can do but wait for better conditions to pedal her round to Morro Bay. We can't afford to pay for accommodation here, so we decide to drive back to Monterey.

The following morning, the coastguard calls with the devastating news that *Moksha* has capsized. We drive straight back to San Simeon, park the car, jump out and run to the end of the pier. All that is visible of *Moksha* is the line of her upturned red hull and the rudder and centreboard pointing skyward. A pocket of air is all that is keeping her from sinking to the seabed. Whereas the day before she had bravely ridden and punched through the white-crested waves, now even the smallest of them washes clean over her exposed belly.

We are forced to sit and wait for the storm to pass. We endure five days of almost constant rain, bullish winds and heavy seas. It is a grim existence. By day we scour the area for equipment – wetsuits, scuba gear, kayaks, rope and all shapes and sizes of flotation devices – that may come in handy in our ever-changing, desperately half-baked plans. At night we find shelter under picnic tables by the beach, shivering and huddling for warmth in sodden sleeping bags. Eventually, on the fifth night, the owner of a beach-front cabin takes pity and lets us sleep in his garage.

The weather finally abates on the six day, giving us an opportunity to kayak out to *Moksha* and ascertain what if anything can be salvaged of her.

Now, at midday, it is raining again. Jason, John and I sit in a loose circle on the beach in our borrowed wetsuits. Casey stands fiddling with a belt buckle to tighten his oxygen tank harness. Jason's wetsuit was made for a giant. He doesn't think it will conserve his body heat for long. John looks nervously at the surf, now diminished from its storm height but still an obstacle, at how it races up the beach and sucks loudly on the shingle in its crackling retreat.

'What do you think then, guys? Should we go from here or throw the kayaks from the pier and jump in after them? I have to speak quite loudly to be heard above the sounds of the sea and the hissing white noise of the rain.

'From here, definitely,' says John, inspecting his paddle. 'At least that way I can be sure of sitting on the thing properly to start with, even if it doesn't last long. I'm going for a practice now. You can watch me go arse-over-tit if you like.' John drags his kayak – which, like the others, is a beginner's floating-board type that one sits on rather than in – down to the water's edge.

'It's not the getting out there that's the problem,' says Jason, who pauses to wipe the rain off his face. 'The problem is what to do after that. *Moksha* weighs what, about a ton and a half with all those supplies? And now she's upside down and waterlogged. Even if the four of us can manhandle her over I can't see her staying upright for long.'

'I don't know what else to try,' I say. 'Oh, here's Ian to make it five of us.' Our friend Ian Satchell from Monterey steps carefully down a steep, rocky slope that separates the picnic area from the beach wearing his wetsuit and carrying scuba equipment. 'Hey buddy! Glad you could make it. We'll take the two-man kayak and strap your tank to the back to save you having to wear it paddling out there.'

'All right man! Let's stick this pig!' says Ian. I fail to comprehend the phrase but his obvious enthusiasm makes me smile. We take both ends of our kayak and carry it down the beach. Some movement on the pier catches my eye and I look over. A white golf buggy tears along it at top speed, dragging behind it two large red buoys. In the driving seat is Eilbhe, evidently enjoying herself. She looks across and waves. A large pair of binoculars hangs on a leather strap from her neck and bounces off her chest as she judders along the wooden planks of the pier.

Ian and I wobble precariously on our double kayak in shallow water and begin paddling out to sea. At the first rolling belt of white water we pass John's upturned yellow kayak going in the other direction, quickly followed by John, arms and legs flailing at all angles. Casey and Jason are already past the line of breakers and are heading for *Moksha*.

All five of us having successfully reached our target, we rise and fall separately on our kayaks on the rain-pocked, undulating swell. The full length of *Moksha*'s round and tapering red hull wallows pitifully and largely submerged. Eruptions of seawater spew up from the centreboard hole after each passing wave, conjuring images of a stricken, sickly whale.

Ian, being the most experienced diver, takes the first foray underneath. After adjusting his mask he slips gently off the back of our kayak and disappears. He resurfaces a minute later holding a heavy blue waterlogged cushion.

'Stupid! Stupid!' he repeats, immediately after disgorging his mouthpiece. I assume he is addressing himself, and perhaps the rest of us by association. These are far from ideal conditions in which to be putting one's head under a heavy floating object.

'Did you get inside the cabin?' asks Casey.

'Yeah, but this is so fucking dangerous,' replies Ian. 'I don't want anybody else going in until I've cleared some of the crap

267

out of there. He replaces the mouthpiece and slips under once more. This time he reappears with a big, knotted bundle of rope.

At the end of Ian's fourth dive he has managed to extract more items that were clogging the entrance to the cabin, including a wooden chart table, more cushions and an assortment of waterlogged plastic bags of food. We secure the items to our kayaks with bungee cord and paddle over to the seaward end of the pier. Eilbhe passes down a rope with which to heave up the salvaged gear and throws down the large red buoys.

'I've done all I can, you guys,' says Ian. He slips off my kayak for the last time and slowly hauls himself up a rusting iron ladder onto the pier. 'I gotta get back to work now.' I am disappointed that he cannot stay longer. The four of us remaining shout our gratitude and wave before paddling back to *Moksha* with the red buoys in tow. We tie them as tightly as we can to *Moksha*'s bow and stern.

'Alright let's try and flip her over,' I shout. All four of us are treading water now, having left our kayaks bunched in a flotilla tied to the rudder.

'I'll stay on the other side to counterbalance after she flips,' says Jason. The rest of us line up along one side and grapple our way onto *Moksha*'s slippery underbelly using whatever hand- and footholds we can find. We lean our full combined weights over but we are not enough. Jason swims around and climbs up next to me. Now she slowly rolls, picking up speed at the pivotal point.

'Yehaa!' We cheer in unison at the sight of *Moksha*'s bright yellow topsides and mast. But the joy is momentary. With the boat waterlogged and full of loose supplies and with the weight of the wind generator and radar reflector on her short mast, *Moksha* is too unstable. She continues to roll in the same direction.

'Watch the mast!' yells John. Casey swims quickly sideways to avoid the mast falling on him in its slingshot trajectory. It hits the water with a heavy thwack! *Moksha* emits a heavy gurgling belch from her bowels as she turns the full revolution to lie capsized again.

'Damn! Alright let's try it again and see if we can hold her long enough to get in and start bailing.' I have little faith in my words but we must try. The idea of losing *Moksha* to the sea is unthinkable. The owner of a salvaging company in Morro Bay told us it might be possible to save her with a floating platform, a crane, flotation bags and expert divers, all at a minimum cost of thirty thousand dollars. There was no other way, they said. We have only five hundred dollars donated by John; therefore there has to be another way.

'Holy shit! Look at this.' John, while treading water, holds aloft a jagged chunk of *Moksha*'s plywood deck, which is attached to a long length of thick braided steel wire. 'It's one of the mast stays!'

'Yep. Here, I've got the other one,' Jason cries from the other side of the boat and holds up another wire and a similar, picture-book-sized piece of plywood, painted bright yellow on one side. The opposite ends of both wires appear still to be firmly attached to the mast. The mystery of *Moksha*'s capsizing, which until now has been an issue of long controversy and thinly-disguised blame, suddenly becomes easier to understand.

The mast was held firm by four wire mast stays: one running to the bow; one to the stern; and two amidships. The strain placed on the bow and stern stays during the storm must have ripped their fastenings from the deck, taking a piece of decking with them. It was a daft mistake to bolt those fastenings through 8mm plywood decking rather than through bulkheads, whoever did it, but I am most at fault because I didn't check. The damage left gaping holes in both fore and aft compartments into which the waves and rain could pour, quickly flooding them. The second crucial mistake was that Casey and John left open the watertight hatches separating the two flooding compartments from the central cabin as well as the sliding hatch, although it is doubtful whether the boat could have avoided capsizing even if they had closed them all.

At 5.00 p.m., the sun dips low, silhouetting the ragged edge of shoreline trees; the temperature begins to plummet. We are all now freezing and exhausted with ashen faces, glazed eyes and bloodless blue lips. Jason is particularly quiet, which worries me, I know he must be struggling against the onset of hypothermia in his thin, ill-fitting suit. We have tried everything we can think of to right *Moksha* and keep her from keeling over again, but to no avail. *Moksha* lies even lower in the water than when we started.

'All that we're doing is making the pocket of air keeping her afloat even smaller. It's no good. Let's call it a day' I insist, 'and try something else tomorrow.'

'Wait,' Casey calls out, 'let me try one last thing. I'm going to dive in and see if I can crack open this emergency canister of air in the forward compartment and close the watertight hatch. It might displace enough water to give us the extra buoyancy we need.'

'All right Casey. But be quick,' I tell him. 'We're all getting too cold now.'

Casey straps himself into his diving gear and disappears under the boat holding a small canister of compressed air in one hand. We wait for some sound of escaping air or a hatch closing but there is no sign of his plan having worked until he breaks the surface again, several minutes later. He signals a thumbs-up and removes his mouthpiece.

'Done it! Now we've got to hold on, two either side, OK. Hold on! Try and stop her from flipping over for as long as you possibly can.' Sure enough, just as Casey predicted,

Moksha begins to rise up out of the water. We hold on for twenty seconds; thirty, forty, fifty seconds; a minute; *Moksha*'s gunwale begins to lift me out of the water.

'Ok, everyone let go! Swim clear!' No sooner have I uttered the words than *Moksha* whips violently round and is righted in a flash. I notice, with a huge sense of relief, that the sliding hatch runners are about six inches above the waterline, which means that *Moksha*'s main cabin cannot instantly flood again. I clamber quickly on deck and jump in through the open hatchway. Jason throws a large white bucket. I catch it and waste no time in bailing heavy bucketfuls of water out of the central cabin, which land with a satisfying splash in the sea where they belong. Jason, Casey and John keep a stabilising hold onto *Moksha*'s sides.

'Hurry up, Steve,' John pleads. 'Give me a go with that bucket. I'm bloody freezing to death.'

'Just a few more, I don't want to risk her tipping over again. Jason, hang on man. How are you doing?' Jason nods that he is all right, but he is shaking uncontrollably, as is John. We take turns to keep warm by bailing until *Moksha* is fully afloat. Casey is the last man out. He closes the hatch firmly shut and we clamber aboard our kayaks and paddle as fast as we can back to the beach.

The sun is down and dusk turns slowly into night. We sit exhausted on the beach around a neat little fire that Eilbhe has built and marvel at the beloved profile of *Moksha*'s silhouette – her long sleek square central cockpit and the gentle slope of her decks – hardly able to believe what we have achieved.

We spent the remainder of John's $500 hiring a tow vessel to bring *Moksha* round to Morro Bay the following day, then borrowed Ian's truck to haul her onto her trailer and drive through the night up to Casey's student house in suburban Palo Alto. The stern end squeezed into Casey's garage and the rest poked out into the driveway. She was a wreck. The stern deck was cracked. The bow was smashed and splintered. Her entire contents, the result of two years of work, were destroyed – provisions, electronics, safety gear, cameras, clothes, books, charts, everything – and the inside surfaces were coated in a thick layer of stinking grey sludge. The neighbours peered in curiosity and scowled in disgust over the neat hedges and through upstairs windows.

We cleaned and salvaged what we could. Casey and his housemates kindly let us keep her there for the time being. It was a miserable time. Christmas approached and everyone went his separate way: Jason disappeared to Guatemala, Casey headed home to Oregon, John got a new posting to Cyprus, Stuart flew back to England and Eilbhe went to stay with April (the primary school teacher who cycled to San Francisco with Jason the summer before last), before returning home to Ireland. I still loved her desperately and asked her to stay. But she felt there was nothing more to discuss.

I took possession of a beaten-up Ford Econoline campervan from a friend, which required major repairs. I nursed it, coughing and spluttering on seven cylinders, all the way to Flagstaff, Arizona, to spend Christmas with a friend, John, and his wolf companion, Alpha. There I found work as a builder's labourer and spent the next three months firing a nail-gun into roofing tiles and clearing snow. In my spare time I learned how to dismantle a 1969 V8 Ford engine in sub-zero temperatures, and I tried not to think too much about Eilbhe.

Throughout the long winter months I did battle with the problem of what I should do next. I looked for a good reason to continue with the expedition but struggled to find it. Loyalty to a concept left me cold; the expedition felt little more than a lonely, pointless, self-indulgent gimmick. Loyalty to Jason? No, team solidarity had died that night at the Fiddler's Green pub in San Francisco. It all came back again to debts: the expedition's fund-raising talks were the only feasible way for me to help repay our debts. I had to go on.

By the middle of March, Jason was back in San Francisco. I flew there to see him. John and Casey had not been in touch since Christmas. *Moksha* was in an even sorrier state in a car park at Stanford University. As I looked at her – her peeling paintwork and splintered bow, grimy and dishevelled, leaves rotting in pools of dark water around her gunwales – I felt another, stronger urge to continue. I couldn't leave her here, broken and filthy.

Jason also felt a strong desire to continue. He had spent a lot of time in Guatemala working among Mayan children, and had conceived of new ways to use the expedition to educate young people via the Internet. This had become his motivation to carry on. We agreed to pull the expedition back onto its feet and pedal to Hawaii together. Jason also had some other pleasing news; the insurance company had finally paid out for his skating accident. The money has been invested in high technology shares and, within a year, the interest earned ought to be more than enough to cover our outstanding debts.

The Presidio Yacht Club
Fort Baker, California: 6 June

I wake to a soft rustling of leaves in the wind. My head is thumping. Oh Jamaican rum! Never again.

I stumble out the side-door of my campervan in search of some cure – water, fresh air. A steep bank covered in tall grass and fennel rises in front of me. To my left, *Moksha* sits forlornly on her trailer, stripped and sanded down to bare wood. She is

273

sandwiched between the hillside and a white, two-storey wooden building that is home to the Presidio Yacht Club.

I walk through a side door into the workshop area where there is a bathroom. After my shower the clubhouse will be open for breakfast. Maybe then my head will stop thumping.

The clubhouse is on the second floor. I am about to climb the stairs when I notice a body. My friend Sam lies spread-eagled and unconscious on the outside terrace.

Ten days ago I trundled across Golden Gate Bridge with *Moksha* in tow, and peered down at Fort Baker – a former military base on the Marin Headlands – for the first time. Very few motorists venture down here, or become sufficiently lost. Despite its prominence at the mouth of San Francisco Bay, Fort Baker is a forgotten relic. The yacht club and small harbour, still military property, are exclusively for federal employees and their boats. Only the caretaker, a retired colonel, is supposed to live here. But the colonel turns a blind eye and lets me live in my van behind the clubhouse.

I love it here. The only drawback is in organising lectures and donations from a windswept outdoor payphone. But how can I complain, living for free within sight of the city, with the Pacific Ocean in front of me and a national park behind.

While I spend my days restoring *Moksha*, Jason bases himself with a friend called Shirley Nice, over in Bernal Heights. He is constantly on the telephone to equipment sponsors, hoping to replace all that was destroyed at San Simeon. He is also designing an Internet curriculum for schools, entitled The Classroom Expedition, which will form a daily sequence of interactive activities during our voyage to Hawaii.

Shirley is our guiding light at this time, helping to transform our haphazard expedition into a coherent non-profit corporation. Both Shirley and Jason have assembled an impressive coterie of professionals – teachers, lawyers, accountants and so on – to assist them in these aims.

I have Sam Smalling. Sam is a short, stout Californian in his late forties with a deep, gravely voice and dark Mediterranean features. In looks and character he is a charming and peculiar admixture of Detective Columbo, Robin Williams and Groucho Marx. A carpenter by trade, Sam is currently renovating *Penelope*, a delightful antique sailboat moored in the harbour. He also lives aboard – the colonel turns his other blind eye – in a tiny cabin crammed to the portholes with bits of wood, engine parts and tools. Half of everything he earns, which isn't much, goes on alimony payments to his ex-wife, following an acrimonious and ultimately unfair settlement administered by a female judge, which rendered Sam deeply suspicious of that sex ('She had her own idea of the penal system,' Sam explained, with eyebrows wriggling in Groucho-fashion; 'If you had a penis, she'd penalise you'). The other half of his income goes on alcohol.

'Hey, Sam, buddy. Wake up man!'

'Brrrrah!' Sam groans and opens one eye. 'Go away will ya! I'm in my happy place.'

I try to drag him inside before the colonel arrives. He is too heavy.

'You go right ahead,' Sam slurs, dreamily. 'Be the early bird... catches the worm. Burremember, izza secon' mouse who getsa cheese.'

'Yeah, whatever you say Sam. Guess you didn't make it as far as *Penelope* last night, huh? Rum and whisky – bad combination. Lemme help you up or the colonel's gonna go apeshit.'

Sam's other eye is purple and swollen shut.

'Jesus! What happened there?' I say.

'Uuuh, another bad combination, man; rum, gravity and concrete.'

I watch Sam slurping coffee up at the clubhouse. He groans and holds a large bag of ice to his black eye.

'You don't happen to have an electric plane on *Penelope* do you? I found a block of white oak to rebuild *Moksha*'s bow but it would take me all day to shape it by hand.'

'Sure. I'll give you a hand with it this afternoon. Workin' all day, Steve! You're gonna give us carpenters a bad name, man. We've got some sailing to do first, soon as I can see where I'm goin'.'

'In *Penelope*? Hey, fantastic! Who else is coming?'

'Oh, just the usual crew, Jack and Bud,' Sam replies with a wide grin.

'That wouldn't be Mister Daniels and Mister Weiser, would it?'

'You know those guys? Well, who would've thunk it!'

That evening, Sam and I make it back into harbour in *Penelope* in the nick of time before a thick San Francisco fog sweeps in under the bridge. I walk back to the van and sit down, feeling suddenly very cold and alone. There is a framed picture of Eilbhe hanging on the wall, which I seem incapable of burying out of sight. I still don't understand what went wrong – it must be more than what happened in Ecuador – and she hasn't felt able or willing to enlighten me, which makes the healing process that much harder because I find myself involuntarily inventing and analysing the endless possibilities, even the most hideous and implausible ones,

I pump up the pressure on my kerosene stove and prepare a warming broth for the pot. Now I wait for it to boil, strumming a few chords on the guitar and watching the steam condense and trickle down the windscreen. Out in the bay the foghorns bellow and bells clang in regular plangent tones that echo around the hills. A dense and spectacular bank of fog rolls over the headlands and pours down to Sausalito like a cheap effect of early cinema.

Richard Brown
Fort Baker: 10 August

Chris Maila, a friend in the Parks Service, tips me off whenever something worth diving for turns up in one his dumpsters. Last week it was lengths of heavy-gauge copper wire that had been torn out of the old army headquarters. A metal merchant over in Richmond gave me $161.60 for the lot, which paid for all the new electrical wire we need for the boat.

The chief electrician of the Parks Service is a great, growling bear of a man called Richard Brown, whom I met when he caught me red-handed in the dumpster. This was fortunate. After I explained my purpose he became enthralled by the expedition and offered to come and show me how to build *Moksha*'s electrical system. I was thoroughly grateful and relieved. I haven't a clue about electricity. Cameraman Kenny cobbled together our electrical system for the Atlantic Ocean. He explained how it worked and I instantly forgot every word.

The new system we require for the Pacific is much more complex. Jason's successes on the telephone have delivered a dazzling array of the latest marine gadgetry including: new solar panels and a wind turbine for power generation; a radar enhancer, which turns *Moksha* into a battleship-sized blip on any radar screen; a radar detector; a satellite transmitter and a waterproof computer for sending daily updates to our website. I accept the use of them, though I submit to the new 'necessities' with some regret – my fondness for simplicity, I suppose.

I have been at a loss all week to discover how best to reciprocate Richard's great kindness. He refuses any payment. He doesn't talk about himself much either, which makes it hard to choose a thoughtful gift. All I knew until yesterday is that he used to be a farmer in South Dakota. Then, quite out of the blue, he revealed his ultimate fantasy: to have every episode of an English television series from the 1980s, *All Creatures Great And Small*, on video.

Even more bizarrely, after I mentioned this to Jason he promptly stumbled upon a full-length film version in an obscure little video store near the top of Haight Street. This morning we borrowed and rigged together two video recorders to produce a pirate copy, but failed to get a decent image.

I returned the rented video to the store, determined to buy it outright. Behind the counter was slumped a young shop assistant with long curly-brown hair who was stoned out of his head.

'Ooh no can do, man. This is the only copy we got for our customers.'

I opened the cassette box and pointed to the last rental date stamped on the card – November sixth, 1989.

'No, this,' I replied, prodding my chest, 'is the only customer you got for your copy. Look, here's sixty bucks. Let's assume that Haight-Ashbury isn't going to get a sudden influx of farmers from the Dakotas. That's like a hundred and thirty-five years worth of rent at the current rate of demand.'

'Hey man, I only started last Monday.' His face is expressionless. He hasn't understood a word. And why should he? This is the Haight. No one makes any sense around here.

'OK, this is my last offer. Seventy bucks. I must have this video. You see there's a part where the vet from Yorkshire walks into the village café and says, 'Sausage and chips please, Rufus'. If you play it backwards it's actually a coded message from aliens who abducted my wife ten years ago and if I don't deliver it to NASA by Friday, I'll never see her alive again.'

'Hey, too bad about the old lady, but I'm just covering for The Man, dude.'

I leave, defeated, with the address of a video distribution company in Michigan.

I race north through the city on my bike and back across Golden Gate Bridge, pick up my slide projector and some T-shirts from the van at Fork Baker, then cycle on to Sausalito. I am almost late for my lunchtime Rotary Club presentation at the exclusive Alta Mira Hotel. I screech to a halt at the entrance and, with a cardboard box of expedition T-shirts still strapped to my back, run inside. The restaurant is an imposingly grand place, with tables of starched linen and dazzling silverware, around which elderly couples sit. They talk softly and emit such an overpowering glow of wealth – gold, diamond, silk, perfume, patent leather and miracles of dentistry – I start to shake. My discomfort intensifies as I realise there are no curtains to darken the room for a slide show and no suitable walls to project it onto. I bravely ad-lib the history and adventures of the expedition for half an hour, barely drawing breath, and finally sit down.

There is a long and uncomfortable silence. Eventually, an elderly lady dripping with pearls lifts her hand and sonorously proclaims, 'Yes, that's all very well dear boy, but now you're poor.' Fortunately, there are a sufficient number of other, more sympathetic plutocrats in the room willing to amuse distant young relatives with a novel T-shirt to make the ordeal worthwhile.

Later that afternoon, back at Fort Baker, *Moksha* is prepped and ready for her final coat of paint. This is an eye-blistering yellow, guaranteed to attract every insect within a half-mile radius to a sticky death. The workload is piling on as we near our departure deadline of 20 September. These days there is little time to sail and sing dirty limericks with the delightful Sam Smalling, which is a great pity. Instead I scurry around giving slide shows, repairing *Moksha* and working with Jason on The Classroom Expedition before flopping into the van to sleep.

Auspicious Occasion
Fort Baker: 12 September

The pace of our preparations grows ever more frantic. We leave in eight days, though it is hard to envisage actually sticking to the schedule. It would be unprecedented.

It never ceases to amaze me how key people simply appear at the ideal moment. Just as Richard Brown was finishing off *Moksha*'s electrical system, a rigger from Sausalito materialised to help design and fit some mast rigging so that we can lower the weight of the wind generator and other electronics in the event of a storm. Furthermore, only days after Jason wistfully remarked how lovely it would be to have a symbolic painting on *Moksha*'s bow, my friend Bonnie from the Cultural Conservancy Centre brought along a Native American artist from the seafaring Quinault Nation in British Columbia.

Jason, the artist in question, with assistance from his adorable grandma Billie, has just completed an exquisite 'Sacred Raven' design painted in bright acrylics.

A real raven flies overhead and crows in approval. This sounds too corny to believe, but it just happened.

Later that afternoon, I climb into the driving seat of my van. The old girl splutters into life. With *Moksha* in tow, I pull away from our cosy nest between the grass bank and the yacht club and proceed cautiously along a dirt road that runs parallel to the waterfront until I come to an old concrete slipway adjacent to the coastguard station.

The evening draws in as Billie performs a sage ceremony and blessing. Another friend Dan stands to attention in his Stewart clan tartans, bagpipes at the ready.

I jump back inside the van and reverse *Moksha* down the slipway until she floats. Dan's bagpipes fill the air with a haunting resonance. I shiver with the power of the moment.

Kenny Brown stands on the harbour wall filming the event. He arrived yesterday, direct from Bosnia, where he is covering the war for the BBC. Next to him stands my father, Stuart, back to lend his crucial support. Stuart has recently been living in Flagstaff, Arizona with my friend John. I am overjoyed that my father has brought John's wolf, Alpha, along with her two wolf-retriever pups, Loci and Kiva.

Moksha's new MicroMarine pedal system works perfectly. Various people take turns at the helm and a curious crowd gathers to watch *Moksha* gliding back and forth in Fort Mason harbour, like a duckling on its first trip to the pond.

Alpha And The Pups
Fort Kronkite: 17 September

Neither Jason nor myself have ever subjected ourselves to fitness training. We are too lazy and too busy and the whole process is usually too dreary. I have, however, discovered one promising technique. Step one is to find an area of wilderness with a deer population – I use the Marin Headlands. Step two is to firmly attach oneself to a pack of dogs – I use a female Artic wolf and two wolf-retriever hybrids, but any self-respecting wolf-descendent will do. Step three is simply to hang on. You not only get to travel over rough ground faster than you thought possible, but you also get to go to very unusual places. I am painfully familiar with at least one area of dense thicket where probably no human has ever been.

I love taking part in this primordial chase, imagining what they must feel and think when the scent of deer first enters their wet noses, making their ears stand erect. We crawl stealthily nearer the herd, shoulder blades rising and falling like pistons, heads hung low, intensely focused. Often I will unclip their leashes and let them spring into action. They always lose the deer pack within seconds but it may be an hour before they come lolloping back with flailing tongues and filthy, mud-splattered bodies.

Having being dragged headfirst through the tall scrubland around Fort Kronkite, I share a breakfast of fruit and bagels with Stuart. We sit on the cliff above the beach, overlooking the Pacific. Alpha and the pups thrash about in the surf below. Kiva the runt is being bullied as usual. But being by nature more of a retriever than her brother, she escapes into deeper water and waits for Alpha and Loci to lose interest. Loci is distracted by a smell. He sprints up the beach to a rotting seal carcass, followed by Alpha. All three roll onto their backs and wriggle in the oily, putrid mess. I suppose it must be a dog's strategy to disguise his own scent although I fail to understand why, from a deer's point of view, the idea of an encroaching seal in the bushes should register as anything other than highly suspicious.

We drive back to Fort Baker in time to greet today's school party. Three coaches are parked along the waterfront, a hundred children piling out of them.

The children are divided into four groups of twelve and the remainder are corralled into a picnic area where they make themselves comfortable on the grass and open their plastic lunch boxes – containing the most vivid and improbable colours of bite-sized foodstuffs, branded with the child's favourite television personality, their list of ingredients employing every single letter of the alphabet. Stuart, Jason, Suzanne Geller (a local teacher and co-designer of our Classroom Expedition) and I go to our agreed stations to prepare for the rotating groups. Suzanne has found a quiet spot at a picnic bench near the clubhouse and puts each child through our questionnaire, which Kenny films. Stuart stands at the jetty alongside *Moksha*, captivating a second group with tales of storms and sharks. Each child has his or her brief turn inside the boat, sitting at the pedal seat then crawling in and out of the sleeping compartment. Jason attends to a third group beside a table crammed with food and equipment. He carefully explains the purpose and use of survival jackets, flare guns and numerous other gadgets, skilfully encouraging each child's imagination by describing the desperate scenarios in which they might be required.

I put my group through a crash course in world geography. One of the daily tasks of participating schools is to plot our progress to Hawaii on a wall chart that we provide. I try to explain the concept of latitude and longitude.

My expectations quickly falter. Many of these nine and ten year-olds have difficulty pointing to their own country on a map of the world. The spelling of simple words, multiplying twenty by five, in fact focusing on anything for more than a few seconds is a monumental effort. Shirley Nice whispers in my ear, 'Be patient, they're excited.'

She is right, but I do despair at times. The standard of American schooling is pretty shocking sometimes, which is one of the many strange anomalies of this, the richest and most influential nation on earth. I've met teenage kids in Oakland (on the east side of San Francisco Bay) who've never heard of the Pacific Ocean. I've heard statements like, 'Gee, you paddled across the Atlantic! Did ya go through the Suez?' Or 'You're going to Peru, huh? Does Peru still exist? Well you know these Middle Eastern countries, they come and go.' And these were the teachers!

Increasing global awareness – which is what the expedition's curriculum tries in its very small way to do - wouldn't matter so much if we lived like Robinson Crusoe. But we don't. We have a global sphere of influence – in all that we consume, and that is what the foreign policies of our countries are currently designed to protect. Understanding countries and their people matters, even if we never go there, because it enables us to see others as we see ourselves rather than as faceless categories we pick up from the news – rebels, communists, collateral damage. Until we learn to think in this way, great nations will continue to be gangsters and smaller ones will remain in various states of prostitution (as Stanley Kubrick once noted) and that's a dangerous world to live in.

And surely anything we teach these kids here today will be more useful than the banalities of soap opera and pop music celebrity.

'Which Spice Girl would you marry, Steve? Which Spice Girl would you marry? Steve, which...' The screams summon me back to the present, slightly terrifying reality – being in charge of a pack of children high on sugar and E-numbers.

'Aargh, I don't know... err, Ginger!' I reply, struggling to think of a name.

'Eeeeergh! You can't choose her, she left!' They squeal in unison. Wrong answer, obviously. My group turn and stampede towards Jason. They drub him with the same piercing salvo.

'Which Spice Girl would you marry Jason? Which Spice Girl would –'

'All of them!' Jason roars. There is open-mouthed, awed silence.

Pacific Postponed
Fort Baker: 21 September

I will remain inside *Moksha* at her berth in the marina for most of the night, yet again, accompanied by the drone of power tools and the glare of powerful floodlights.

Today is Monday. We were supposed to have departed yesterday morning at the climax of a week-long wave of effort that hardly broke for sleep.

At 8.00 p.m. on Saturday night, ten hours before launch, I was busy in the workshop fabricating a bread-baking dish for our pressure-cooker (having been sent an email with instructions on how fresh bread can be made at sea from a Mrs Diane Hoff in Sweden). Scott Morrison arrived for a final inspection of the stainless steel propellers and steel housing he fabricated for *Moksha*'s pedal system. He is deservedly proud of his beautiful work, upon which he has engraved the words 'The Dog's Bollocks'.

He returned from *Moksha*'s berth with one of the pedal-drive units under his arm. Disaster! After only a week of immersion in salt water, electrolytic corrosion had eaten through the aluminium casing, leaving several pea-sized holes. He tipped the unit upside down. Seawater poured from the holes, from where there should only be lubricating oil for the shaft and cogs.

A new pedal-drive unit is being couriered from the MicroMarine factory. Every metal part of the pedal system will then be given three coats of anti-corrosion paint. More zinc anodes are being installed, and a length of copper wire to channel all electrolysis to the sacrificial zinc. The delay will cost us a week.

The bursting of our departure bubble was a stunning blow, but was quickly followed by a feeling of immense relief that Scott had discovered the problem in time. All I could think to do was take him straight to the clubhouse bar and buy him a beer.

By this time, people were already arriving for our last-night send-off party. JimBo Trout was tuning up his guitar with the rest of the band, the Fishpeople. I made a brief announcement, apologising for the fact that we wouldn't be leaving just yet, after all, but that since we were all here we might as well make a night of it. And so we did. We danced and drank and ate sushi and threw Hawaiian leis (garlands of fresh flowers) around each other's necks and drank and danced some more. Even Alpha and the pups were allowed to join in, until Alpha began howling in a very different key to JimBo's bluegrass and Loci wolfed down the spare ribs.

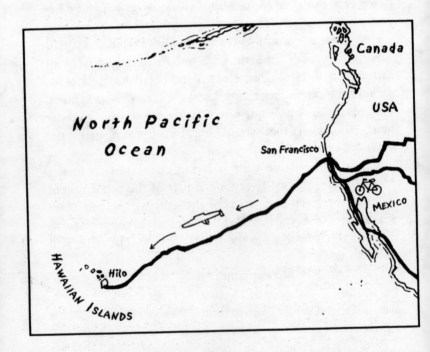

North Pacific
Ocean

Canada

USA

San Francisco

MEXICO

HILO

HAWAIIAN ISLANDS

CHAPTER 7
THE PACIFIC OCEAN

ROUTE LEGEND

PEDAL BOAT

7. The Pacific Ocean
(September – November 1998)

Another Ocean, Another Hangover
Fort Baker: 28 September

5.00 a.m.: departure day is here again and this time it's for real. Alpha and the pups stand beside me in the workshop, barking furiously at the sound of a Parks Police car crackling along the gravel drive outside. I listen for the familiar sound of a car door opening and heavy footsteps. These usually precede a parking ticket on my van's windscreen.

The car continues up the hill without stopping. I continue my work, weighing batches of flour and dried yeast and sealing them in plastic bags. I feel shattered and horribly hungover. Why leave it until now to prepare bread-mix? Why get steaming drunk and go without sleep before a major ocean voyage? It's a very silly habit.

6.00 a.m.: more barking is triggered as our electrician Richard Brown arrives to see us off. The voyage is supposed to begin at seven. The dear man must have woken at four in order to make it here in plenty of time. He holds a flask of coffee in one hand. 'Okedoke,' he says patiently, 'I'll wait in the car.'

6.45 a.m.: I climb the stairs to the clubhouse, where Jason and the others lie curled asleep in sleeping bags on the floor. I flick the lights on and off.

'Last call for Hawaii passengers – boat leaves in fifteen minutes!' Several bodies squirm and grunt sub-human replies.

10.15 a.m.: Jason finally steps out of the yacht club and saunters along the dirt road clutching a bundle of loose clothes and a computer. He stops briefly for a final sensation of land then strides purposefully down the gangplank. The awful farewells begin. I kiss Shirley and shake hands with the colonel and other friends. 'Thanks for everything Sam,' I say, stretching out my hand. 'You'll have to do better than that buddy,' Sam replies and gives me a great bear hug. Lastly I hug my father. 'Be safe,' he says with moistened eyes.

Jason steps down into *Moksha* first. I slip the mooring lines and jump in after him. Shirley tosses me a cold can of Sprite. I take a few gulps and hand the rest to Jason. It is our last cold drink for two thousand miles. He pedals and steers us around the other boats in the harbour.

I take out the Turks and Caicos conch shell for the traditional farewell blow, stand in the open hatchway and inhale deeply.

'Ppppppppppph.' My first attempt is a high-pitched fart. I try again. The second blast barely reaches the crowd on the shoreline. The third, thankfully, is a resonant, lip-tickling trombone. The crowd responds with cheers and waves. I wave back and smile. My head throbs.

Jason pedals out of the harbour. We glide under Golden Gate Bridge, passing close by one of its colossal red limbs. The ocean swell begins. I gaze up at the traffic on the bridge and beyond it, to the overcast sky. Now I look ahead at an open, featureless expanse of blue.

Penelope circles *Moksha* one last time before heading back. Sam Smalling grins and waves from the helm. Kenny leans precariously over the bow rail with a camera on his shoulder.

Stuart stands holding a cigarette and stares, all pride and emotion. We wave them goodbye.

Jason continues to pedal and steer south-west and looks much better than he deserves after last night's drinking performance. I feel strangely calm and unmoved. I look around the central cabin for something useful to do. The area around the passenger seat is a chaotic heap of provisions, mostly last-minute bags of fresh food, mixed with computer cables, clothing and paperback novels. I begin to reorganise storage lockers to accommodate them but am quite suddenly overcome with tiredness and nausea. Abandoning all work, I wriggle my way into the rat-hole for sleep. I dream that I have fallen asleep on a boat in Fort Baker. The boat accidentally slips its mooring and sweeps me unwittingly out to sea. I wake myself up screaming, 'Whoaah! Where am I? Help!'

We swap places every few hours and the coastline falls from sight. The only way to visually mark distance now is the uniform horizon about three miles away in all directions. Our world is again reduced to this - tones of blue, grey and white. We try to keep our heads up and peer over the short, choppy waves to the horizon to avoid being sick. Lunch and dinner disappear into the ocean just the same. *Moksha* rolls and pitches like a staggering drunk as the wind freshens. It starts raining just before dark.

The rain stops the following morning but the day remains grey and cold. Everything is damp. We both feel sicker than ever. Our backs and knees ache from the effort of pedalling and our shoulders are sore from collisions with the cabin walls.

The only escape from the misery is in sleep.

For the next five days we gradually pull away from the coastal weather systems, which are cold, capricious and confused, and slip deeper into the full-bodied and more stable Pacific Ocean. Our ears adjust to the new intricacies of balance and our appetite returns. Marine creatures occasionally provide a welcome distraction: two seabirds fighting over a fish; a small pod of dolphins satisfying their curiosity; a large tiger shark that we found languidly flapping a ventral fin at the surface, as if inviting us in; a migrating finback whale, which surfaced and exhaled a great plume of mist and disappeared again, leaving a stale odour in the air. But mostly we spend long hours pedalling and staring vacantly through the window or reading books.

There are many things that trigger flashbacks to the Atlantic Ocean. I'll be cursing and fumbling to retrieve something that I've dropped on the wet, sloshing floor of the boat and I'll think to myself – oh yeah, I remember this.

In other ways things are very different. I don't know if it's simply the passage of time, if we've matured over the last four years, or whether perhaps we're just more confident and relaxed this time because we know what we're in for, but Jason and I are getting along much better on this voyage.

Jason sits on the passenger seat opposite me, tending to a pot of breakfast porridge heating on the stove. He stirs the pot with a large wooden spoon, while pouring in more fresh water from a plastic container with his other hand. His hips and shoulders gyrate to maintain balance as *Moksha* rolls and slides over each wave.

'I was just wondering, Jason,' I begin. 'How do you feel about us being together on this boat again?' He puts the water container down and stares up at the cabin roof while considering his reply.

'I, um, I can't begin to compare the two voyages. It's like chalk and cheese really, completely different. My relationship with you on the Atlantic was... it's a vague memory, mostly bad. I've tried to forget. I just remember finding it really hard to be on the same boat with you... almost the whole time. I thought you were arrogant.'

'Arrogant! Really? I just remember being pretty scared and stressed out.' The revelation that he thought me arrogant comes as quite a shock.

'Well I wish you could have told me that,' Jason adds.

'But you cut yourself off, completely.' I say. 'Besides, I don't think I could admit I was scared, not even to myself.'

'I guess we had our own ways of dealing with it. But it would have helped matters if we could have talked about how stressful it is to live like this.'

'Yes. It is brutal, isn't it?' I agree. Jason continues stirring his pot.

Wow! Four years – that's how long it took for us to acknowledge the blindingly obvious. Hold the front pages – sharing a tiny, constantly moving, cramped wooden box with another person for four months on an ocean is a hugely stressful existence! Why should we have kept that from one another? What were we afraid of, admitting a weakness?

It is shameful how little we exchanged thoughts and fears on the Atlantic. It was a harsh and solitary regime from the very beginning – two-hour pedal shifts during daylight and four-hour shifts at night – a no-discussion, no-excuses pattern of behaviour. There was no need to talk, understand, or trust. We sacrificed everything companionship ought to be in favour of a mechanical certainty – you just do your two hours and I'll do mine.

But on this voyage we are finally opening up. We have so far established no assigned roles or schedules at all. We take turns to pedal and sleep, cook and make fresh water. There is no suspicious calculation of who may have done more, and yet everything is done well and we have probably spoken more in one week than we did in four months on the Atlantic. I know how well Jason slept, whether he feels hungry, tired or sick, and when he feels inspired to cook or plot a course. There is eye contact, sincerity, conversation and humour – all of which makes this voyage already a stunning success.

In fact it reminds me of another outstanding week of my life – the Christmas camping trip to Mount Shasta with Eilbhe,

Therese, JimBo and the others, where we lived in an atmosphere of unconditional trust that inspired us all to do our best. We turned competition on its head and strove to work for each other. And it strikes me that it requires no special effort. There is no particular skill or secret to enable friends to behave this way. It happens naturally, like a mother with her child, when the fear of being exploited and the thought of taking advantage become equally ridiculous.

Who knows how long it will last – especially if the bastard stiffs me on my porridge ration! But I am grateful that it happens at all.

Jason carefully brings breakfast to the boil. He gives a final stir and, with a loud clattering of pots and tins, pulls two aluminium eating bowls from a storage-well by the passenger seat. Two-handed tasks must be done quickly between waves. His left arm whips back to its bracing position on the cabin wall, ready for the next hissing, foaming collision. Today it is the short, aggressive class of wave with that awkward, vindictive streak. The next one comes in low and hard and breaks at the last second with a deep thud against *Moksha*'s packed belly. Jason's eyes follow an arching, glistening bucketful of ocean that flies superbly in through the hatchway. It lands in the porridge with a triumphant 'flop'. He shakes his head and looks at me. I giggle and he smiles back. Then he stands up in the open hatchway, scoops the spoiled porridge into the ocean and starts again.

On the evening of our ninth day at sea, fresh winds and twelve-foot swells sweep down from the north. We welcome them at first and steer diagonally down the rumbling blue hills with good advantage on our south-west heading.

Soon it becomes more frightening. The wind howls and whips up sharp, cresting waves with the intensity of a sudden rainsquall, though the night sky is clear and starry.

The wind is really blowing now. Waves build into huge, confused seas. I remain calm while preparing dinner. I even write an update on the computer and email it on to our website coordinator, then I squirrel myself down in the rat-hole and try to sleep, hoping that the weather will have improved when I surface again.

Jason wakes me just after midnight. My first sense is of the thundering gale. I wrestle myself semi-consciously into the central compartment. Jason begins yelling instructions.

'You'll have to be careful with some of these waves.' He sounds very excited, or worried. 'Probably feels worse than it is, but some of them could've capsized us. It's hard to tell at night. I've been doing all right on a heading of 210°-ish, but don't go as far over as 240° or 270°. That's too close to broaching. There's some big ol' breakers out there.'

I strap on my sandals, settle into the pedal seat and grip the steering handles. Jason is already fast asleep in the rat-hole. Wind howls in through the partially open hatchway. The air is damp and cold. I strain my tired eyes to focus on the red glow of the compass light. It seems to hop around the cabin in a crazy dance. What did he say, the other side of 210°?

I start on a heading of 180°. *Moksha*'s stern suddenly lifts, the bow tips down and we hurtle forward. My stomach reels as a mountain of ocean sweeps us up. We accelerate downhill amid a frenzy of buffeting white foam. It's like being trapped in a demented car wash.

I am down in the trough, between waves, in the sucking blackness: only the compass light can be seen. Is that 180°, or 350°? Another wave scoops us up like a twig. *Moksha* is swept along almost on her side.

'Screw this!' I cry. I'm going to throw out the sea anchor (our new, heavy nylon parachute-shaped version) and let the boat drift safely perpendicular to the waves. I scramble to the hatchway and poke my head outside. It would also be better to lower the mast, I think. I unfasten the mast line from its cleat and lower the mast to its horizontal, locked position. The boat is immediately more stable, although the lowered mast now sits on top of the ventilation hatch above the pedal seat. That's fine by me, I'm ventilated enough!

I throw out the sea anchor on a length of heavy line attached to the stern.

Damn! In my haste I threw the sea anchor out on the windward side. Instead of drifting away from the boat, the sea anchor disappears underneath the boat and the line is caught around the propeller.

'Shit! Bollocks!' I continue swearing and unclamp the pedal system, lift it from its steel housing, and wrestle with the tangled rope. The clanging and scraping of metal finally wakes Jason. He turns and lifts his head, angrily looking for an explanation.

'I was coping fine with it,' he protests. 'I'll carry on at the helm if you can't.'

'What, pedalling?' I reply, equally furious. 'I'd rather drift safely. Why risk capsizing in this for a few extra miles? Do you think I'm going to feel any safer lying in the rat-hole, waiting for you to capsize us? I'd rather sit it out till morning, if only I could sort out this fucking sea anchor. I'll be fine, go back to sleep.'

Annoyingly, he does. I slowly heave in the mass of rope and retrieve the dripping parachute. I hurl it all back over the leeward side.

Idiot! The sea anchor drifts quickly away but now the rope is snarled on the roof. Either I haul the whole lot back again or start messing about outside. I'm not going out there. I start to retrieve the line again, but the strain of pulling in the sea anchor against the wind and waves exceeds my strength. I curse loudly and Jason wakes again. This time I ask for help.

It takes our combined strength to pull in the deployed sea anchor. I am back where I started, except the main compartment is now swamped with water and covered in a huge pile of wet rope. Jason wriggles back into the rat-hole for a third attempt at sleep.

I stay awake through the hellish night, steering as best I can diagonally down the waves. The moon appears. I keep looking over my shoulder for the next glistening avalanche of water.

Jason hauls himself from the rat-hole at 6.00 a.m., turns around and reaches for the video camera beside him. He points it at my exhausted face. I sit dripping wet and in silence, wearing a waterproof top and life jacket. He checks our position on the GPS.

'Outstanding progress!' he exclaims. 'We've travelled forty-five miles in the last twelve hours.'

The wind abates over the next two days and I begin to enjoy myself again. The only lingering remnant of the storm is a big ocean swell. When, at regular intervals, we rise up onto the summit of each great, elongated mound, the surreally beautiful pattern of parallel lines – of hills and valleys – is all that can be seen under the blue sky, nothing but these great rippling spines of water. It is a marvellous, bizarre sensation, like riding the peristaltic waves on the skin of a colossal snake.

I stand in the open hatchway at dawn to appreciate the scene. The sun rises in a haze of yellow to the east. The moon sets in a blush of pink to the west. We ride the serpent that slithers in between.

I decide to make some bread for breakfast. On the inside cover of my diary is a page entitled 'Diana and Stein Hoff's

Recipe For Pressure-Cooked Bread', with the instructions written by hand. I empty a bag of dried bread mix (containing 600g of flour, 6g of dried yeast and a handful of chopped nuts and seeds) into a mixing bowl wedged safely beside the passenger seat. I stand and reach over into the ocean with a measuring jug, scoop out 100ml of seawater, and add it to the dry mix, followed by 200ml of fresh water from a plastic container and a large tablespoon of oil. I mix the bowl well.

I resume pedalling for forty minutes while waiting for the dough to rise. Then I transfer myself back to the passenger seat, place a wooden board on my lap, scoop the dough out onto it and kneed for about twenty minutes. I put the dough and board to one side while I place a metal platform into the bottom of the pressure cooker, into which I then pour 500ml of seawater. Finally I grease my steel baking dish (customised to fit snugly inside the pressure cooker), put the dough inside and lower the dish into the cooker, where it sits on the platform. I let the dough rise for a further twenty minutes then light the stove and pressure cook for thirty minutes.

The loaf is pale and wet when I lift the lid. I lift the dish out with its wire handle and leave it beside me to dry. The central cabin fills with steam and the delightful aroma of freshly baked bread. I carry on pedalling.

Jason is soon awake. Sunlight glints across the rat-hole hatch as Jason pushes it fully open and pulls himself onto the passenger seat. He picks up the bread and holds it in front of his nose.

'Mmh, smells excellent. Morning skipper. Lovely morning.'

'Yeah, a beauty isn't she.'

We change places. He falls into the pedal seat and grubs around in a locker for music. I stand surveying the bright blue sky and ocean and start pumping the desalinating machine for fresh water. The silky blues of J.J. Cale singing 'After Midnight' bellows from mini-speakers attached to a Walkman – instantly erasing the familiar sounds of sea and wind but the music abruptly stops.

'Too sombre,' says Jason, 'not strong enough to kick-start the day. How about some Smashing Pumpkins? Oh no, empty box, must've lost that one. Aha! Blondie. That'll do.' He inserts the new tape and presses a button on the Walkman beside him. The opening lyrics of 'One Way or Another' scream out like a petulant witch and stream into my veins, infusing me with a new, nervous energy. Jason pounds enthusiastically at the pedals and sings along, emphasising with malice every teeth-clenched 'get-cha!' We carry on like this for several minutes. It is the nearest we can get out here to 'losing it' on the dance floor.

Music is hugely important to us. Other priceless goods include what remains of a cabbage and a small rack of spices. We ration ourselves to one divinely fresh and crunchy cabbage leaf per day. Stupidly, we only brought one cabbage. We have started growing sprouts in glass jars for a source of fresh food when the cabbage is gone. The selection of spices gives variety to our criminally-bland stock of main meals donated by the manufacturers. These are all soy-based, vegetarian and dehydrated meals of three different kinds: Chicken á la King, Pasta Primavera and Chilli con Carne. The only edible one is the chilli, the rest are foul. Thus our challenge is to find imaginative ways of flavouring chilli every evening for the next few months. The only alternative rests upon Jason locating a thirty pound bag of pea soup hidden somewhere in the rear storage compartment. It has already acquired mythical status – The Holy Gruel!

Later, in the afternoon, a wind freshens from the west, making pedalling a struggle for me. Jason stands and sings to the waves while pumping for fresh water. A sharp, vicious wave leaps up and covers him. He spits out what he caught in his mouth and suddenly turns around.

'Did you hear that?'

'Hear what?'

'A woman's voice, I swear she was right behind me, laughing!'

'Yeah I remember hearing things on the Atlantic. Sometimes it was a crowded party, or police sirens. Once there were police sirens and opera at once – that was a trip.'

The radar detector emits a loud bleep, warning of another vessel. A heavily-laden container ship appears on the horizon. It looks to be heading straight for us.

I alter course and pedal furiously to avoid it. The vessel, *Darne*, rumbles past at top speed, bound for Japan. We have tried, on six separate occasions, to make radio contact with passing ships, but without success. I try again. No response. I try again.

'Go ahead,' crackles a high-pitched Asian accent.

'*Darne*, this is pedal boat *Moksha*. Can you confirm you have us on radar, over?' There is a long pause.

'Yes.'

'*Darne*, this is *Moksha*. That's good to hear. Could you tell us how far away you picked us up, over?' There is another long pause.

'Yes.'

'*Darne*, this is *Moksha*. What distance did you pick us up, over?'

'Okay.'

I give up. I watch *Darne* steaming away into the opposite horizon. There ploughs another fifty thousand tonnes of cold steel in the hands of a lad from Manila. I suppose we ought to be grateful that this one was awake.

Day 14: Hamsters
11 October

I am very tired; I have been pedalling against the wind for four hours. Pedalling into the wind is more exhausting than the extra energy spent. It is the gnawing humiliation of watching the same bubble in the water beside me for two whole minutes, showing that I am a hamster on a wheel, going nowhere.

Our desalinator has been leaking for several days. Jason has spent hours trying to locate the fault. Now it has broken completely. The loss of the desalinator would have been a life-threatening situation on the Atlantic Ocean, but thankfully we now have a smaller, emergency unit to fall back on. This spare, pocket-sized pump takes four times longer to produce our daily gallon of fresh water and is not supposed to last for very long.

The psychological reaction is interesting. The prospect of running out of water creates an immediate, gripping thirst. We discuss cutting our water use in half, while examining each other for signs of panic. There are none yet. The entire deck of the boat is designed to collect rainwater, though we don't know how practical this would be to rely upon.

'So, what will we do if this one breaks down?'

'Dunno. Let's have a cuppa tea and think about it,' Jason replies. We fall about, giggling like schoolchildren.

The sea is calm enough for us to enjoy a civilised dinner – for once not having to wedge ourselves against the cabin walls with our knees as we eat. A bottle of Glenlivet whisky shuttles back and forward for dessert.

'What's this?' I remark. 'The Dean Martin theory of water conservation?'

I offer the rat-hole to Jason for a whole, uninterrupted night's sleep. I intend to pedal on until I'm too exhausted then rig up a hammock in the central cabin. He smiles, recites the old line about looking into the mouths of gift-horses and smartly retires. He shuffles feet first into his snug cocoon and is instantly asleep, reminding me of a documentary on butterfly metamorphosis, played in fast reverse.

Two hours later, thoroughly bored and tired, I abandon my pedalling plans. I start up the laptop computer and program it to receive the latest weather bulletin. It reports that Hurricane Kay is veering away from our course and will dissipate in the tropics. Greatly relieved, I unravel the heavy canvas hammock and slot the aluminium poles into their brackets on both sides of the cabin.

This sleeping arrangement is not one of my better designs. The hammock is suspended above the pedal-drive and is therefore higher above sea level than the rat-hole, which amplifies *Moksha*'s rolling motion. The hammock picks up every pitch, roll, hiccup and fish fart in the surrounding sea and transfers it directly to me. One could find a better night's sleep sharing a deluxe waterbed with Mr and Mrs Walrus on their honeymoon night.

I give up trying to sleep at dawn and clamber down from the rolling torture machine. It is stowed away and the kettle is boiled for tea. I cut a slice of yesterday's bread, skewer it with a fork then burn it on the gas stove to make toast.

The morning sky is overcast. A cold wind blows in from the west. I put on a coat and look up. It is just a rainsquall. A thick, grey cloud consumes the sky and a patter of rain approaches across the sea. Water!

I drop everything, fly through the hatchway and begin scrambling about the deck to uncork the water-collection holes, then jump back inside to look for suitable pots to place under their corresponding outlets. Water is soon gushing from both tubes. The first pot is too salty. I ditch it overboard. The next three are drinkable.

The shower is intense and short-lived. I collect almost a gallon of water in ten minutes, saving us about four hours of pumping with our tiny, emergency desalinator. I taste it again and realise the water is still quite salty. The ideal situation, I suppose, is to have a rain shower when the sea is very calm, so that waves don't wash over the gunwales and contaminate the run-off. This very rarely happens.

The commotion wakes Jason, who emerges from a ten-hour sleep feeling reborn. He tastes a sip of my rainwater, purses his lips and winces slightly.

'It'll be OK for cooking,' he says, with touching diplomacy.

Day 21: Sundays
18 October

I've been thinking a lot about England, wondering whether still to call it home, and where specifically in England home might be? My family home, the place where I grew up, was in the middle of the country near Wolverhampton, which is about as far away from the sea as an Englishman can live. It was a beautiful old Georgian house with a large rambling garden dominated by a sprawling Lebanon cedar tree. I still find myself back there in dreams, even though I left home over thirteen years ago after finishing school.

I travelled and worked my way through North America in my gap year before university, and it wasn't long after I began my degree when the family unit sort of imploded; my sister went to live abroad, my parents divorced, my father lost his job, then most of his pension, and the family home was sold. We have all been fairly rootless ever since.

The closest place to 'home' would be Salcombe, on the south coast of Devon, where my sister now lives with her husband and two children. I can't ever imagine owning my own house there, the prices are exorbitant, but perhaps I could live on a boat in the estuary.

Today is Sunday. My perfect Sunday goes like this: I wake at sunrise on my sailboat in Salcombe Harbour. I sit out on deck to enjoy the morning sun and watch the wading birds on the mud flats, then row ashore in a dingy and walk to a friend's farm to exercise his horse.

We gallop across damp, steaming fields and pick a path through fragrant woods to the beach, where we race along the surf line. I row back across the estuary to town for an oozing bacon and egg sandwich at Captain Morgan's, with a pot of tea and a fat newspaper. Later, there is a surprise gathering of friends, with lots of children. We go to the beach, play games and devour a picnic of sushi and champagne. I fall asleep among the dunes with the love of my life, her cheek warm on my chest and her soft hair ruffling in a gentle breeze, tickling my chin.

There is a big family meal in the evening with roast wild duck, potatoes and vegetables, treacle tart and custard for dessert. Card games and storytelling last into the early hours with coffee, brandy and cheese.

This particular Sunday starts like this: Jason's voice echoes from the rat-hole, 'Steve, you awake?' It's 7.00 a.m. I am wearing a salty, damp T-shirt, a wet sleeping bag over that, and over that I seem to be wearing a small yellow boat that rolls violently on the Pacific Ocean, eight hundred miles from land. I have had two hours of 'sleep' on the rolling torture hammock, having been tossed around like a rag doll. The last three weeks have been a near-constant life of assault and battery.

Water sloshes about on the floor, along with an empty sachet of hot chocolate and a wool sock. Outside, the wind howls across grey-blue hills of white-capped waves. It starts raining. I could pump a little plastic machine for twenty minutes, to make enough water for a cup of tea, but I don't want one that much. A wave squeezes in through the slightly open hatchway, injecting half a gallon of cold water on my head. Most of it trickles its way down my body inside the sleeping bag.

One day I will have my perfect Sunday. And when I do, I will have it in memory of this one.

We have been at sea now for almost a month and are roughly halfway to Hawaii. Our progress is over forty miles a day on average, much as we expected, although when Jason last checked the GPS a few hours ago it reported that we'd made less than ten miles in the last ten hours of pedalling, despite a following wind. We must be in one of those weird counter-currents. There was also an hour of stoppage when we took turns to dive and scrub thousands of gooseneck barnacles off the hull. I reacted to the news with great disappointment.

'Well, you've just got to enjoy it,' said Jason. He's right. I am still too anxious about progress.

A month at sea has taken its toll on our bodies and the equipment. Jason feels very tired and nauseous at the moment. He is taking restorative mineral and salt powders, suspecting some kind of deficiency. I feel all right, but take the powders anyway. Common sense tells me that it won't be long before I'm lacking whatever he's lacking.

The dreaded salt-sores are also beginning to appear in bright red bulges on our skins. They seem to get worse as we head further south into tropical waters. We dive in for a swim several times a day to keep cool (no sharks have been sighted since the big tiger shark early in the voyage), thus a permanent film of salt clings to our skins and rubs into open pores. Infection inevitably follows. A body scrub with a freshwater flannel seems to keep them at bay. But since the primary water-maker broke and left us with only the small emergency unit – which itself is starting to leak – fresh water has become a very precious commodity. This inspired me to experiment with boiling seawater in the pressure-cooker. I place flannels inside it, which rest on the raised platform we use for bread making, and the result is a hot freshwater towel – like they give you in Asian restaurants and on airplanes.

No amount of food crammed down our throats appears able to compensate for the disappearance of flesh from our bones. We are slowly wasting away with the struggle of constant motion. Happily though, there have so far been no serious cuts, broken bones or, for that matter, burnt testicles.

Our pedal-drive units are also casualties. Several hours of last night were spent fiddling around in the dark in a desperate search for spare parts. We are now down to the third and final unit, but only half way to Hawaii.

It is no one's fault. In fact, the donated MicroMarine units are a big improvement on any pedal system we have used before. But since we don't have twenty thousand dollars to custom-build a tougher stainless steel version, we have to make-do with the alloy product designed for a recreational market. Not many people want to pedal two-tonne machines across violent oceans, whereas they do enjoy pedalling around lakes keeping their hands free for the fishing line. What is amply robust for the latter pursuit cannot be expected to withstand the forces at work out here.

The propeller shaft on the first unit snapped in two within ten days; the second one was stripped of its gear teeth. We pray that the final unit will do better, but we will probably need to keep fixing it with unbroken components from the first two. Failing that there are the emergency oars – a dreadful prospect. We tried rowing *Moksha* once, at the Bay View Boat Club in San Francisco. It was a terribly cramped and painful experience over a distance of only two hundred yards.

The leak in our emergency water-maker gets worse. Unless we can find the fault and fix it, we are going to have to start praying for rain and create some other, imaginative device for distilling freshwater with bits of God only knows what. The trouble is, we can't even unscrew the pump cylinder to find where the problem lies. Our tool kit carries no clamps or wrenches wide enough to fit around it. It is fastened far too tightly to loosen by hand. The panic level starts to rise.

'Ah! I know,' says Jason. He reaches over to the metal arm used to clamp our video camera to a fixed position on the boat. There is no piece of equipment I detest more on this voyage, because I'm forever banging my head against it.

To our immense relief, the camera clamp exerts sufficient grip and leverage to twist open the cylinder. Inside, Jason discovers a disconnected intake pipe. The life-threatening crisis is solved. It is simply a case of reattaching a flimsy plastic clip. He replaces both the pipe and holding clip, screws the cylinder back on and pumps the desalinator once again. The lifesaving liquid begins to drip slowly from the freshwater outlet pipe. It works perfectly. My relationship with the video camera clamp is transformed.

Jason returns to his open laptop computer, into which he had been typing his daily report before stopping to fix the water-maker. He transmits his message with the satellite link-up and downloads messages that are being received.

'Hey, there's an email here from my old man.' He reads it, smiling. 'Wow! He's got hold of another water-maker. Oh God! He's been in touch with the bloody Pentagon for us. He says there's a US Navy destroyer ready and waiting to rendezvous with us to hand over the new water-maker. He's standing by for our decision and coordinates. Fuckinell Dad, nice one!' Jason looks up at me, with a big grin. 'How exciting. What do you think? It's a bit much really, isn't it?'

'Yeah, just a bit,' I agree. 'Amazing though. It's good to know we have someone like Sebert watching over us. But let's not bother the US Navy just yet, eh.'

'Nope, we're in good shape,' he says. 'Actually, I'm feeling a lot better today, at least physically. I'm a bit concerned about my mind though,' he continues, scratching his head and smiling. 'Do you remember me telling you about the voices?'

'The laughing woman?'

'Yeah, and the big shark that turned out to be bubbles.'

'And the deadly scorpion fish?' I add.

305

'Oh yeah, the deadly scorpion fish, which turned back into a floating flip-flop,' he says and laughs. I nod in sympathy and add an expression of pained embarrassment.

'Well, last night the strangest thing happened.' He carries on. 'I was pedalling away just fine in the darkness, looking at the compass. The heading was 240°. Suddenly, the 2 on the 240 sprouted a huge set of teeth and took a chunk out of 270's backside! From then on it was just a ragged 27.'

I shake my head and laugh. Prolonged hallucinations are almost commonplace for us now. I am more concerned for my own sanity, determined not to repeat the mistakes of the previous voyage by clinging too doggedly to the idea of progress towards land. I keep thinking about what Jason said earlier - 'You've just got to enjoy it'. Those words pierced me. I know he is right. And I am enjoying it; certainly a lot more than the last voyage. I just have to keep reminding myself, whenever I notice myself becoming anxious, that I have a simple choice: either to continue cursing foul winds, staring obsessively at charts and measuring distances, or to relax and enjoy it. Whichever one I choose, Hawaii – that first smell of wet earth and green hills, that first juicy pineapple – won't come any quicker. The weather won't be more obliging. The ocean continually offers me that choice: anxiety or acceptance.

Picture a sewing machine. The needle of a sewing machine penetrates the fabric at its own speed. All it requires is guidance. If you pull at the material and try to hold on to it, what you end up with is a tangled mess of errant thread. The same happens if you try to push the material through too fast, in a hurry. I often find myself doing one or the other, either holding back or forcing forward the fabric of living process, pulling or pushing, reminiscing or fantasising, coveting or wanting, unable merely to lay my hands upon it and pay attention.

Life – my education, role models, the media, careers and peers – has taught me a great deal about wanting something more. At times like this I wish I had better prepared myself to make the best of a situation that cannot be improved.

We change places. I sit down at the passenger end. The computer has been left on for me to write my own daily message. I stare at the screen for ten minutes, struggling to find some inspiration. Our daily updates contain many ideas and introspections but precious little news, for the good reason that hardly anything ever happens. Day changes to night and back again and the vast, liquid desert shifts in its endless variations on blue and white. Even the air temperature refuses to fluctuate any more. It is always damp and warm.

All I can think about is England. I begin typing. 'My mind wanders home. It must be well into autumn there. Has there been a frost and those crisp, cold mornings? Have the wasps given up their sluggish struggle? Are geese making 'Vs' for the south? Do apple orchards sag with fat speckled fruit? What colour are the leaves? Can you smell them, damp and rotting? Do children drag their feet through the leaf-drifts on their way to school, talking of Halloween and bonfires? Are the streetlights turned on before you get home? Are milkmen and postmen searching for woolly sweaters for the early-morning round? Or have they worn them all the rotten summer too? Is the fire back in the hearth, coal ordered and wood stacked? Have the birds and lawnmowers gone silent? Isn't it strange, how we take for granted what we have and value what we lack? Presently, in the sub-tropical Pacific, I'm as curious about my home as I ever was about the world.'

Day 38 of the voyage: we rake along at a speed of fifty miles per day in the trade winds. Hawaii is now less than seven hundred miles away. The emergency water-maker is holding out but the final pedal unit is sounding strange: no longer a smooth whir, but a raspy grind. At least our position is such that, even if we drifted on the current, the chain of islands that is Hawaii would probably catch us as the outstretched fan of a sea anemone catches a particle of food.

Jason is sweating profusely as he squirms his way out of the rear compartment, having spent more than an hour digging around for food supplies and rearranging chaotic heaps of garbage bags, spent gas canisters and other miscellaneous stores. Whatever became of the legendary pea soup mix remains a mystery.

He passes over bags of Chilli con Carne, chocolate bars and a large tin of rice, which I stow in the storage lockers beside the passenger seat. Then he climbs out and dives headfirst into the blue with a resounding splash that leaves me rocking.

Jason hauls himself back on board feeling euphoric, transformed, and sits on the roof. Water drips from his dangling leg onto the cabin floor. I ought to jump in as well. I am sluggish today, sensing that dreadful, now familiar descent into chronic fatigue.

My lethargy is more mental than physical. I think it has a lot to do with routine. I have become too habitual, doing the same thing day after day. It is stagnancy, a loss of imagination, and the solution is to force myself out of the rut, stimulate myself, do something different – like dive under the boat to scrape away the barnacles and algae that now carpet the hull.

The longer the safe and familiar routine goes on, the harder I find it to stir myself into action. The crucial trigger is more a discomforting level of self-disgust than anything positive. It helps to have the glistening blue ocean outside and the effect of diving in is miraculous. One minute I'll be pedalling away in a state of robotic boredom. But having made the effort – having felt the boom on my eardrums as my head hits the water and the sheer exhilaration of swimming in cobalt blue water three miles deep – my heart will be pounding as I climb back on board. Then the experience of pedalling is utterly different. Suddenly, life is full of new possibilities: I'll throw on some music – The Red Hot Chili Peppers, full volume; I'll take out the cherry wood hash pipe that Sam Smalling made for me and before long Jason and I will be talking nonsense in ridiculous German accents.

In the late afternoon it starts to rain. We both scramble out on deck for a freshwater shower – eyes shut tight, facing the sky, mouths open wide and arms outstretched in messianic devotion, worshipping every precious drop. I laugh out loud as the cold rain pummels my skin and trickles down my body.

If only I could capture this intensity of joy, this delight in simple pleasures, and keep it on land, my life would become an endlessly divine experience. Every hot shower would be a miracle; every cold drink, fresh vegetable and comfortable chair would be a cause for radiant happiness.

But of course it won't be. The rain will again become largely an inconvenience and the rest will be taken for granted. That is the tragedy of familiarity. And that, I suppose, is the value of venturing into the wilderness every so often. Nothing is appreciated so well as when it becomes rare or even lost.

There ought to be a law making it compulsory to spend a month in the wilderness every few years. The month time period is significant. As we approach our fortieth day at sea, Jason and I have been discussing the biblical references to 'forty days and forty nights'. I used to believe it was just an ascetic ordeal, a kind of penance for sin. But I think the real value of isolation goes beyond the physical hardship, and indeed beyond anything you can conceive of.

After almost forty days my mind appears more settled, no longer constipated with the thoughts of the busy world. Back there, there's always another target to reach. I'm constantly aiming for something. Targets validate my entire life – life is target practice. Out here the only target is the other shore, which is so vastly distant at walking speed that it's meaningless.

The aim of the expedition itself – to go around the world by human power – means even less. The target may as well not exist from one day to the next, leaving only this blue void. It takes my mind, which believes it is nothing without goals, all this time to stop striving, cease looking for reasons, things to aim for in an aimless void. And the moment of surrender comes: this unexpected and unspeakable moment in the rain, when I am no one in particular, with nothing to aim for, and everything is perfect as it is. This is my Moksha, my freedom.

A few nights later, just after 1.00 a.m., Lucky Lester the flying fish lands on board. Previous flying fish that we have encountered have all deserved the nickname Unlucky something or other – for crashing into the only hard surface within a thousand square miles. This one glides straight through the open hatchway and lands safely in my lap. We both nearly die of fright. I toss him back into the dark ocean and he vanishes in a phosphorescent swirl.

The last few days have been a miserable continuum of squalls and contrary winds from the south-east. Unless we can manage, somehow, to claw our way south we could miss the big island of Hawaii altogether. Or we might find ourselves in one of the treacherous channels between islands that funnel the wind and squeeze the waves into terrible seas.

The struggle south is hard on body and mind. We sweat profusely and stop frequently to jump into the ocean and cool off. Not surprisingly, the pedal seat is starting to 'hum', as Jason puts it. It is the perfect word to describe the resonant stench on board.

Day 45: the weather continues to be unstable, with heavy rain showers and winds from the south-east. The weather bulletin speaks of shear lines and ridges, but it's all Swahili to me.

We head due south to try and get closer to the latitude of the Hawaiian Islands, now four hundred miles to the south-west.

I check our GPS late in the following afternoon and discover that we have pedalled only three miles in the last twenty-four hours of constant effort southward. In the same period we drifted sideways (westward) twenty-nine miles!

Tensions build as we strategize our approach to Hilo – the only harbour on the east coast of Hawaii. It is a very small target that we cannot afford to miss. The coastline north of Hilo is an unbroken line of huge cliffs stretching to the fearsome Alenuihaha Channel, between Hawaii and Maui. To the south are more cliffs and an active volcano, Kilauea, which continually spills molten lava into the sea. Below the island is, well, nothing – next stop the islands of Kiribati, two thousand miles to the south-west.

There is a pungent smell of male competition in the air – to be the one to save the day. Jason favours being in line with Hilo's latitude of 20°N when we are still a hundred miles out. I prefer a more gradual slide south. I think we are bound to encounter the odd, helpful day of north-easterlies, whereas he suspects they have been permanently displaced by winds from the south and east. I probably ought to let go and trust in Jason to get us to Hilo. He, after all, trusted me to find Miami.

Day 47: it is lucky Friday the thirteenth! The wind is force three from the north-east. Yes, the north-east! We dare to set our hearts on dry land in a week.

Day 49: we continue to make excellent progress with following winds. Hawaii should be in sight in a few days. It can't arrive soon enough, especially now that we've eaten all the chocolate M&Ms, the last jar of peanut butter has been

ceremoniously licked clean, and Jason is pedalling through the day in women's underwear. The sight of this big hairy bloke in the nude was unpleasant enough, without having to suffer him in red rose-patterned knickers with a dainty red bow on the front. He claims they help reduce salt-sores and chafing, but that doesn't explain the evident pleasure in his eyes, the worrying smile, or how he came to own a pair of rose-patterned knickers with a dainty red bow on the front in the first place.

Day 53: no sight of land as yet with thirty-five miles to go, only a blanket of cloud and the eerie, orange glow of the volcano, Kilauea, erupting to the south-west. The presence of land is also felt in confused, lunging waves – a result of collisions between waves coming in to shore and those that have already hit and rebounded back – made worse by a strong north-east wind that sculpts the waves into tall, sharp forms with rolling heads of surf. We fly before them at top speed. We will undoubtedly make land tomorrow, whether we like it or not. The only crucial question is where that will be – in safe harbour or at the cliff face.

I stand in the open hatchway and stare out at the furious, roaring tumult. I am filled with a great sense of privilege and appreciation for all the people who made this all possible – those who helped to build and repair *Moksha* along the way; those who gave their time, money or just a bed for the night and asked for nothing in return. I hope that we gave something back, some added measure of self-belief and confidence, perhaps. I hope that we inspired people to think, 'Well if you can do all that, what must I be capable of?'

Mid-afternoon the following day, the GPS indicates we are merely seven miles from Hilo Harbour. We surf along the face of great rolling swells under a bloated, thunderous sky.

Incredibly, we cannot see the gigantic heap of rock rising from the sea in front of us. The island remains hidden behind a mass of low cloud.

An hour later, Jason stands outside, straddling the bow deck with his hand pointed ahead, arm outstretched, while his other hand curls around his mouth, and cries 'Land Ahoy!' I stumble from the pedal seat and stand in the open hatchway.

'Where? I can't see anything?' I keep looking. 'Oh there!' There are a few specks on the horizon. Soon they grow larger. Black and sinister dagger shapes, spindles of lava rock, slowly materialise through the grey mist. They merge into a saw-toothed line that we guess to be Leleiwi Point. A massive barge, laden with containers, crawls out of the mist on the starboard side, heading for Hilo.

Suddenly, the veil lifts. A staggeringly enormous slope of land rises from the sea. Its colour is an electrifying, lush green. I scramble back into the pedal seat and continue pedalling, bristling with joy, while Jason grabs the video camera and stands in the open hatchway. We stare at the thrilling, motionless mass of solid colours and gradually pick out its detail – green cotton-bud forests of trees; specks of cattle on smooth pasture; houses with rusting corrugated roofs; black steaming rocks.

The ocean quickly changes colour from cobalt blue to muddy brown – from sediment washed out to sea by days of heavy rain.

A sport-fishing vessel appears. My father is on the foredeck, dancing and waving. A woman dressed in a grass skirt and bikini dances next to him. My God! It is Nancy Sanford, our old friend from St Petersburg, Florida. We both laugh and wave. Nancy jumps into the air and waves back. A third person has a professional film camera on his shoulder. I know it can't be Kenny. He emailed us yesterday to say he was stuck in a curfew in a hotel room in Baghdad – leaning out of an open window with his camera, waiting for cruise missiles to give him a scoop for the evening news. The man puts the camera down and vomits over the side of the boat. The desperate sound of retching reaches us. I recognise his bald head and white beard. It is Jake, a film producer from San Francisco.

Stuart's voice crackles out on our VHF speaker. He instructs us to follow his vessel, *Force Play*, into Hilo Harbour. We are to dock at the jetty of the Nani Loa Hotel. Hawaiian maidens will be waiting to greet us with garlands of flowers, he says! We have complementary rooms there for the night and all we can eat. The news is unspeakably fabulous.

Jason and I swap duties. I pedal the final half-mile, while Jason tidies himself and digs out the conch shell for the traditional signal of journey's end. He looks happy but subdued, equally thrilled and disappointed. It is the end of the voyage, an end to the simple hardship and the beginning of complicated comfort.

Tomorrow we will begin trying to pay for it all, finding somewhere to live and somewhere to prepare *Moksha* for the next leg to Kiribati. There is another expedition newsletter to produce and distribute to three thousand supporters, school visits must be organised and so on and on – but not today. This evening is for eating fresh pineapple and dancing with hula girls, for digging our feet into warm sand and for swapping stories with Stuart and our friends over a cold glass of beer.

The following morning at 3.00 a.m., I wake for my pedal shift only to find myself in a hotel bedroom in a different world – a world that doesn't move. I chuckle at the glorious sensation of crisp cotton sheets next to my skin. An air conditioner hums gently by the window.

I walk outside into the hotel garden and stand at the shore. The air is still and fragrant. The sea strokes over black rocks, leaving puddles. I brush my hand down the trunk of a mighty palm tree and feel its rough, scaly texture. I heave a great sigh and wrap my arms tightly around it and enter into its creaking sway.

Walking through the parking lot I hear a delicate pre-dawn twittering of birds in the canopy. I stand entranced and listen to their exquisite conversation. Perhaps someone will alert the police that a deranged and emaciated Gollum-like creature is lurking among parked cars. I am not concerned. This is bliss. I only wish that life could always be filled with this infinite sense of gratitude and wonder.

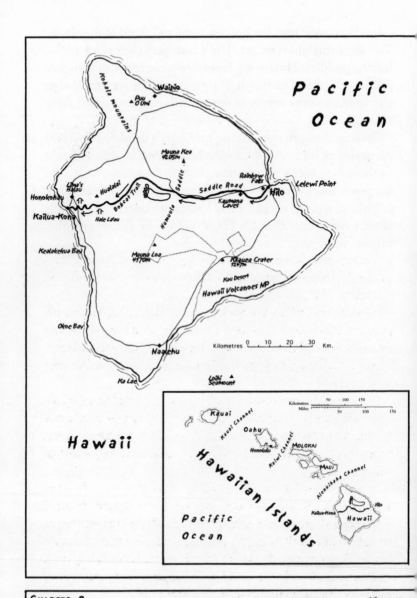

8. Hawaii
(December 1998 – May 1999)

After a month on land, I'm managing to hang on to the spirit of that blissful state in which I arrived, a task made easier on this tranquil paradise island.

Jason is shortly to fly back to Rye, Colorado, where his partner April is a teacher, to continue developing the expedition's network of schools. He plans to return in March, when we will begin preparing *Moksha* for her onward voyage to Kiribati.

My nomadic existence continues here with an enviable selection of places to stay each night. My favourite place is the black sand beach at Punalu'u, on Hawaii's southern shore, where we keep *Moksha*. I call it my *pu'uhonua*, my place of refuge.

In pre-colonial days, when Hawaiian society was subject to a strict code or *kapu*, an offender could be buried, burned alive, stoned, clubbed or strangled to death for committing as trivial a crime as allowing his or her shadow to fall on a chief's house. A woman could expect a death sentence for eating pork or bananas. But if you could avoid capture long enough to reach a designated pu'uhonua, you were safe.

Punalu'u is breathtakingly beautiful place. A steep beach of jet-black volcanic sand separates a palm-fringed, inland lagoon from a wild, surf-strewn bay on the seaward side. Freshwater springs bubble up through cracks in the swirling patterns of solidified black lava at the far end of the beach. Rare Hawksbill turtles can usually be found resting or dragging themselves wearily onto shore. Directly behind the beach, set back and almost hidden by an encroaching forest, is a traditional Hawaiian *halau* – a large open structure with an arching grass roof.

The *halau* serves as shelter for a row of traditional Polynesian outriggers belonging to the Ka'u Sailing Club Association. *Moksha* sits proudly alongside them, nestled comfortably in the black sand.

We discovered the place soon after we arrived at Hilo and began visiting schools around the island. At Na'alehu School, just a few miles north of Punalu'u, we met Kiko Johnston-Kitazawa, a gentle giant with an impressive red-brown beard, who runs the sailing club.

Last weekend I shared the beach with Kiko and a group of about twenty teenage students from Konawaena School, who came to learn the art of Polynesian sailing. It took several hours to lash a wooden outrigger and mast correctly to each canoe before taking to the water. Beginners started in the lagoon and graduated to the ocean. On Saturday night there was a large campfire and barbecue and the teenagers from Konawaena, all native Hawaiians, sang harmonious traditional songs. A rather scary-looking, rugged native, his dark brown skin covered with green tattoos, later arrived with a flashlight. The students ran to him and greeted him (what seemed to me a most improbable name) as Uncle Ernie.

Uncle Ernie led us all onto the beach and proceeded to use his flashlight beam as a pointer to the stars, sweeping it across the heavens like a light sabre in his Polynesian navigation lesson. He showed us Hokupa'a (the North Star), Makali'i (the Pleiades), Hokule'a (Arcturus) and many others the names of which I forget.

The art of navigation without instruments is a truly awesome skill, still practiced and passed on throughout the islands of Polynesia, from Hawaii to New Zealand and from the Tuamotus to New Caledonia. It requires an almost supernatural intuition, as well as a lifelong apprenticeship in building mental maps of the stars and planets. The Polynesian navigator also takes his directions from the clouds, from the wind, from the patterns of waves, even from the fish in the sea and the birds in the sky. The way that a seabird flies back to its nest filled with food, for example, is different to the way that it flies away from home, hungry and looking for food – thus telling the mariner the direction of land. Using only these natural observations he can guide his vessel across thousands of miles of open-ocean to a specific island.

Whenever I need more money I hitch-hike seventy miles north to Kona, midway up Hawaii's western shore, where there is a large commercial boatyard alongside Honokauhau Marina. There is always cash-in-hand work there – fibreglassing, antifouling and so on, which boat owners will gladly pay good money to avoid. Part of the interest earned from Jason's accident compensation has (and nothing, after all these years of debt and fund-raising, keeps a smile on my face more than this) paid off our remaining debts, which leaves me needing to earn only enough money to feed myself.

At the end of a day's work, usually covered in tiny, madly irritating fibreglass dust, I'll retire to a small, secluded beach nearby. After a swim I'll stand at the water's edge and let the dying sun – often a spectacle of bruised yellows and purples in a volcanic haze – dry me off before carefully brushing myself down with a handful of dry grass. The tiny particles of glass fall off with the film of salt that has dried to my skin.

This beach is my second home. Sleeping outside in West Hawaii is delightfully easy, since the temperature never falls below 70°F. I wake to the sound of the ocean and dive in for a swim among the corals and countless colourful fish. I bring along a sleeping mat and canvas bag containing breakfast – usually papaya and sweet potato bread, which I tie to a tree overnight. My overnight bag also contains a change of clothes and a kitchen kit with utensils, honey, lemon, soy sauce, tofu, balsamic vinegar, rice, nuts, chillies, mustard, dried mushrooms and herbs. This enables me to create dinner on the beach or at a friend's house, after only a quick stop at the fish and veggie market. With a few exceptions, the only items I feel confident of finding in their refrigerators, cavernous though they may be, are antique jars of pickles!

I would stay at Honokauhau beach more often, but it can be quite dangerous. Young men sometimes arrive late at night, twisted on booze and drugs. They don't take kindly to the presence of a *haole* (white man).

As an occasional treat I am invited to stay at the home of a wealthy British ex-patriot, Jonathon, who lives in a large villa in the hills above Kona. This is also where I go to visit my father, Stuart, who is clearly (and unsurprisingly) happy to spend his days playing backgammon and drinking beer by the pool with Jonathon and his many colourful friends.

As much as I dearly love my father and appreciate the support he has given at every stop on our journey, I keep hoping that one day he will find somewhere to settle down, maybe with a lovely woman. He is sixty years old and, to put it nicely, has never treated his liver or lungs with much respect. His fragile health concerns me. There is no prospect of financial security, social health care or comfort in the years ahead as the expedition continues to Kiribati, the Solomon Islands, Indonesia and overland through Asia. He lives on a very small pension. On the other hand, I know how much he enjoys the travelling lifestyle, hustling for donations, winning people over and living on his wits with (as he puts it) 'barely a pot to piss in'. I don't worry too much. Stuart is a remarkable character and a born survivor, although I wish Jonathon would forbid him using his motorised scooter. He's had it for three weeks and has already crashed twice, both times requiring hospital treatment for cuts and bruises.

The Journey Continues
Kailua Kona: 23 April

Jason returned in March 1999 with three friends: Scott, 36, from San Francisco, who made *Moksha*'s propellers; Edie, 26, a school teacher from Monterey; and Travis, 17, a schoolboy from Colorado. He invited them here for 'a holiday and a bit of a walk', which, they were shocked to discover, was in reality a ninety-mile hike across Hawaii. I invited a sixth companion, Avery, who works as a waiter in Kona and has a good knowledge of the natural history of Hawaii.

It began at sea level in Hilo, where we had landed, climbed almost seven thousand feet to the black lava plateau (or cleavage, as I prefer to think of it) between the two mighty bosoms of Hawaii's goddess-volcanoes, Mauna Kea and Mauna Loa, and down again to sea level to Kona, from where we are due to depart. The hike thus served to fill in the gap in our human-powered journey.

We were all either unfit, over-weight or both, and had no knowledge of the terrain or the poorly-marked series of tracks across the lava fields, much of which was a designated bombing range for the US Air Force. We each carried towering rucksacks weighing about eighty pounds full of food, warm clothing and water – there being no settlement or natural water source along the five-day route.

Scott and Travis wanted to turn back to Hilo after three hours but were eventually persuaded to keep going. Avery frequently distracted us from our sore feet by stopping to point out plants with interesting legends attached – such as the Naupaka, a white flower with five petals fused together into a half-circle. 'This is the mountain Naupaka,' Avery patiently explained. 'There's also a beach Naupaka. The two were once lovers, joined together as a full circle, but the Goddess Pele (Mauna Loa) became jealous and banished them to separate parts of the island.' But before the sentence was over, we had already collapsed in a sweaty heap and were suckling furiously on our water canisters like starving lambs.

On we plodded, mile after mile, panting heavily in the thin air and burning sun. Travis had a lot of pain in his knees and Edie developed quite serious ruptured blisters on her feet, but everyone seemed more fortified by their achievement the further we went. By the third day Scott was transformed. He amused us all with endless jokes and chimpanzee impressions. He had boundless energy, even after we added weight to his pack in the hope of slowing the bastard down.

As we sat around our campfire on the final night, at the edge of the lava plateau high above Kona, Travis spoke for all of us when he said, 'It's good that we all stayed together. It wouldn't have been the same if one of us had dropped out.' His words touched me deeply. This is the feeling of community and solidarity that, for me, makes any adventure – and life in general – worthwhile.

I sat in our circle, watched the crackling fire and listened to the scraping of dinner plates and the easy banter of our now familiar group. This was a victory, I thought to myself, but also extremely hard. It was a narrow victory, and that's what fascinated me. The phrase 'being on the edge' has become an unfortunately overused cliché but it nonetheless defines what we experienced and witnessed on the march. The edge is the place where we learn about ourselves. It lies between the comfort zone and the precipice of crushing defeat.

The following month we towed *Moksha* from Punalu'u up to Kona. A wonderful woman called Laurie-Anne let us squeeze the pedal boat into a narrow gap between her garage and garden wall, much to the neighbours' bemusement. It wasn't long before we commandeered the garage as well for equipment checks, food preparations and other supplies. Jason created an office and a bedroom there, in a tiny annex to the garage, which he shares with a family of rats in the rafters.

I have been busy on minor repairs and the installation of new equipment, including an electric water-maker, satellite phone and an alcohol cooking stove. Jason resumes his focus on the educational program, school visits, supplies and provisions.

I sometimes spend the night on the floor of Laurie-Anne's garage, rising early to work on *Moksha* before cycling to Honokauhau for paid work at the dockyard. But mostly now I stay at the home of an extraordinary woman called Nancy Griffith, thirty miles to the south, near the town of Captain Cook.

Captain Cook
Kealakekua Bay: 24 April

5.00 a.m.: 'Rhu-eu-euuuuuuuu-errh!'

'Fucking rooster!'

The first opportunity for a lie-in in weeks – ruined!

I step outside onto a wooden balcony, dressed in the shorts that I slept in, and inhale the fragrant dawn. Beyond the neighbour's roof, and framed on two sides by blossoming plumeria, a patch of the Pacific Ocean glimmers in the distance. Specks of white surf seem to crystallise on its blue satin cloth then dissolve... and re-emerge again. Birds chatter around a magnificent jacaranda tree in the garden, which flowers like a frozen display of purple fireworks. I stretch out my hand and pick off a bulging pod from a tamarind tree, crack the brown shell and suck on the sweet sticky fruit.

'Rheu-oooo-errh!'

'God damn that bird!' Nancy's voice comes bellowing down the hall. 'You've crowed your last sunrise, buster! Hey Steve, you up?'

'Yeah. I got back late, hope I didn't wake you up.'

'Nope. Want some papaya? I brought a whole bunch down from the farm. Couldn't reach the bananas though. Maybe you could take the jeep and cut some down later. There's a machete in the garage. Oh, and collect some avocados for lunch – check 'em for ants first.' The screen door opens and Nancy's beaming face offers a welcoming smile. 'We've got to swap that rooster for Charlie's hen today or the neighbour's gonna shoot 'im for sure.'

It is a rare pleasure when one meets a person with great natural presence – but Nancy Griffith is such a person. Aged somewhere in her late sixties, Nancy is a most extraordinary character. She has a fascinating face, with piercing eyes and high, rosy cheeks. It is powerful yet peaceful, both fearsome and serene. There is enormous strength in it, and also much joy and suffering.

She talks often of her departed husband Bob, the father of their two children, who in many ways was her inspiration. Bob and Nancy Griffith circumnavigated the world three times together, small children included. One circumnavigation followed the route of Captain James Cook, the great British navigator and explorer, and another time they were shipwrecked on a deserted atoll in the South Pacific for sixty-seven days. Bob also built a wooden raft similar to Thor Heyerdal's *Kon Tiki*, which they sailed from San Francisco to the Marquesas Islands. And in the 1960s they wrote the first

'How To' book about the cruising life, entitled *Blue Water*. The Griffith family were pioneers of the nomadic sailing lifestyle.

Nowadays it is common to encounter people, whose home is their vessel, docked at any lively harbour around the world. Some are retired and bask on million-dollar palaces. Others make ends meet with casual work, scavenging wood and canvas for repairs to keep themselves afloat. There must be several thousands of them. But when Bob and Nancy started it was practically unheard of.

Other women of Nancy's age are busy with grandchildren, baking pies and sitting on the board of school governors. Not Nancy. Before it mysteriously went up in flames and sank last year, she was the captain of a hundred-foot cargo vessel that delivered supplies throughout the Cook Islands of the South Pacific. 'And if those bastards at the insurance company in Tahiti ever pay up, I'm going to buy a bigger one,' she swears.

After a light breakfast of fruit and pancakes on the balcony, I descend the wooden steps to the garden. Nancy has asked me to clear out a shed full of old rigging and boat fittings, so that it can be used for seedlings and garden tools.

I sit on a fence at the edge of the garden and watch one of Nancy's hens fussing about on a tree branch. There are so many advantages to being settled, I think to myself. There, ahead of me, is a compost heap ready for growing vegetables. Over there are fruit trees and a chicken coop. The warm, comfortable house behind me is a place to relax whatever the weather; where one can keep a wall full of books, a cupboard full of clothes, a room full of musical instruments, a kitchen full of foods. Settlement enables one to become deeply immersed in things.

The life of the adventure traveller is, in comparison, an altogether shallower existence. It is a continual process of survival: finding food; making shelter and keeping warm; making a buck here and there; a life spent skimming along the surface of people and places. A nomad finds it difficult to become deeply involved in anything, because survival demands a competence in so many different skills rather than an expertise in one thing in particular. One must also carry everything, which adds to the difficulty of developing specific interests.

And being a nomad means saying goodbye to friends, over and over again. Everywhere is quicksand for the heart and the deeper in love one sinks with places and friends, the harder it is to move on again. I'm so sick of the pain of goodbyes that I've started avoiding them altogether, preferring just to disappear, however shallow it makes me look. Perhaps shallowness is part of the bargain of any great ambition, travelling or otherwise, because great ambitions require obsessive single-mindedness and obsession exacts its price – the highest being the neglect of those we profess to love the most.

'Should I settle or should I roam?' This question is never far from my mind. One settles in order to sink deeper into skills and places and relationships. One roams to remedy being stuck, to skim along the surface, to re-sharpen dulled wits and regain perspective. I am lucky enough to have had the choice, and yet the question remains. They are two very different lives – the nomad and the settler – and I wonder whether the time has come to finally choose the latter. I also often wonder, if I had been more self-assured eight years ago in Paris, perhaps less anxious to prove myself, what other alternatives to middle-class normality I might have chosen; a less spectacular, more practical kind of simplicity, I suspect. I might have become involved in a sustainable community project, or organic farming, something wholesome and useful.

Later, having cleared out the shed, I decide to go for a swim. I take a set of mask, snorkel and fins and walk from Nancy's house down the driveway, turn right and continue along a narrow, tree-lined lane. The road comes to a deadend at a low, curving seawall in front of a stony beach. A woman and her young child sit weaving grass hats in flimsy deckchairs in the shade. Further along the wall, a small group of boys with surfboards sit upon it and dangle their feet over the edge. They watch and wait for the waves to build, chatting loudly, hoping to impress two young girls who lean against a parked car and exchange coquettish whispers.

Two old ladies in long floral dresses stand nearest to me on the road. One fiddles with her coral necklace. The other folds her massive saggy arms and stares seaward. Everyone stares seaward, at nothing specific. It's that elemental fixation, like a campfire's flame.

On the opposite side of the road is a much higher wall built of smooth, rounded rocks each about the size of a football. A flight of steps is built into the wall, leading up to a raised rock plateau about forty feet square. This impressive mound structure forms the foundations of the sacred *heiau* or temple of Kealakekua.

Captain James Cook stood at this spot two hundred and twenty years ago. He climbed these steps for his ordination as the god Lono – Lord of The Sun and of Wisdom, 'The One who caused the earth to grow green'. Imagine that, the moment that the son of a farm labourer from Yorkshire became a Hawaiian god.

Did he look upon it as a fortunate case of mistaken identity? At that point in Cook's incredible life, he was eager to re-supply his vessel, *Resolution*, and sail north to the Bering Straits for a second attempt at discovering the fabled North-west Passage. This was the kind of worship he craved, to be the one to find a shorter trading route between the two great oceans, Pacific and Atlantic. The navigator who delivered this prize, he surely knew, could expect a level of power and public devotion way beyond the imagination of these savages with their feather hats and crude ornaments.

I doubt that Cook climbed these steps naively, with a sense of awed respect for Hawaiian religion. A god, after all, can negotiate pretty good trading terms. Entire villages could be harnesses into butchering and drying meat, felling timbers, collecting water, making clothes and so on, all with the least loss in exchange of his own goods. I imagine that Cook was delighted to impersonate Lono, at least for a while.

Here he stood, probably sweltering under his white wig and blue officer's uniform. He must have looked terrifyingly impressive to the islanders, with his other-worldly white skin and decorated with polished buckles and shiny buttons. These people had never encountered metal or glass. Their materials were bone, wood, coral and stone. Imagine the mystery of first seeing glass, the divine sorcery of a ship's cannon in action, or a sailor's musket. And anchored out in Kealakekua Bay was the awesome sight of 'Lono's' ship – one-hundred-and-ten-feet long, thirty-five feet wide. One hundred and twelve crew would have been busily reefing its enormous white sails.

I walk through a gap in the seawall, down a rock-strewn path to a narrow stretch of sand, put on my snorkelling gear and walk through surf into the sea. The water is luxuriously warm and clear. I swim out with my head down, breathing from my snorkel. Long, shimmering tentacles of light stream down to the sandy bottom forty or fifty feet below. I am mesmerised. It is like flying through the Aurora Borealis.

After a while I lift my mask onto my forehead and look back at a small crowd of day-trippers arriving at the seawall. I must have swum a third of a mile.

A large black dorsal fin slices through the water ahead of me. The fin vanishes underwater. I watch the surface for it to reappear, slowly rotating. Another fin breaks the surface and turns slowly towards us. Now there are four fins. Two of them breach together and I see the entire length of the dolphins' bodies arch and then disappear, leaving barely a ripple. I am ecstatic. I put the mask back over my eyes and dip my face underwater to see where they went. My rasping snorkel-breath resonates through my head.

Suddenly, from deep underwater amid the shifting streams of light, dozens more dolphins appear. They glide in close formations of threes and fours, weaving and encircling each other. Now they rise all together. The sea surface becomes a rippling flurry of fins, tails and churning water. My heartbeat thumps rapidly through me.

The dolphins vanish just as quickly as they came. I continue swimming.

After another hour I reach the northern shore of Kealakekua Bay. Here is a spectacular reef, an impossibly colourful forest of corals, some shaped like brains and others with long, delicate, tree-like fans, all teeming with fish. I wallow over it and peer down through my mask, utterly transfixed.

I clamber ashore, remove my snorkelling gear and lie exhausted on a hot, flat rock. A white stone monument rises above the bushes inland. It is a memorial cenotaph for Captain Cook and marks the spot where 'the ablest and most renowned navigator this or any country hath produced' (according to his superior, Lord Palliser) was bludgeoned to death.

It is generally understood that Cook was killed when the natives saw him bleed after being wounded in a skirmish, thereby exposing him as a fake, not a god after all. Personally, I think that suspicions must have been rife well before that, not least because Cook was forced to return to Kealakekua within a week of first leaving when *Resolution* broke her mast in a storm. In addition to his other divine attributes, Lono was considered to be the god of the weather. Perhaps he never knew that.

But it was Cook's second mistake that was to prove his undoing. He failed to understand the importance of his trading commodity – iron nails. The ship's blacksmith had pounded dozens of them into sharp blades, which Cook then presented to the chief in part-exchange for wood and supplies. Metal weaponry was a vastly superior technology to anything Hawaiians had known before. Crucially, the chief's rivals determined that they should also have it. So one night they stole one of *Resolution*'s rowing boats and promptly set fire to it in order to extract the metal. Cook's rather ungodly response was to try to kidnap the chief and hold him hostage until the missing boat was returned. The kidnapping plan was bungled, hence the skirmish, the blood, and the death of my country's greatest ever explorer.

Here he fell, possibly with the final irony of having one of his own ship's nails embedded in his chest, and that burning desire, the search for the fabled North-west Passage, that immense vision and skill, all of that was suddenly gone.

'I had ambition not only to go farther than any man had ever been before,' wrote Cook, 'but as far as it was possible to go.'

It occurs to me, as I lie here, that this may be as far as it is possible for me to go too. This great endeavour, once embarked upon, seems to have bound me to itself and its consequences, and kept me acting again and again. I have seldom come upon a space, a time like this, between one act and the next, between one voyage and the next, when I might stop to ask myself who I really am. I have proved that I have the courage to do it. Do I also have the courage not to do it?

Later that evening, I drive up to Kona to see Jason. I find him in Laurie-Anne's garage, almost hidden behind a desk piled high with papers, charts and electronic equipment. The garage floor is littered with plastic bags of food, ropes, survival gear and an assortment of tools. More of our stuff has spread onto Laurie-Anne's freezer, barbecue and garden furniture. Two orange sea anchors hang from a pitchfork and packets of spare fuses sit on top of upturned flowerpots.

Not knowing how else to put it, I come straight to the point. I tell him that I've decided not to continue.

'I was wondering why you looked so happy,' he replies and smiles. 'I'm really pleased for you, Stevie. It must have been a difficult decision to make.' His voice wavers. He seems emotional but not at all surprised.

'Yes and no,' I say. 'It was easy in the sense that it feels the right thing to do, but of course hard because I don't want to let anyone down.' He pauses for a long time before answering.

'Well, to be brutally honest, I'd have been very fucking disappointed in you if you'd carried on much longer. We got along pretty well on the last voyage but the ocean really isn't your bag, is it?'

'It's not just the ocean, mate, It's the whole thing. I don't know how to explain it really. I guess I just don't see the point in travelling like this anymore. Being on Hawaii has made me realise I need a better balance, being more deeply involved in people and things than I can as a traveller. I've done all I can do, proved what I needed to prove, learned what I needed to learn, and that's it.' I shrug my shoulders and lift my hands. 'Time to do something else.'

'Well. If you change your mind... you know, let me know. I think we've both come to the conclusion that *Moksha* is just too damn small for two people and I'm happy for you to do the next voyage to Tarawa if you like. I could do the one after that.'

331

'I appreciate that mate, but I don't think I'll change my mind. It's not something you could do half-heartedly. Fortune favours the brave, isn't that what they say? But I think it takes a pretty dim view of the semi-committed.'

'Yeah.' He smiles at me with great affection and put his hand on my shoulder. 'But don't forget that other saying, what was it? Anyone destined to hang on land – '

'Will never drown at sea.' We laugh together. 'This next voyage is all yours, Jason. I'll stick around to see you off safely and then figure out what to do next. Maybe I'll find some nice quiet place in the country and write a book.'

The Goodewind
6 May

I am aboard *Goodewind*, a classic 1929, fifty-two foot cutter jointly owned by Nancy Griffith and her friend Terry Causey, about one hundred and twenty five miles south-west of Hawaii.

If only I had a boat like this, I think to myself. A few months at sea would be no great hardship. I nestle my head into the crackling folds of *Goodewind*'s jib sail, which has been gathered and tied to the bow rail to create a body's length of luxurious, albeit noisy, cushioning. I set my cup of coffee down on the dry teak deck but keep my hand there for a while, just to be sure that it won't slide away as the boat yaws and rolls.

Goodewind flops about in a torpid stupor and the mainsail, reined-in on a close haul, alternately drops flaccid, fills and snaps taut like an angry chambermaid changing bed sheets. There is a sense of indignation in *Goodewind*'s creaking sighs, an impetuous longing to be released before this warm, steady wind and prove her rightful dominion. The vessel's frustration is mirrored in Nancy, her skipper. She can barely restrain herself from crying out, 'Curse this unnatural, wicked sloth!

Hoist the jib, un-reef that mainsail. To hell with escorting pedal boats, set the lady free!'

Moksha, with Jason and Kenny inside, waddles silently and patiently through the shimmering blue about a hundred feet off our starboard side. I have watched her disappear once before, from the quayside at Monterey, but I never saw how she looked at sea. She is perfect for her purpose, a little too square and boxy perhaps, but low and sleek and strong as a bullet. The thought of seeing her disappear soon, perhaps forever, sends me into a slight panic. Of course I knew the moment would come, but I thought nothing of it. I am not prepared. What if Jason shouts over, 'Last chance to change your mind, Steve? I stowed enough food for two just in case. You coming?' What should I do then?

Stuart ambles along the deck towards me, his hand intermittently resting on the handrail for support. He wears a white expedition T-shirt and long, fawn corduroy shorts that end at his knees. The deep brown tan of his skin almost hides the old naval tattoos on his arms and lower legs. I stare at the varicose veins bulging from his calves as he addresses me.

'Hi son,' he begins, gently. 'We just had a message from Jason on the radio. He's ready to say goodbye now. Kenny's packing up his camera gear, then they'll head over to us and we'll pick him up.'

Kenny has been pedalling and living aboard *Moksha* with Jason for the three days since we left Kona. I had a private conversation with him by radio late last night, when he was alone on pedalling duty and I was on watch at the helm of *Goodewind*. 'Are you glad to have a go after all these years of filming us, over?' I asked him.

'Oh aye.' He replied with his usual, unadorned brevity. 'It's great fun.'

333

'Shall we head back now then, leave you and Jason to carry on to Tarawa?'

'Fuck no, don't ye dare!' His voice spluttered in staccato through the radio speakers. 'It's great for a few days like, but it's a ridiculous way to cross an ocean.' The microphone picked up his wheezing, heavy exhalations and the gentle whirring sound of the pedal drive as he worked.

Jason waves from *Moksha* to signal his readiness to make the transfer. I discard the remainder of my coffee in the ocean and sense a dread that knots my stomach as I walk along the deck to where Nancy has laid out a rope ladder. Kenny appears in *Moksha*'s open hatchway with a large black bag as we come alongside. He passes the bag carefully to me, climbs up the ladder and stands unsteadily on deck. Jason takes his bowline, steps along *Moksha*'s gunwale onto the bow deck, and loops the line around a cleat on *Goodewind* to hold *Moksha* alongside. Nancy leans over the rail and offers her hand to wish him luck. He takes it and goes further, reaching up to plant a kiss on her cheek, then loses balance and almost falls overboard. He laughs. The rest of *Goodewind*'s crew take their turn to say goodbye. I am the last one. I crouch on the deck floor and reach under the rail to grasp Jason's outstretched hand.

'Take good care of yourself, my friend.' The words almost refuse to leave my dry, quivering mouth. 'Remember to keep that safety line clipped around your ankle, even when it's calm.' He nods and swallows hard. He looks up at me with a solemn expression and a wide-eyed, penetrating gaze and squeezes my hand.

'Are you sure you're OK with this?'

'Yes. Yes.' I nod and smile. 'I'm sure.'

'Thanks. Thanks for everything.'

Jason slips the bowline and pushes off. Then he stands and waves from the open hatchway. Nancy wastes no time in turning about. On her orders the crew is sent in all directions

– two to the boom to unreef the mainsail, one to the bow to guide the jib and another to the base of the mast to haul on the jib sheet.

We turn sharply into wind and begin to keel over. I feel an increasing, vibrating tension of wind against sail as *Goodewind* shivers and strains up to speed. Jason is still standing and waving. I watch him slowly shrink and lose his features. He becomes smaller and smaller, until he is indistinct from the little yellow sliver that bobs up intermittently with the swell. I continue doing battle with a lump in my throat and keep a firm grip on *Goodewind*'s handrail, almost sure that my shaking legs will soon give way. Kenny is filming me. I expected that he would.

'How are you feeling, Steve? Any regrets?' I force myself to smile and put on a brave face.

'Well... my first thought is, um... actually... I'm chuffed to bits!' It began as a throwaway line for the camera but now I laugh, delightfully, wholeheartedly, because I realise that it is deeply true.

I'm sad to see *Moksha* go, and my friend, but really, overall, I couldn't be happier. I spent eight years entirely wrapped up in this trip and six months of my life in that little pedal boat. I know exactly what I'm missing. And if I decide to cross an ocean again, I'll probably try a sailboat. Making use of the wind is such a good idea.

I sit alone for a while longer on a wooden locker under *Goodewind*'s bristling mainsail. She bounds and slices through the dark, swelling ocean. The sun descends behind us and its last long rays catch the sparkling showers of waves that burst off the bow and leave their fizzing trail of white scum. While Jason prepares for the first of many nights alone at sea, we are sprinting back to land.

My mind wanders back to Paris, recapturing the summer of 1991: my tiny apartment on Rue Aristide Briand; what I wore; who my friends were; the person I was then. I smile at the thought of that earnest, ambitious young man, who went to work on the train each morning, to his office on the sixth floor, dressed in one of his two suits and one of his five ties. He was an optimist, a romantic and an idealist, but he also had a gnawing fear of death – not of death itself, more of the thought of dying in the knowledge that life had only been mediocre. And he had a terrific sense of urgency, I remember, that compelled him to do the most extraordinarily adventurous thing he could think of.

And how it grew! The expedition defined my existence for so many years until... when? I don't think I ever questioned what I was doing until Jason came to San Francisco to tell me that our expedition partnership was over. Not that I blame him for anything. In fact, he was helpful. He forced me to question everything, although it wasn't until we got to Hawaii, when our debts were paid and options became available, that the answer became clear. The only mediocre future now would be to carry on pedalling.

'Hey, Steve.' Nancy's head pops up from the galley hatchway. 'You're on watch at the helm with your dad. Wind's supposed to get up a bit later so keep on your toes. We could reef in the mainsail a pinch or two if you like.'

'No, it's OK Nancy,' I reply. 'Let the old girl go.'

9. Salcombe
(2000 –)

Jason pedalled on alone through the tropical Central Pacific, crossing both the International Date Line and the Equator. The winds were generally favourable and the sky a daily mixture of sun and sudden, thunderous showers. There were no shipping lanes. What tested Jason's courage and endurance most of all was the Equatorial Counter-Current, a band of east-flowing water that he had to cross before he could continue south-west to Tarawa, in the Kiribati Islands. He pedalled for nearly three weeks through the blistering, windless heat of the Doldrums, without going anywhere. But eventually, on 15 July, after 73 days at sea, he reached Tarawa with (as he amusingly described it) 'chronic salt-sores and mild schizophrenia'.

A year later, Jason invited *Moksha*'s original builder, Chris Tipper, to accompany him on the next 1,000-mile stretch from Kiribati to the Solomons. The ocean behaved faultlessly throughout the three-week journey, by all accounts, and the biggest challenges faced (by Jason's reckoning) were Chris's rotten-smelling feet and atrocious cooking.

Jason's partner, April, took over from Chris for the final Pacific leg across the Coral Sea to Port Douglas, Australia. The Coral Sea has a reputation for being one of the trickiest stretches of water in the world, and their attempt to cross it so late in the season added to the challenge. Almost constant south-easterly winds threatened early on to blow them onto the reefs east of Papua New Guinea and, later on in the voyage, onto the Great Barrier Reef. April, from Colorado, had never been in a boat before and throughout the voyage she suffered terribly from seasickness.

After a month at sea they faced catastrophe, as they could do nothing more to halt their drift onto the Barrier Reef. April's health had deteriorated with her inability to hold down food. Kenny Brown arrived into Port Douglas just in the nick of time to commandeer a vessel, race out through the reef and bring them back to safety.

A year later, in July 2001, Jason cycled with a group of young men and women across Australia to Darwin, on the north coast. *Moksha* arrived at Darwin later that year as deck cargo on a freighter, and has been in storage there ever since.

The next leg of the journey, delayed for several years through lack of funds, is due to begin as this book goes to print. Possibly the most hazardous, challenging and fascinating phase of the expedition so far, it involves pedalling *Moksha* 500 miles north from Darwin to the island of Timor, then using kayaks and bicycles to travel the length of Indonesia and across the Malacca Straits to Singapore. This is another bold, never-previously-attempted phase of the journey, and all the more exciting for me because I will be involved. Well, I've been writing this book in sedate, soft-shitting comfort for four years. It's about time I got back out there for a little adventure. From thereon, who knows? I believe Jason will finish the entire circumnavigation one day, maybe by 2008-9, but whether I'll be there alongside him or among the spectators cheering him across the line at Greenwich is hard to say.

I am pleased to be able to relate happy endings for the other principal characters in this odyssey. My father Stuart developed the sailing bug and managed to talk his way onto many a fine vessel as an able deckhand, ploughing through the cruising triangle between San Francisco, Acapulco and Hawaii. He returned to England in September 2001 and found himself a cosy bungalow on the idyllic south coast of Devon (within twenty miles of where I now live) and a local pub serving good bitter. He rescued a greyhound from the dog pound to keep him company and reacquainted himself with his grandchildren. He was last heard declaring, 'They'll have to take me out of here in a box.'

Kenny Brown produced four one-hour documentaries about the expedition, which were snapped up by the Discovery Channel (Europe). After covering more conflicts for the BBC in Palestine, Afghanistan, Iraq, Columbia and the 9/11 tragedy in New York, Kenny felt he had witnessed enough war for the time being and took a degree in film studies in Los Angeles. He is now back in Iraq with the BBC, the last I heard, trying to repay his student debts.

I left Hawaii soon after the *Goodewind* voyage and floated around the world for about a year in search of a community I could call 'home'. From Hawaii I flew to New Zealand, where I cycled around the islands and spent several months helping to establish a Buddhist retreat. I went on to Australia for three months, and eventually made my way back to Europe. I found some idyllic places and wonderful people, but nowhere felt right for me.

I returned to England and to Salcombe, where my sister and her family have lived for many years. By this time, my mother Sylvia, who had remarried, was also living there. My stepfather offered me a job as a ferryman, which, strangely enough, was a dream I harboured as a child.

I drive an open, wooden boat between some ancient steps and a slipway on the opposite beach. The distance across the estuary is only two or three hundred metres, depending on the tide.

It took me a long time to really settle into it. Where is the achievement, after all, in driving a ferryboat back and forth across the same stretch of water all day long? Then one day it dawned on me that if the expedition taught me anything, it is that you can't depend on the accomplishment of goals or journeys - however great or small - for your happiness. You just have to enjoy them all, and from beginning to end, because happiness is the acceptance of the journey as it is now, not the promise of the other shore.

I get all sorts of passengers: Salcombe townsfolk from one side; the 'Bearlanders' of East Portlemouth from the other, who take the ferry daily to work or to go shopping; parents on holiday, who clatter down the steps loaded with buggies and beach balls and picnics; their excited children, who lean over the side and giggle at every splash and spray; hikers wearing thick socks and boots, determined to walk the coastal path as far as Start Point Lighthouse or Torcross; young lovers, who tenderly hold hands; old men with knees that won't bend, too proud to take a helping hand, who never fail to remind me of a time when the fare was a penny.

Yesterday, a middle-aged couple with red faces and muddy shins walked down the slipway wheeling their bicycles.

'Having a good ride?' I asked, lifting the bikes onto the ferry.

'Phew, that was hard going!' said the woman, still trying to catch her breath. 'Great fun though – we've come all the way from Ivybridge.'

It was their first big ride in many years, the man said. They were looking forward to a lunch break once they got to East Prawle.

I drove them across the estuary and helped them off the other side. I wished them good luck. They thanked me. I watched them climb back onto their bikes and felt a touch of envy as they wobbled off down the lane.

Acknowledgements

Having pedalled to Hawaii and written a book, I have to say that the latter was harder to achieve. Mentally and emotionally the two have much in common, being glacially slow, largely solitary journeys during which you must focus on the job at hand or risk losing your mind contemplating the vast distance to 'the other shore'. My first acknowledgement is to those throughout my life – the list is too long to print – who have inspired and fortified the belief that as long as I keep going I'll get there in the end.

I extend heartfelt thanks to: reviewers who suffered earlier versions of the manuscript – Lola Broomberg, Michael 'Doko' Hatchett, Matthew Oakley, Therese Ortolani, Madeline Poole, Nancy Sanford, Sylvia Shortman, David Craig, Nicky Eaton and Ben White; to Eilbhe Donovan for her beautiful maps; to my agent Jacqueline Burns and my editor Jennifer Barclay who gave gentle and detailed guidance in how to breathe more life and humanity into the narrative; to all at Summersdale Publishers, who are a joy to work with; to Nicholas Crane for his boundless enthusiasm, help and suggestions, including a cracking book title; to His Holiness The Dalai Lama for his lovely foreword.

Many thousands of individuals and hundreds of sponsor companies have enabled Expedition 360 – the first human-powered around the world expedition – to keep moving forward since Jason and I began at Greenwich in July 1994. I'm sure that Jason will pay tribute to his own collection of key people when he finally publishes his account, but my special thanks go to: my father Stuart Smith, my mother Sylvia Shortman, Kenny Brown, Maria Gale, Patricia Rogers, Chris Tipper, Hugo Burnham, David Goddard, Sebert and Gillian Lewis, Alan Boswell, Tony Izard, Bill Parnell, Margaret Quass, Spencer Drummond, Chris Court, Chris Lees, Martin Gascoigne, Charlie Brooks, Vasco Pinto Basto, Francisco Ramada, Mark Shenstone, all at Turtle Cove, Providenciales, the crew of the USCS Charles L. Brown, Nancy Sanford, Kimberli Swan, Richard and Susan Pudsey, Tom and Suzie DeBusk, Jeff Debevec, John Thude, Pete and Regina Wolff, Deanna and Norm Ferrera, Bill Pence and Penny Rix, Barbara Bourns, Arf Pitney, Therese Ortolani, JimBo Trout, Abigail Hare, Carla, Kim Cook, Roger Kauffman, Ryan Sandau, Ken Danylchuk, Sherwood Bishop, the Daggett family, Lucky Congdon, the O'Flaherty family, Robbie Lopez, Sam Smalling, Suzanne Geller, Billie and Jason Lacy, Bonnie, Nancy Griffith, Laurie-Ann Thrasher, Betti and Diego Sax-Falconi, Shirley Nice, Sarsfield and Barbara Donovan, Eilbhe Donovan, April Abril, Lima Tamasese, Scott Morrison, Bill Bercik, Chris Maila, Richard Brown, John Oman, Ian Satchell, Jane Koca, Casey Dunn, John Walker, Dan Klug, Darren Witt and Sher Dhillon. Finally I promised Chad Benson a mention, just for being the cheeriest soul in Salcombe.

Anyone interested in the on-going adventures, sponsorship or educational opportunities of Expedition 360 should visit the website at www.expedition360.com

Stevie Smith is the founder of Expedition 360 – the first attempt to circumnavigate the world using only human power. He has given hundreds of lectures to audiences in the UK, France, Spain, Portugal, the United States and Canada, in schools and universities and at sports shows including the Montreal Cycling Festival.

Prior to the expedition, Stevie spent four years as a consultant in environmental research, specialising in European and global policy issues in London, Paris and Brussels. He holds a Master's Degree in Environmental Technology from Imperial College, London. While writing the book, Stevie worked as a ferryman in the idyllic coastal town of Salcombe, South Devon.

The expedition has been largely funded through the promotional efforts of Stevie, his expedition partner Jason Lewis and members of the support team, most notably Stevie's father Stuart. It received widespread media coverage across Europe and North America, and was the subject of three documentaries broadcast by Discovery Networks Europe.

www.expedition360.com

'A journey of great courage and determination'
His Holiness The Dalai Lama

'One of the last great firsts'
Nicholas Crane

'One of the greatest small-scale expeditions of the twentieth/twenty-first centuries'
John Pilkington

'Not only a human-powered but also a humanising trip'
Lord Yehudi Menuhin

'Remarkable, heroic, funny, inspirational'
Geo Plein Air Magazine

'Half of me reckons that Steve Smith is bonkers… the other half is deeply envious at the thought of him experiencing the world by being so deeply and naturally a part of it.'
Jonathon Porritt

'Pedalling to Hawaii shows that anything is possible'
Sir Ranulph Fiennes

World Records:

- Longest Continuous Human-Powered Journey (ongoing)

- First Human-Powered Atlantic Crossing East–West from Continent to Continent

- First Unassisted In-Line Skate Across North America (J. Lewis)

- First Pedal-Powered Crossing from US Mainland to Hawaii

Total Cost: £140,000

Previous Experience:

Stevie Smith:

- 1 day crewing sailboat round the Isle of Wight
- Once cycled 50 miles with school group
- No camping experience. Never pitched a tent

Jason Lewis:

- 3 days crewing sailboat off Dorset coast
- Never cycled more than 3 miles
- Fair camping skills acquired from army cadets

Training Strategy:

None. Why prolong the agony?

OTHER TRAVEL TITLES FROM SUMMERSDALE

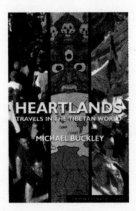

Heartlands

Travels in the Tibetan World

Michael Buckley

£7.99 Paperback

A glimpse into the troubled soul of hidden Tibet.

Reaching Lhasa is the dream of all Tibetan pilgrims, but China's brutal occupation has reduced this ancient civilisation to a shadow of its former self. If you want to discover real Tibetan culture, you have to go elsewhere on the plateau – to Ladakh, Bhutan or Outer Mongolia.

Exploring these remote regions in a series of trips, Michael Buckley embarks on a quest to come to grips with Tibetan ways, from the celebrated spirituality to the downright bizarre, and finds himself balanced somewhere in between magic and reality. A fascinating and personal journey of discovery, Buckley rubs shoulders with hardy nomads, encounters giant phalluses and stuffed kangaroos, cycles snowbound passes, chats to the Dalai Lama and survives interrogation by Chinese police.

Darkly funny, informative and inspired, Buckley's account of these amazing lands makes invaluable reading.

Good Vibrations

Coast to Coast by Harley

Tom Cunliffe

£7.99 Paperback

A motorcycle the size of Roz's Betty Boop would have been beyond the dreams of the craziest pack leader at the Ace Café on London's North Circular Road in the monochrome days of rockers, Nortons, Bonnevilles and Marianne Faithfull, when 'good' was middle class, 'bad' misunderstood and the motorcycle offered stark hope to a generation of inarticulate searchers...

Tom Cunliffe and his wife Roz take life in the saddle and onto the American highways and byways astride the quintessential 'dream machine' - the Harley-Davidson.

Bikes Betty Boop and Black Madonna are chrome steeds for an extensive road-trip: from Maryland on the east coast to San Francisco on the west (and then back again), they thunder their way over the sun-beaten plains, through scorching Death Valley, neon Las Vegas, the deep South and everywhere in between.

With flashbacks to the sixties, the eclectic assortment of moonshiners, bikers hard and not-so-hard, cowhands, Sioux Indians, strippers, bible-bashers, war veterans, southern gents and the occasional alligator delivers a unique insight into the diversity of the USA.

An easy-riding peepshow into today's America through British eyes and between the handlebars of the great Harley-Davidson.

Off the Rails

Moscow to Beijing on recumbent bikes

Chris Hatherly and Tim Cope

£7.99 Paperback

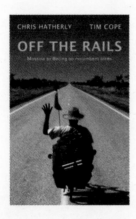

Twenty years old and possessed by a burning desire to challenge themselves in an extraordinary way, Tim Cope and Chris Hatherly plan an epic journey across the vast expanse of Russia, Siberia and Mongolia, to end in Tiananmen Square, Beijing. Not content with such an adventure, however, they also decide to undertake it by recumbent bicycle.

Tim and Chris are not just fearless adventurers but philosophers on wheels, open to every experience from the voice of the steppes to encountering the nomads of the Gobi desert. An often funny, moving and inspirational tale of living out a dream, *Off the Rails* is also the story of their tumultuous relationship as two opposing wills battle it out in the midst of heat, snow and hunger.

Tim Cope and Chris Hatherly received the Australian National Geographic Young Adventurer of the Year Award and the Spirit of Adventure Award for their travels.

'A journey beyond the limit of endurance. An amazing true story'
Sydney Morning Herald

The Trail to Titicaca

A Journey Through South America

Rupert Attlee

£7.99 Paperback

It seemed like a mad enterprise: three inexperienced cyclists setting out to pedal 6,500 miles up the Andes, from Tierra del Fuego to Lake Titicaca. After nearly a year and against the odds – contending with grasshopper storms, deserts of volcanic ash and trigger-happy police – the trio succeeded in their objective, also raising tens of thousands of pounds for the Leukaemia Research Fund.

Battling with the language barrier, an addiction to chocolate and fuelled by copious amounts of vino, this is the story of the physical and emotional ups and downs experienced by three friends: the romantic, the stoic and the writer. Their journey tells of the awe-inspiring wilds, history and peoples of Chile, Argentina and Bolivia. What started as the adventure of a lifetime evolved into a voyage of discovery, comradeship and humour.

'A great read, but be warned, it'll sow the adventure seed in your mind and you may want to do the trip yourself'

Maximum Mountain Bike

'Any book, peppered as it is with snippets of historical and geographical background so far removed from our own, must surely be worth a read'

Geographical Magazine

www.summersdale.com